dessert

CATHY BAELLO
FEB. 20 '06
U.K

desserts

igloo

Published by Igloo Books Limited
Henson Way
Kettering
Northants
NN16 8PX
info@igloo-books.com

This edition printed in 2005

ISBN 1-84193-311-2

Printed in China

Author: Victoria Chow
With thanks to Yew Yuan Chow and James Mitchell

Project management by Metro Media Limited

Contents

Introduction

Everyone's favourite part of the meal is dessert, and whether your taste is for fresh fruit or rich chocolate, classic cake or creamy puddings, this book will help you create mouth-watering treats with which to truly indulge yourself.

Almond cake, Banana cake or the classic Chocolate cake – Cakes & Muffins is the first chapter and what better place to start? From the traditional to the unfamiliar, there is a wide selection to be found here. So whether you are preparing for a child's birthday, an anniversary, or just a treat to cheer yourself up after a hard day you are guaranteed to find what you are looking for.

However, perhaps you are more tempted by a Bakewell tart? Or perhaps delicious Chocolate éclairs or Banana empanadas? If so, then turn to the Pastries chapter where all these can be found, as well as such tasty treats as Custard tarts, Plum cobbler and Jalousie.

Sometimes, though, you need something filling and comforting and the Puddings section certainly provides plenty of that. Scrumptious Sticky toffee pudding or Semolina, tasty Tiramisu or Tapioca pudding, satisfying desserts or tasty treats – this is the section for curling up and enjoying an evening in.

The chapter for Soufflés, Mousses, Custards & Pancakes can provide you with a charming Crème caramel, a ravishing Raspberry mousse and appetising Apple pancake stacks. And whether you are looking for teatime treats or after-dinner winners, the Biscuits section has more than enough to charm and delight. Apple brownies, Almond shortbread or Fruity roulade, the choice is yours.

If all this talk about sweet things is leaving you hot and bothered then turn to the Ice-Creams, Sorbets & Cold desserts section, where Turkish delight ice-cream, Watermelon sorbet and Frozen cherry ripples are guaranteed to refresh you.

And from a basic Banana split to exquisite Exotic fruit parcels, the Fresh Fruit chapter has delectable delights in all the colours of the rainbow. Pineapples, pears and passion fruit, mangoes and melons, whether tropical fruit or everyday, are all sure to please.

Cakes & muffins

Whether you are looking for a tasty teatime treat or that perfect cake for a special occasion, this chapter is sure to provide you with plenty of inspiration. From the traditional Coffee & walnut cake, Rich fruit cake or Dundee cake to the indulgent Chocolate & coconut roulade, Wild strawberry sponge or Rose mousse gâteau, there is a recipe here to suit most occasions and tastes.

Mocha layer cake

SERVES 8

INGREDIENTS:

200g/7oz self-raising flour
¼ teaspoon baking powder
25g/1oz cocoa powder
100g/4oz caster sugar
2 eggs
2 tablespoons golden syrup
150ml/¼pt sunflower oil

150ml/¼pt milk

For the filling:
1 teaspoon instant coffee
1 tablespoon boiling water
300ml/½pt double cream
25g/1oz icing sugar

- Preheat the oven to 180°C/350°F/Gas mark 4.
- Lightly grease three 18cm/7in cake tins.
- Sift the flour, baking powder and cocoa powder into a large mixing bowl. Stir in the sugar.
- Make a well in the centre and crack in the eggs and add the syrup, oil and milk. Beat the liquid with a wooden spoon, gradually mixing in the dry ingredients to make a smooth mixture.
- Divide the mixture between the prepared tins.
- Bake in the oven for 35 to 45 minutes or until springy to the touch. Leave in the tins for 5 minutes, then turn out on to wire racks to cool completely.
- Dissolve the instant coffee in the boiling water and place in a bowl with the cream and the icing sugar.
- Whip until the cream is just holding its shape. Use half of the cream to sandwich the 3 cakes together. Transfer to a serving plate.
- Spread the remaining cream over the top and sides of the cake.
- Chill until ready to serve.

Pound cake

SERVES 6-8

INGREDIENTS:

375g/13oz butter (softened)
375g/13oz caster sugar
1 teaspoon vanilla essence
6 eggs (lightly beaten)

375g/13oz plain flour (sifted)
1 teaspoon baking powder
125ml/4fl oz milk
Icing sugar for dusting

- Preheat the oven to 180°C/350°F/Gas mark 4.
- Lightly grease the base and side of a 23cm/9in round cake tin and line the base with baking parchment.
- Cream the butter and sugar in a small bowl with an electric beater until the mixture is light and fluffy.
- Beat in the vanilla essence, then add the eggs gradually, beating thoroughly after each addition. Transfer to a large bowl.
- Using a metal spoon, fold in the sifted flour and baking powder alternately with the milk. Stir until the mixture is just combined and almost smooth.
- Spoon the mixture into the tin and smooth the surface. Bake for 1 hour. Leave in the tin for 10 minutes before turning out on to a wire rack to cool.
- Lightly dust with icing sugar before serving.

Frosted mint cheesecake

SERVES 6

INGREDIENTS:

75g/3oz butter (plus extra for greasing)
150g/5oz caster sugar
100g/4oz plain flour
225g/8oz full fat soft cheese
150g/5oz natural yogurt

75ml/3fl oz crème de menthe
2 tablespoons water
1½ teaspoons gelatine
1 egg white

- Preheat the oven to 180°C/350°F/Gas mark 4. Grease a 20cm/8in flan ring, and line with a sheet of aluminium foil.
- Make the shortbread mixture by using a wooden spoon to cream the butter with 50g/2oz sugar until smooth. Stir in the flour and knead the mixture until smooth.
- Press the shortbread mixture into the base of the prepared flan ring. Bake in the oven for 18 to 20 minutes, then cool in the ring.
- Beat the cheese with a wooden spoon until smooth, then gradually whisk in the yogurt, 25g/1oz sugar and the mint-flavoured liqueur.
- Place the water in a bowl and sprinkle in the gelatine.
- Stand the bowl over a saucepan of hot water and heat gently until dissolved. Leave to cool slightly, then stir into the cheese mixture.
- Whisk the egg white until stiff, then fold into the cheesecake mixture.
- Pour the mixture over the shortbread base. Open freeze for at least 8 hours.
- About 1 hour before serving, remove the cheesecake from the freezer and place on a serving plate.
- Place the remaining sugar in a saucepan over a medium heat until it turns

→

← brown and caramelizes, then pour over the cheesecake in a lattice pattern. Place in the refrigerator for 45 minutes before serving.

Rich chocolate cake with cherries

SERVES 6–8

INGREDIENTS:

400g/14oz dark chocolate (broken into pieces)
2 tablespoons instant coffee granules
75ml/3fl oz kirsch
4 eggs (separated)

175g/6oz butter
50g/2oz self-raising flour
Pinch of salt
125g/4oz caster sugar
450g/1lb fresh cherries (stoned)

- Preheat the oven to 190°C/375°F/Gas mark 5. Line the bottom of a deep 20cm/8in square cake tin with greaseproof paper, then spread the pan evenly with butter.
- In a heavy-based saucepan set over a low heat, melt 225g/8oz dark chocolate with 1 tablespoon coffee granules and half of the kirsch, stirring occasionally, until smooth. Off the heat, stir in the egg yolks, one at a time, then return the pan to the heat and stir the mixture briefly until the yolks are warmed and have thickened the chocolate slightly. Off the heat, beat in the butter, by tablespoons, stirring until smooth. Stir in the flour.
- Beat the egg whites with the salt until they form soft peaks. Sprinkle on 50g/2oz sugar and continue beating until they form stiff and shiny peaks.
- Fold the warm chocolate mixture delicately into the meringue and turn the batter into the prepared tin. Bake in the oven for 25 to 30 minutes.
- Set the pan on a rack to cool for at least 45 minutes before unmoulding.
- While the cake is cooling, place the cherries in a saucepan with the remaining sugar and 2 tablespoons of the remaining kirsch. Cook the mixture over a medium low heat, partially covered, for 30 to 40 minutes, stirring occasionally. Uncover the pan for the last 10 minutes or so. The cherries should reduce to a thick compote.
- Allow the cherries to cool, then chop roughly.
- Invert the cake on to a serving platter and remove the paper.
- Using a spoon, trace a circle in the centre of the cake, then scoop out the top part of the cake within the circle, leaving at least 1cm/½in of cake at the bottom.
- Add the scooped-out cake to the cherries and stir together well. Return the mixture to the hole in the cake, smoothing out.

- In a heavy-based saucepan, melt the remaining chocolate, coffee granules and kirsch and 3 tablespoons water, stirring occasionally, until smooth.
- Allow to cool slightly, then spread evenly over the top and sides of the cake.
- Refrigerate until 30 minutes before serving.

Devil's food cake

SERVES 6

INGREDIENTS:

250g/9oz self-raising flour
1 teaspoon bicarbonate of soda
225g/8oz butter
400g/14oz dark muscovado sugar
1 teaspoon vanilla essence
3 eggs
100g/4oz dark chocolate (melted)
125ml/4fl oz buttermilk
225ml/8fl oz boiling water

For the icing:
300g/11oz caster sugar
2 egg whites
1 tablespoon lemon juice
3 tablespoons orange juice

- Preheat the oven to 190°C/375°F/Gas mark 5. Lightly grease 2 x 20cm/8in shallow round cake tins and line the bases with baking parchment.
- Sift the flour and bicarbonate of soda together into a bowl.
- With a wooden spoon, beat the butter and sugar together in a bowl until pale and fluffy. Beat in the vanilla essence and the eggs, one at a time, beating well after each addition. Add a little flour to the mixture if it begins to curdle.
- Fold the melted chocolate into the mixture until well blended. Gradually fold in the flour, then stir in the buttermilk and boiling water.
- Divide the mixture between the tins and level the tops. Bake in the oven for 30 minutes, until springy to the touch.
- Leave to cool in the tin for 5 minutes, then transfer to a wire rack and leave to cool completely.
- Place the icing ingredients in a large bowl set over a pan of gently simmering water. Whisk, preferably with an electric beater, until thickened and forming soft peaks. Remove from the heat and whisk until the mixture is cool.
- Sandwich the 2 cakes together with a little of the frosting then spread the remainder over the top and sides of the cake.

Lemon delicious

SERVES 4

INGREDIENTS:

50g/2oz butter
175g/6oz caster sugar
3 eggs (separated)
1 teaspoon grated lemon zest

50g/2oz self-raising flour (sifted)
50ml/2fl oz lemon juice
175ml/6fl oz milk
Icing sugar to dust

- Preheat the oven to 180°C/350°F/Gas mark 4. Brush a 1 litre/1³/₄pt ovenproof dish with oil.
- Using an electric beater, beat the butter, sugar, egg yolks and lemon zest in a small bowl until the mixture is light and creamy. Transfer to a medium-sized bowl.
- Add the flour and stir with a wooden spoon until just combined. Add the lemon juice and milk and stir to combine.
- Place the egg whites in a small bowl. Using an electric beater, beat until firm peaks form. Fold in the pudding mixture with a metal spoon until just combined.
- Spoon into the ovenproof dish and place the dish in a deep baking dish. Pour in boiling water to come about one third of the way up the side of the pudding dish.
- Bake for about 40 minutes. Dust with icing sugar.

Alaskan blueberry coffee cake

SERVES 8

INGREDIENTS:

350g/12oz plain flour
175g/6oz caster sugar
2¹/₂ teaspoon baking powder
1 teaspoon salt
50ml/2fl oz vegetable oil
175ml/6fl oz milk

1 egg
250g/9oz blueberries
100g/4oz demerara sugar
¹/₂ teaspoon ground cinnamon
50g/2oz butter

- Preheat the oven to 190°C/375°F/Gas mark 5. Grease a greased deep 20cm/8in round cake tin.

- In a medium-sized mixing bowl, blend together 250g/9oz flour with the sugar, baking powder, salt, oil, milk, egg and 225g/8oz blueberries. With a wooden spoon, beat thoroughly for 30 seconds and spread in the prepared cake tin.
- Combine the remaining flour, demerara sugar, cinnamon and butter. Sprinkle over the batter and top with the remaining berries.
Bake in the oven for 30 to 40 minutes.

Mud cake

SERVES 6–8

INGREDIENTS:

225g/8oz butter
225g/8oz dark chocolate (chopped)
2 tablespoons instant coffee powder
175ml/6fl oz hot water
150g/5oz self-raising flour
150g/5oz plain flour
50g/2oz cocoa powder
½ teaspoon bicarbonate of soda

550g/1lb 4oz caster sugar
4 eggs (lightly beaten)
2 tablespoons vegetable oil
125ml/4fl oz buttermilk

For the icing:
150g/5oz unsalted butter (chopped)
150g/5oz dark chocolate (chopped)

Preheat the oven to 160°C/325°F/Gas mark 3. Lightly grease a deep 23cm/9in round cake tin and line with baking parchment, making sure the paper around the side extends at least 5cm/2in above the top edge.
- Put the butter, chocolate and coffee in a pan with the hot water and stir over a low heat until smooth. Remove from the heat.
Sift the flours, cocoa and bicarbonate of soda into a large bowl. Stir in the sugar and make a well in the centre. Combine the eggs, oil and buttermilk, add the dry ingredients and, using a large metal spoon, slowly stir them in. Gradually stir in the butter mixture.
Pour the mixture into the tin and bake for 1½ hours. Remove from the oven. If the top looks raw, bake for another 5 to 10 minutes, then remove. Leave in the tin until completely cold, then turn out.
- For the icing, combine the butter and chocolate in a saucepan and stir over a low heat until melted. Remove and allow to cool slightly. Spread over the cake and serve.

Bermuda cheesecake

SERVES 6–8

INGREDIENTS:

75g/3oz butter
400g/14oz caster sugar
250g/9oz biscuit crumbs
500g/1lb 2oz cream cheese

75g/3oz cocoa powder
1½ teaspoons vanilla essence
2 eggs
250g/9oz sour cream

- Preheat the oven to 180°C/350°F/Gas mark 5.
- Melt the butter in a pan, stir in 25g/1oz caster sugar and the biscuit crumbs, mixing thoroughly. Press mixture over the base of a 20cm/8in round tin and chill while preparing the filling.
- Beat the cream cheese until smooth. Beat in 350g/12oz sugar, then gradually add the cocoa powder, 1 teaspoon of the vanilla essence and the eggs. When smooth, pour into the crumb crust and bake for 35 minutes.
- Combine the sour cream with the remaining sugar and vanilla essence. Spread the mixture over the top of the cheesecake and bake for another 10 minutes.
- Remove from the oven, cool and chill overnight.

Seed cake

SERVES 6–8

INGREDIENTS:

100g/4oz butter
150g/5oz caster sugar
2 eggs
150g/5oz flour (sifted)
25g/1oz cornflour

2 teaspoons caraway seeds
1/2 teaspoon baking powder
50g/2oz glacé cherries (finely chopped)
½ teaspoon vanilla essence

- Preheat the oven to 170°C/325°F/Gas mark 3. Grease a 20cm/8in round cake tin and line with baking parchment.
- Beat the butter and sugar together until white, then add each egg separately.
- Gradually stir in the flour, cornflour, caraway seeds, baking powder, cherries and vanilla essence.
- Pour the mixture into the prepared cake tin and bake in the oven for 1¼ hours. Turn on to a wire rack to cool.

Panforte di Siena

SERVES 12

INGREDIENTS:

100g/4oz split whole almonds
100g/4oz hazelnuts
75g/3oz mixed peel
50g/2oz no-soak dried apricots (finely chopped)
50g/2oz glacé pineapple (finely chopped)

Grated zest of 1 orange
50g/2oz plain flour
2 tablespoons cocoa powder
2 teaspoons ground cinnamon
150g/5oz caster sugar
175g/6oz honey
Icing sugar for dredging

- Preheat the oven to 150°C/300°F/Gas mark 2. Line a round 20cm/8in cake tin with baking parchment.
- Toast the almonds under the grill until lightly browned and place in a bowl.
- Toast the hazelnuts until the skins split. Place on a dry tea towel and rub off the skins. Roughly chop the hazelnuts and add to the almonds with the mixed peel.
- Add the apricots and pineapple to the nuts with the orange zest and mix well.
- Sift the flour with the cocoa and cinnamon, add to the nut mixture and mix. Place the sugar and honey in a saucepan and heat until the sugar dissolves, then cook gently for about 5 minutes or until the mixture thickens and begins to turn a deeper shade of brown. Quickly add to the nut mixture and mix evenly. Turn into the prepared tin and level the top, using the back of a damp spoon. Cook in the oven for 1 hour. Remove from the oven and leave in the tin until cold. Before serving dredge the cake heavily with sifted icing sugar and serve in thin slices.

Coffee & walnut cake

SERVES 8

INGREDIENTS:

100g/4oz butter (softened, plus extra for greasing)
300g/11oz caster sugar
2 eggs (lightly beaten)
200g/7oz flour (sieved with 1

tablespoon baking powder)
150ml/¼pt strong coffee
200g/7oz shelled walnuts (finely chopped)
Butter for greasing

→

←
- Preheat the oven to 180°C/350°F/Gas mark 4. Grease a 20cm/8in square cake tin.
- Cream the butter and sugar together in a large mixing bowl until light and fluffy, then beat in the eggs.
- Add the flour alternately with the coffee until the mixture is soft and smooth.
- Add the nuts and mix well.
- Pour the mixture into the prepared cake tin and bake in the oven for 1 hour. Leave to cool in the tin for 10 minutes, then turn out on to a wire rack to cool completely. Serve with after-dinner coffee.

Diabalo cake

SERVES 8

INGREDIENTS:

75g/3oz dark chocolate
4 eggs (separated)
100g/4oz caster sugar
175g/6oz butter
150g/5oz flour (sifted)
¼ teaspoon salt
1 teaspoon vanilla essence

For the filling:
450g/1lb dark chocolate
475g/1lb 1oz cream
2 tablespoons coffee liqueur

For the frosting:
225g/8oz caster sugar
125ml/4fl oz hot coffee
175g/6oz dark chocolate
1 tablespoon liquid glucose
50g/2oz butter
1 tablespoon coffee liqueur

- Preheat the oven to 180°C/350°F/Gas mark 4. Grease a 38 x 25cm/15 x 10in Swiss roll tin and line with baking parchment.
- Melt the chocolate in a heatproof bowl set over a saucepan of simmering water.
- Beat the egg whites in a medium-sized bowl until foamy white and double in volume. Beat in half of the sugar, 1 tablespoon at a time, until the meringue stands in soft peaks.
- Beat the butter in a large bowl, gradually add the remaining sugar and continue beating until well blended. Beat in the egg yolks until smooth, then the cooled chocolate. Sift the flour and salt into the chocolate mixture and stir to blend. Add the vanilla essence.
- Stir a third of the meringue mixture into the chocolate mixture until blended.
- Spread the batter in the prepared tin.
- Bake in the oven for 15 minutes, or until springy. Cool in the tin for 5 minutes, then turn out on to a wire rack. Remove the parchment and allow to cool.

For the filling, break the chocolate into small pieces. Combine with the cream in a saucepan. Heat slowly, stirring constantly, until the chocolate melts. Remove from the heat and stir in the coffee liqueur. Pour into a bowl and chill for 1½ hours. When chilled, beat until still and thick.
Cut the cooled cake in half crossways and use the chocolate cream mixture to sandwich the halves together.
For the frosting, heat the sugar and coffee in a saucepan until the sugar dissolves. Break the chocolate into small pieces and add to the saucepan with the liquid glucose. Heat to boiling, stirring constantly, and cook for 5 minutes.
Remove from the heat and add the butter and coffee liqueur. Beat for 5 minutes, until mixture begins to thicken. Quickly spread over the cake. Chill for at least 1 hour before serving.

Butterfly cakes

SERVES 4–6

INGREDIENTS:

100g/4oz butter (softened)
150g/5oz caster sugar
175g/6oz self-raising flour
125ml/4fl oz milk
2 teaspoons vanilla essence
2 eggs

125ml/4fl oz double cream (whipped to soft peaks)
100g/4oz strawberry jam
Icing sugar for dusting

Preheat the oven to 180°C/350°F/Gas mark 4. Line a 12-hole shallow muffin tin with paper cases. Put the butter, sugar, flour, milk, vanilla essence and eggs in a bowl and beat with an electric beater on a low speed for 2 minutes, or until well mixed. Increase the speed and beat for another 2 minutes, or until smooth and pale.
Divide the mixture evenly among the cases and bake for 20 minutes, or until cooked and golden. Transfer to a wire rack to cool completely.
Using a small sharp knife, cut shallow rounds from the top of each cake. Cut these in half. Spoon ½ tablespoon cream into the hole in each cake, then top with a teaspoon of jam. Position two halves of the cake tops in the jam to resemble butterfly wings. Dust the cakes with icing sugar before serving.

Tennessee white fruit cake

SERVES 10–12

INGREDIENTS:

1 large coconut (grated)
450g/1lb candied pineapple (chopped)
450g/1lb sultanas (chopped)
450g/1lb red glacé cherries (chopped)
250g/9oz green glacé cherries
(chopped)
250g/9oz candied citron peel (chopped)
500g/1lb 2oz ground almonds
450g/1lb ground pecans

350g/12oz flour
500g/1lb 2oz caster sugar
350g/12oz butter
7 eggs
75ml/3fl oz buttermilk
½ teaspoon bicarbonate of soda
Pinch of salt
200ml/7fl oz whisky
Juice of 1 large orange

- Preheat the oven to 140°C/275°F/Gas mark 1. Butter a 23cm/9in cake tin and line it with 2 layers of buttered baking parchment.
- Dredge the coconut, fruit and ground nuts with 225g/8oz flour. Cream the sugar and butter together until the mixture is pale and fluffy and beat in the eggs, one at a time. Mix well after each addition. Beat in the buttermilk, bicarbonate of soda, salt and the remaining flour and mix well. Add the whisky and orange juice and stir well. Lastly, fold in the fruit and nuts.
- Pour the cake mixture to within 5cm/2in of the top and place 2 layers of baking parchment over the top.
- Bake in the oven for 3 hours. For the last hour of baking remove the parchment.

Spiced banana muffins

SERVES 4–6

INGREDIENTS:

75g/3oz plain wholemeal flour
50g/2oz plain white flour
2 teaspoons baking powder
Pinch of salt
1 teaspoon mixed spice
50g/2oz demerara sugar
50g/2oz margarine
1 egg (beaten)

150ml/¼pt milk
Grated zest of 1 orange
1 ripe banana
25g/1oz porridge oats
25g/1oz chopped hazelnuts

Preheat the oven to 200°C/400°F/Gas mark 6. Line a 12-hole muffin tin with paper cases. Sift together both flours, the baking powder, salt and mixed spice into a bowl, then tip the bran remaining in the sieve into the bowl. Stir in the sugar.

Melt the margarine and pour it into a mixing bowl. Leave to cool slightly, then beat in the egg, milk and grated orange zest.

Gently fold in the dry ingredients. Mash the banana with a fork, then stir it gently into the mixture, being careful not to over mix.

Spoon the mixture into the paper cases. Combine the oats and hazelnuts and spread a little of the mixture over each muffin.

Bake for 20 minutes until the muffins are well risen and golden. Transfer to a wire rack and serve warm or cold.

Fruit salad cake

SERVES 6-8

INGREDIENTS:

175g/6oz roughly chopped dried fruit salad mixture
250ml/9fl oz hot tea
Butter for greasing
225g/8oz wholemeal self-raising flour

1 teaspoon grated nutmeg
50g/2oz muscovado sugar
3 tablespoons sunflower oil
75ml/3fl oz skimmed milk
Demerara sugar to sprinkle

Soak the dried fruits in the tea for several hours or overnight. Drain and reserve the liquid.

Preheat the oven to 180°C/350°F/Gas mark 4. Grease an 18cm/7in round cake tin and line the base with non-stick baking parchment.

Sift the flour into a bowl with the nutmeg. Stir in the muscovado sugar, fruit salad mixture and tea. Add the oil and milk and mix well.

Spoon the mixture into the prepared tin and sprinkle with Demerara sugar. Bake for 50 to 55 minutes or until firm. Turn out and cool on a wire rack.

Lemon & saffron cake

SERVES 8-10

INGREDIENTS:

*175g/6oz butter (softened, plus extra
for greasing)*
Grated zest and juice of 1½ lemons
275g/10oz caster sugar
5 large eggs (separated)
50g/2oz ground almonds
275g/10oz self-raising flour (sifted)

For the syrup:
150ml/¼pt lemon juice
350g/12oz caster sugar
Large pinch of saffron
300ml/½pt water
*Crème fraîche or Mascarpone cheese,
to serve*

- Preheat the oven to 170°C/325°F/Gas mark 3. Grease a 23cm/9in cake tin and line with baking parchment.
- In a large mixing bowl, beat together the butter, lemon zest and sugar until thoroughly combined, then mix in the lemon juice, a tablespoon at a time. Beat in the egg yolks together with the ground almonds, then fold in the flour.
- Whisk the egg whites in a large bowl until soft peaks form. Stir a quarter of the egg whites into the butter mixture, then fold in the remainder with 2 tablespoons cold water.
- Pour the mixture into the prepared cake tin and smooth the top.
- Bake for 50 to 60 minutes or until the cake is cooked in the centre. Leave the cake in the tin and allow to cool for 30 minutes.
- To make the syrup, put the lemon juice, sugar, saffron and water into a heavy-based pan. Dissolve the sugar over a low heat, then bring to the boil. Set aside until the cake is cool. Drizzle the syrup over the cake and leave to soak for 30 minutes. Serve with crème fraîche or Mascarpone cheese.

Chocolate roulade

SERVES 6

INGREDIENTS:

150g/5oz dark chocolate
2 tablespoons water
6 eggs
175g/6oz caster sugar
25g/1oz plain flour

7g/¼oz cocoa powder
Icing sugar for dusting

For the filling:
300ml/½pt double cream (whisked)
75g/3oz strawberries (sliced)

- Preheat the oven to 200°C/400°F/Gas mark 6. Line a 38 x 25cm/15 x 10in Swiss roll tin with baking parchment.
- In a small saucepan, melt the chocolate in the water, stirring constantly over a medium heat. Leave to cool slightly.
- Place the eggs and sugar in a bowl and whisk for 10 minutes or until the mixture is pale and foamy. Whisk in the chocolate in a thin stream. Sift the flour and cocoa together and fold into the mixture. Pour into the tin and level the top.
- Bake in the oven for 12 minutes. Dust a sheet of baking parchment with a little icing sugar, turn the roulade on to it and peel off the lining parchment. Roll up the roulade with the fresh paper inside. Place on a wire rack, cover with a damp tea towel and leave to cool.
- Unroll the roulade and spread with the cream. Scatter with the strawberries and re-roll. Place on a plate and dust with icing sugar. Serve sliced.

Rich fruit cake

SERVES 8-10

INGREDIENTS:

450g/1lb sultanas
375g/13oz raisins (chopped)
225g/8oz currants
225g/8oz glacé cherries (quartered)
250ml/9fl oz brandy (plus 1 tablespoon to glaze)
225g/8oz butter
200g/7oz demerara sugar

2 tablespoons apricot jam
2 tablespoons treacle
1 tablespoon grated lemon zest
4 eggs
300g/11oz plain flour (sifted)
1 teaspoon ground ginger
1 teaspoon mixed spice
1 teaspoon ground cinnamon

- Put the sultanas, raisins, currants and cherries in a bowl with the brandy and soak overnight.
- Preheat the oven to 150°C/300°F/Gas mark 2. Lightly grease and line a deep 23cm/9in round cake tin.
- Beat the butter and sugar in a large bowl with an electric beater to just combine.
- Beat in the jam, treacle and lemon zest. Add the eggs, one at a time, beating after each addition.
- Stir the fruit, flour and spices alternately into the mixture.
- Spoon into the tin and smooth the surface. Tap the tin on the bench to remove any air bubbles. Level the surface with wet hands.
- Bake for 3 to 3¼ hours. Brush the surface with the extra tablespoon of brandy. Cover the top of the cake with baking parchment and wrap in a tea towel. Cool completely in the tin.

Strawberry shortcake

SERVES 4

INGREDIENTS:

450g/1lb strawberries (sliced)
¼ teaspoon honey
2 teaspoons orange juice
50g/2oz caster sugar
450g/1lb flour
4 tablespoons baking powder

½ teaspoon salt
Grated zest of 1 orange
50g/2oz butter
50g/2oz solid shortening
100g/4oz sour cream
600ml/1pt whipping cream

- Preheat the oven to 200°C/400°F/Gas mark 6.
- Combine the strawberries, honey and orange juice in a mixing bowl and leave to stand at room temperature for 1 hour.
- Sift the sugar, flour, baking powder and salt together into a medium-sized bowl. Add the orange zest, butter and shortening and work into the flour mixture thoroughly.
- Lightly mix in the sour cream with a fork to form a soft dough. Roll the dough out 2.5cm/1in thick on a lightly floured board and cut into 4 even circles. Place on a baking tray and bake in the oven for about 20 minutes or until golden.
- To serve, top with berry mixture. Whip the cream into soft peaks and serve with the shortcake.

Plum cake

SERVES 10-12

INGREDIENTS:

450g/1lb butter
450g/1lb brown sugar
12 eggs
450g/1lb plain white flour
225g/8oz ground almonds
450g/1lb sultanas

450g/1lb raisins
450g/1lb currants
225g/8oz mixed peel
Grated zest and juice of 1 lemon
175ml/6fl oz whisky

- Preheat the oven to 180°C/350°F/Gas mark 4. Line a 30cm/12in round cake tin carefully with baking parchment.
- Cream the butter in a large bowl. Add the sugar and beat until soft and light. Add the eggs one at a time, beating well between each one.
- Mix half the flour and the almonds with the fruit and peel.

- Stir the other half of the flour into the cake mixture, then carefully stir in the fruit with the lemon juice and zest and mix thoroughly.
- Pour the cake mixture into the tin, smooth the top and bake for 2 hours. Allow the cake to cool in the tin. Poke holes in the cake with a skewer and pour the whisky over it.

Creole Christmas cake

SERVES 16–20

INGREDIENTS:

175g/6oz prunes (roughly chopped)
175g/6oz raisins
175g/6oz currants
100g/4oz glacé cherries (halved)
100g/4oz candied peel (chopped)
250ml/9fl oz dark rum
175g/6oz butter (plus extra for greasing)
175g/6oz dark molasses sugar (sieved)
4 medium eggs (beaten)
200g/7oz self-raising flour

3 tablespoons molasses
1 tablespoon vanilla essence
50g/2oz root ginger (peeled and chopped)

For the topping:
450g/1lb icing sugar (sifted)
3 tablespoon glucose syrup
50g/2oz butter (softened)
3 tablespoons dark rum
25g/1oz dried cranberries to decorate

- Put the prunes, raisins, currants, cherries and peel in a lidded container and add the rum. Cover and leave to stand for at least 24 hours, stirring occasionally until most of the rum is absorbed.
- Preheat the oven to 150°C/300°F/Gas mark 2. Grease and line an 18cm/7in round cake tin with baking parchment.
- Using a slotted spoon, drain and weigh out 450g/1lb of the soaked fruit. Transfer to a blender or food processor and blend to a thick purée.
- Beat together the butter and sugar until creamy. Beat in the eggs, a little at a time, adding some of the flour if the mixture starts to curdle. Add the remaining fruit and any rum juices to the bowl along with the fruit purée, molasses, vanilla essence, ginger and remaining flour. Using a large metal spoon, gently fold the ingredients together until evenly combined.
- Turn into the prepared tin and bake in the oven for 3 hours or until firm. Leave to cool in the tin.
- To decorate the cake, put the icing sugar in a bowl and add the glucose syrup, butter and rum. Beat with an electric whisk until the mixture is smooth, creamy and softly peaking.
- Put the cake on a flat serving plate and swirl the icing over the top and sides using a palette knife. Scatter the cranberries over the top.

Molasses cake

SERVES 8–10

INGREDIENTS:

1.1kg/2½lb plain flour
250g/9oz butter (plus extra for greasing)
250g/9oz sugar
2 teaspoons ground ginger

1 tablespoon bicarbonate of soda
3 tablespoons warm water
225ml/8fl oz sour milk
450g/1lb molasses

- Preheat the oven to 190°C/375°F/Gas mark 5. Grease a 23cm/9in cake tin.
- Put the flour in a large basin and rub in the butter until the mixture is quite smooth, then mix in the sugar and the ginger.
- Dissolve the bicarbonate of soda in the warm water and stir the sour milk and molasses.
- Add to the mixture to make a fairly sticky dough.
- Work the dough thoroughly. Place in the prepared cake tin and bake in the oven for 50 minutes. Leave to cool in the tin for 30 minutes.

Cinnamon sugar buns

SERVES 4–8

INGREDIENTS:

300g/11oz pizza base mix
200ml/7fl oz hot water
50g/2oz butter (melted, plus extra for greasing)

100g/4oz brown sugar
1½ teaspoons ground cinnamon
75g/3oz flaked almonds
2 tablespoons golden syrup (warmed)

- Put the pizza base mix into a bowl, add the hot water and mix to form a dough.
- Knead thoroughly on a lightly floured surface for 5 minutes, until smooth and elastic.
- Roll out the dough on a lightly floured surface to form a rectangle 35 x 23cm/ 14 x 9in. Brush all over with some of the melted butter, reserving a little for later. Mix the sugar with half the cinnamon and two-thirds of the almonds. Sprinkle over the dough.
- Starting from a long side, roll up like a Swiss roll. Damp the edge with water and press down firmly to seal the roll. Cut the roll into 8 equal slices. Put the slices flat and push down with the palm of your hand to form neat pinwheels.

- Generously butter a 23cm/9in round sandwich tin and coat with a little of the remaining sugar and cinnamon. Arrange slices of the roll in the tin. Brush all over with the remaining butter and sprinkle with the remaining cinnamon sugar and flaked almonds.
- Cover with a lightly oiled polythene bag and leave to prove in a warm place until doubled in size. Preheat the oven to 190°C/375°F/Gas mark 5. Bake in the oven for 25 minutes. Drizzle with the warmed golden syrup while still hot.
- Stand on a wire rack to cool. Serve hot or cold.

Chocolate Swiss roll

SERVES 6

INGREDIENTS:

Butter for greasing
3 eggs
100g/4oz caster sugar
25g/1oz plain flour
15g/¹/₂oz cocoa powder

For the filling:
250ml/9fl oz cream
1 tablespoon icing sugar (plus extra for dusting)
¹/₂ teaspoon vanilla essence

- Preheat the oven to 200°C/400°F/Gas mark 6. Lightly grease the base and sides of a 38 x 25cm/15 x 10in Swiss roll tin. Line with baking parchment, extending over the 2 long sides.
- Beat the eggs and 75g/3oz caster sugar in a small bowl with an electric beater until thick and creamy. Sift together the flour and cocoa and, using a metal spoon, gently fold into the mixture.
- Spread the mixture into the tin and smooth the surface. Bake for 10 to 12 minutes, or until the cake is just set.
- Place a tea towel on a work surface, cover with baking parchment and sprinkle with the remaining caster sugar. When the cake is cooked, turn it out immediately on to the sugar. Roll the cake up from the short side, rolling so the parchment is on the inside. Stand the rolled cake on a wire rack for 5 minutes, then carefully unroll and allow the cake to cool to room temperature. Trim the ends with a knife.
- Beat the cream, icing sugar and vanilla essence until stiff peaks form. Spread the cream over the cooled cake, leaving a 1cm/¹/₂in border all around. Re-roll the cake, using the paper as a guide. Place the roll, seam-side down, on a tray.
- Refrigerate, covered, for 30 minutes. Lightly dust with icing sugar and serve sliced.

Norwegian apple cake

SERVES 12

INGREDIENTS:

4 large Bramley apples
Juice of ½ lemon
3 eggs
250g/9oz caster sugar
150g/5oz butter (plus more
for greasing)
200ml/7fl oz single cream

200g/7oz plain flour (plus more
for dusting)
3 teaspoons baking powder

- Preheat the oven to 200°C/400°F/Gas mark 6. Butter a 30 x 20cm/12 x 8in roasting tin, dust with flour and set aside.
- Peel and core the apples, cut into slices and sprinkle with the lemon juice.
- Whisk the eggs with 225g/8oz sugar until the mixture creams and thickens. Put the butter with the cream in a pan and bring to the boil. Pour this into the egg mixture while whisking. Sift in the flour and baking powder and fold in carefully with the whisk to make sure there are no lumps.
- Pour this batter into the prepared tin, then arrange the apple slices overlapping on the top. Sprinkle the remaining caster sugar over the top and bake for 25 minutes, when it is golden brown around the edges. Leave to cool in the tin.

Caramel apple sauce cake

SERVES 8–10

INGREDIENTS:

50g/2oz butter
150g/5oz demerara sugar
150ml/¼pt apple sauce
2 eggs
225g/8oz flour
1 teaspoon ground cinnamon

½ teaspoon ground nutmeg
¾ teaspoon baking powder
¼ teaspoon salt
100g/4oz raisins
100g/4oz chopped pecan nuts

- Preheat the oven to 180°C/350°F/Gas mark 4. Grease a 20cm/8in square baking tin.
- Melt the butter and sugar in a medium-sized saucepan. Remove from the heat and stir in the apple sauce. Whisk in the eggs until well blended.
- In a mixing bowl, stir or sift together the flour, cinnamon, nutmeg, baking

powder and salt. Stir in the raisins and pecan nuts. Add the dry ingredients to the saucepan and stir or whisk until just blended.

- Pour the batter into the tin and bake in the centre of the oven for 25 minutes until the top springs back when lightly touched. Leave to cool in the tin on a wire rack for at least 10 minutes before cutting into squares.

Children's birthday cake

SERVES 10–12

INGREDIENTS:

275g/10oz butter (plus extra for greasing)
275g/10oz caster sugar

5 eggs
350g/12oz self-raising flour
Grated zest of 2 oranges

- Preheat the oven to 160°C/325°F/Gas mark 3. Grease a 3.6 litre/6pt ovenproof glass mixing bowl and line the base with baking parchment.
- Beat together the butter, sugar, eggs, flour and orange zest. Turn into the bowl and level the surface. Bake for 1 hour 10 minutes until just firm. Loosen from the bowl with a knife, then turn out and leave to cool on a wire rack.
- This is the perfect base cake for brightly coloured icing for a children's birthday.

Banana & apricot Chelsea buns

SERVES 9

INGREDIENTS:

175ml/6fl oz warm skimmed milk
1 teaspoon dried yeast
225g/8oz plain flour
2 teaspoon mixed spice
1/2 teaspoon salt
50g/2oz caster sugar
25g/1oz margarine (softened, plus extra for greasing)
1 egg

For the filling:
1 large banana
175g/6oz ready-to-eat dried apricots
2 teaspoons muscovado sugar

For the glaze:
25g/1oz caster sugar
2 tablespoons water

→

←

- Lightly grease an 18cm/7in square tin.
- Put the warm milk in a jug and sprinkle the yeast on top. Mix well and leave for 30 minutes.
- Sift the flour, spice and salt into a mixing bowl. Stir in the caster sugar, rub in the margarine, then stir in the yeast mixture and the egg. Gradually mix in the flour to make a soft dough, adding extra milk if needed.
- Turn out the dough onto a floured surface and knead for 5 minutes until smooth and elastic. Return the dough to the bowl, cover with a damp tea towel and leave in a warm place for about 2 hours, until doubled in bulk.
- To prepare the filling, mash the banana in a bowl. Using scissors, snip the apricots into pieces, then stir into the banana with the sugar.
- Knead the dough on a floured surface for 2 minutes, then roll out to a 30 x 23cm/12 x 9in rectangle. Spread the banana and apricot filling over the dough and roll up lengthways, like a Swiss roll.
- Cut the roll into 9 buns. Place, cut side down, in the tin. Cover and leave to rise for 30 minutes. Preheat the oven to 200°C/400°F/Gas mark 6 and bake for 20 to 25 minutes.
- To make the glaze, mix the caster sugar and water in a small saucepan. Heat, stirring, until dissolved, then boil for 2 minutes. Brush the glaze over the buns while still hot.

Chocolate & banana roll

SERVES 6

INGREDIENTS:

25g/1oz cocoa powder (sifted)	*250g/9oz Mascarpone cheese*
150ml/¼pt milk	*1 tablespoon maple syrup*
4 medium eggs (separated)	*3 tablespoons double cream*
100g/4oz caster sugar (plus 2	*1 banana (sliced)*
tablespoons for dusting)	*1 teaspoon vanilla essence*

- Line a 33 x 23cm/13 x 9in Swiss roll tin with baking parchment.
- Mix the cocoa powder with 3 tablespoons milk to form a paste. Heat the remaining milk in a small pan, then slowly pour on to the cocoa paste and stir together to combine evenly. Cool for 10 minutes.
- Preheat the oven to 180°C/350°F/Gas mark 4.
- Whisk the egg yolks with the sugar in a freestanding mixer until pale, thickened and mousse-like. Gradually mix in the cooling chocolate milk.
- Whisk the egg whites in a bowl until they form stiff peaks. Gently fold a third into the chocolate mixture, to loosen slightly, then fold in the remainder.
- Turn into the prepared Swiss roll tin and bake for 25 minutes until the mixture

has risen and is just firm to the touch. Turn out on to a sheet of baking parchment dusted with 2 tablespoons caster sugar and remove the baking parchment lining. Cover with a warm damp tea towel to prevent the sponge from drying out.

Put the Mascarpone into a bowl and stir in the maple syrup and cream. Put the banana slices in a small bowl, pour on the vanilla essence and stir to mix. Remove the tea towel from the chocolate sponge and, using a palette knife, spread half the Mascarpone cream over the sponge. Scatter the banana on top. Starting at the shortest end, roll up the chocolate sponge. Slide on to the serving plate and serve in slices with the rest of the Mascarpone cream.

Orange pecan crown cake

SERVES 8

INGREDIENTS:

75g/3oz butter (softened, plus extra for greasing)
100g/4oz caster sugar
1 egg
½ teaspoon vanilla essence
100g/4oz plain flour (sifted)
½ teaspoon baking powder
½ teaspoon bicarbonate of soda
Pinch of salt
75ml/3fl oz buttermilk

Grated zest of 1 large orange
75g/3oz finely chopped stoned dates (rolled in 2 tablespoons flour)
75g/3oz pecan nuts (finely chopped)
Icing sugar (sifted)

For the rum syrup:
175ml/6fl oz orange juice
50g/2oz sugar
2 tablespoons rum

- Preheat the oven to 180°C/350°F/Gas mark 4.
- In a mixing bowl, cream together the butter and sugar thoroughly. Add the egg and vanilla and beat until the mixture is light and fluffy.
- Sift together the flour, baking powder, bicarbonate of soda and salt, then beat the flour mixture into the creamed mixture alternately with the buttermilk. Stir in the orange zest.
- Mix together the dates and pecans. Add them to the batter and mix well.
- Turn the batter into a greased deep 20cm/8in cake tin and bake in the oven for 50 minutes.
- With a skewer, poke several holes down through the cake to the bottom of the cake tin.
- Stir together the syrup ingredients, then slowly spoon the syrup over the warm cake, letting it soak in.
- When cool, cover or wrap tightly and allow the cake to stand for 2 to 3 hours before serving.

Almond cake

SERVES 8

INGREDIENTS:

175g/6oz almonds (blanched)
Grated zest of 1 lemon
3 eggs (lightly beaten)
175g/6oz plain flour

175g/6oz butter (plus extra
for greasing)
175g/6oz granulated sugar

- Preheat the oven to 170°C/325°F/Gas mark 3. Grease a 23cm/9in tart tin.
- Pound the almonds in a large mortar with the lemon zest. Add the remaining ingredients gradually, pounding them together to form a thick paste.
- Spread the paste evenly into the prepared tart tin and bake in the oven for 1 hour, or until the cake is golden on top.

Wild strawberry sponge

SERVES 8

INGREDIENTS:

Butter for greasing
150g/5oz caster sugar (plus extra for
dusting)
5 eggs
150g/5oz plain flour

For the topping:
350ml/12fl oz double cream
450g/1lb wild strawberries

- Preheat the oven to 190°C/375°F/Gas mark 5. Line the base and sides of a 23 x 30cm/9 x 12in Swiss roll tin with baking parchment. Brush the paper with melted butter and dust with caster sugar.
- Put the caster sugar and eggs into a heatproof bowl over a saucepan of simmering water. Whisk the mixture until it is light and fluffy. Take off the heat and continue to whisk until the mixture is cool again. Sieve in about one-third of the flour at a time and fold it into the mousse using a large metal spoon.
- Pour the mixture gently into the tin. Bake in the oven for 12 to 15 minutes, or until it feels firm in the centre.
- Lay a piece of baking parchment on a work surface and sprinkle with the extra caster sugar.
- Turn the cake out on to the paper. Remove the lining parchment from the cake and allow to cool.

For the topping, whisk the cream until softly whipped. When the cake is cold, spread whipped cream on top, sprinkle with wild strawberries and serve.

Apple cinnamon muffins

SERVES 6-12

INGREDIENTS:

400g/14oz apple sauce
275g/10oz self-raising flour
2 teaspoon ground cinnamon
100g/4oz demerara sugar
350ml/12fl oz milk

2 eggs
1 teaspoon vanilla essence
150g/5oz butter (melted, then cooled)
50g/2oz walnuts (finely chopped)

Preheat the oven to 200°C/400°F/Gas mark 6. Lightly grease a 12-hole muffin tin.
Place the apple sauce in a bowl and break up with a knife.
Sift the flour and cinnamon into a separate bowl and add the sugar. Make a well in the centre. Whisk together the milk, eggs and vanilla essence in a jug and pour into the well. Add the melted butter.
Fold the mixture gently with a wooden spoon until just combined. Add the apple sauce and gently stir through. Do not over mix – the batter should be lumpy.
Fill each muffin hole in the tray with the mixture. Bake for 20 to 25 minutes.
Allow to cool in the tray for a few minutes before removing.

White truffle cake

SERVES 12

INGREDIENTS:

50g/2oz white chocolate
2 eggs
50g/2oz caster sugar
50g/2oz tablespoons plain flour (sifted)

For the truffle topping:
300ml/1/2pt double cream
350g/12oz white chocolate (broken into pieces)
250g/9oz fromage frais
Cocoa powder for dusting

Preheat the oven to 180°C/350°F/Gas mark 4. Grease a 20cm/8in round springform tin and line the base with baking parchment.
In a heatproof bowl set over a pan of simmering water, melt the white chocolate.

→

←

- Whisk the eggs and sugar in a mixing bowl for 10 minutes, or until very light and foamy. Fold in the flour with a metal spoon. Then fold in the melted white chocolate.
- Pour the mixture into the tin and bake in the oven for 25 minutes, or until springy to the touch. Leave to cool slightly, then transfer to a wire rack to cool completely. Wash and dry the cake tin and return the cold cake to it.
- To make the topping, place the cream in a pan and bring to the boil, stirring to prevent it from sticking to the bottom of the pan. Cool slightly, then add the white chocolate pieces and stir until melted and combined. Remove from the heat and set aside until almost cool, stirring, then stir in the fromage frais. Pour the mixture on top of the cake and chill for 2 hours.
- Remove the cake from the tin and transfer to the serving plate. Dust with cocoa powder and serve.

Dundee cake

SERVES 10

INGREDIENTS:

175g/6oz butter
175g/6oz caster sugar
4 eggs
50g/2oz ground almonds
300g/11oz self-raising flour
½ teaspoon salt
1 teaspoon baking powder

100g/4oz currants
100g/4oz sultanas
100g/4oz raisins
50g/2oz candied mixed peel (chopped)
25g/1oz whole almonds (blanched and split)

- Preheat the oven to 240°C/475°F/Gas mark 9. Line a 20cm/8in cake tin with baking parchment.
- Beat the butter and sugar to a light, fluffy cream and then beat in the eggs, one at a time, along with the ground almonds.
- Sift the flour with the salt and baking powder and gradually add it to the creamed mixture along with the fruit and peel. Put the mixture in the prepared cake tin, smooth it over and arrange the split almonds on top.
- Place in the oven on the middle shelf. Immediately reduce the heat to 170°C/325°F/Gas mark 3 and bake the cake for 1½ hours.

Neapolitan ribbon cake

SERVES 4

INGREDIENTS:

600g/1¼lb sponge cake mix
Yellow, red and green food colouring

100g/4oz apple sauce
50ml/2fl oz crème de cacao liqueur

Preheat the oven to 180°C/350°F/Gas mark 4. Grease 3 x 23cm/9in square sandwich cake tins.
Make up the cake mix according to the directions and divide into three. Colour one portion yellow, one pink and one green.
Pour into the prepared cake tins and bake for 15 minutes, or until springy. Loosen and turn out on to wire racks to cool completely.
Cut each layer in half crossways through the centre.
Combine the apple sauce and crème de cacao in a small saucepan and heat slowly.
To assemble the cake, place one green strip on to baking parchment. Spoon some apple syrup over. Top with a yellow strip, and spoon apple sauce over. Repeat with the remaining cake strips and apple sauce.

Peach Swiss roll

SERVES 6-8

INGREDIENTS:

3 eggs
100g/4oz caster sugar
75g/3oz plain flour (sifted)

1 tablespoon boiling water
100g/4oz peach jam or puréed peaches

Preheat the oven to 200°C/400°C/Gas mark 6. Grease a 30 x 20cm/12 x 8in Swiss roll tin and line with baking parchment.
Combine the eggs and sugar in a bowl. Beat with a hand-held electric whisk until thick and mousse-like.
Carefully fold in the flour with a large metal spoon, then add the boiling water in the same way.
Spoon into the prepared tin, spread evenly to the edges and bake for 10 to 12 minutes until the cake springs back when lightly pressed.
Spread a sheet of baking parchment on a flat surface, sprinkle it with caster sugar, then invert the cake on top. Peel off the lining parchment.

→

←
- Neatly trim the edges of the cake.
- Spread the cake with the peach jam or puréed peaches and roll up quickly. Hold in position for a minute, ensuring the join is underneath. Cool on a wire rack.

Banana cake

SERVES 12

INGREDIENTS:

Butter for greasing
475g/1lb 1oz plain flour
1 tablespoon baking powder
½ teaspoon salt
50ml/2fl oz vegetable oil
2 eggs

125ml/4fl oz milk
1 teaspoon vanilla essence
225g/8oz bananas (mashed)
2 tablespoons caster sugar
225g/8oz vanilla yogurt

- Preheat the oven to 180°C/350°F/Gas mark 4. Grease 2 x 20cm/8in round cake tins.
- Sift together the dry ingredients into a large mixing bowl.
- Blend the oil, eggs, milk and vanilla essence until smooth in a separate bowl, then stir in the bananas. Add to the dry ingredients and stir well.
- Pour equal amounts into the prepared tins. Bake in the oven for 20 minutes, then cool completely on a wire rack. Sprinkle with caster sugar.
- Spread the yogurt on one layer and use to sandwich the cakes together.

Raspberry & lavender pavlova

SERVES 8

INGREDIENTS:

3 egg whites
200g/7oz lavender sugar
1 teaspoon cornflour
1 teaspoon raspberry vinegar

300ml/½pt Greek yogurt
450g/1lb fresh raspberries
150ml/¼pt double cream

- Draw a 23cm/9in oval on a piece of non-stick baking parchment and place on a baking tray. Preheat the oven to 180°C/350°F/Gas mark 4.

To make the meringue, whisk the egg whites in a large bowl until very stiff. Add 50g/2oz lavender sugar and whisk until stiff. Add the remaining sugar, reserving 15g/¹/₂oz for the topping, and whisk again until the meringue forms soft peaks. Fold in the cornflour and vinegar. Pile or pipe the meringue into the oval marked on the baking tray. Make a dip in the middle to hold the filling. Bake in the oven for 5 minutes, then lower the heat to 130°C/250°F/Gas mark ¹/₂ for a further 45 to 50 minutes.

Leave to cool slightly, then carefully peel off the paper. When the meringue is completely cold, whip the cream with the remaining sugar until it just holds its shape, then fold in the yogurt. Roughly crush half of the raspberries and fold into the cream mixture. Pile on top of the pavlova.

Push the remaining raspberries through a sieve and drizzle over the pavlova.

Chocolate & coconut roulade

SERVES 8

INGREDIENTS:

175g/6oz dark chocolate (broken into pieces)
5 eggs (separated)
175g/6oz caster sugar (plus extra for dusting)
1 tablespoon water

15g/¹/₂oz (sifted)
300ml/¹/₂pt double cream
50g/2oz creamed coconut (finely chopped)
25g/1oz flaked coconut (toasted)

Preheat the oven to 180°C/350°F/Gas mark 4. Grease a 33 x 23cm/13 x 9in Swiss roll tin and line with greaseproof paper.

Melt 100g/4oz chocolate in a heatproof bowl set over a saucepan of simmering water. Leave the chocolate to cool.

Whisk the egg yolks with the sugar until pale and fluffy. Add the water, melted chocolate and cocoa and whisk well to combine. Stiffly whisk the egg whites and lightly fold into the mixture. Turn the mixture into the prepared tin and level the surface. Bake for 20 minutes, until well risen and firm to the touch. Remove from the oven, leave in the tin and cover with a sheet of greaseproof paper and a damp tea towel. Leave at room temperature overnight.

The next day, dust a large sheet of greaseproof paper with caster sugar. Turn the cake out on to the paper and remove the lining paper.

Stiffly whip the cream and fold in the creamed coconut. Spread half of the cream over the chocolate mixture and roll up, like a Swiss roll.

Cover the roll with the remaining coconut cream and arrange the toasted coconut down the centre. Melt the remaining chocolate and drizzle over the roll. Leave to set before serving.

Brandied chocolate cake

SERVES 8-10

INGREDIENTS:

100g/4oz dark chocolate (broken into small pieces)
2 tablespoons strong black coffee
4 eggs
100g/4oz caster sugar

100g/4oz plain flour (sifted)
Butter for greasing
4 tablespoons brandy
Whipped cream or ice-cream, to serve

- Preheat the oven to 180°C/350°F/Gas mark 4. Grease a 20cm/8in springform tin.
- Melt the chocolate in a heatproof bowl set over a pan of simmering water. Stir in the coffee and put aside until cooled.
- Beat the eggs, gradually beat in the sugar and continue beating until soft and creamy. Fold in the flour alternately with the cooled chocolate mixture.
- Turn into the prepared tin and bake in the oven for 30 to 35 minutes. Leave in the tin to cool for 10 minutes before removing. While the cake is still warm, sprinkle brandy over and then chill overnight.
- Serve with whipped cream or ice-cream.

Meringue cake with peaches

SERVES 8

INGREDIENTS:

100g/4oz butter (plus extra for greasing)
300g/11oz sugar
4 eggs (separated)
4 tablespoons milk
½ teaspoon vanilla essence
100g/4oz flour (sifted with 1 teaspoon baking powder)

Pinch of salt
25g/1oz shelled walnuts (chopped)
225ml/8fl oz double cream (whipped)
2 tablespoons icing sugar
2 peaches (peeled, stoned and diced)

- Preheat the oven to 180°C/350°F/Gas mark 4. Grease 2 x 20cm/8in sandwich tins and line the bases with baking parchment.
- In an electric mixer bowl, cream the butter, slowly add 100g/4oz sugar and beat until light and fluffy.
- Beat in the egg yolks, one at a time, then add the milk and vanilla essence.

- Add the flour, beating slowly until mixed. Continue beating for at least 2 minutes.
- Divide the batter between the 2 tins, smoothing the tops with a spatula.
- Beat the egg whites with the salt until stiff. Add the remaining sugar, a tablespoonful at a time, beating constantly. Continue to beat until the mixture is like marshmallow and feels smooth when you pinch it. Spread the meringue over the cake batter in the tins, then sprinkle 1 layer only with chopped nuts. Bake for 30 minutes.
- To assemble the cake, whip the cream and sweeten it with the icing sugar. Fold in the peaches. Place the layer without nuts meringue-side down on a serving plate. Spread with all of the peaches and cream. Place the second layer on top, nut-side up. Refrigerate for at least 20 minutes before serving.

Banana & lime cake

SERVES 10

INGREDIENTS:

Butter for greasing
300g/11oz plain flour
1 teaspoon salt
1½ teaspoons baking powder
175g/6oz muscovado sugar
1 teaspoon grated lime zest
1 medium egg (beaten)
1 medium banana (peeled and mashed
with 1 tablespoon lime juice)
150ml/¼pt natural fromage frais
100g/4oz sultanas

For the topping:
100g/4oz icing sugar
2 teaspoons lime juice
½ teaspoon lime zest (finely grated)

- Preheat the oven to 180°C/350°F/Gas mark 4. Grease and line a deep 18cm/7in round cake tin with baking parchment.
- Sift the flour, salt and baking powder into a mixing bowl and stir in the sugar and lime zest. Make a well in the centre and add the egg, banana, fromage frais and sultanas. Mix thoroughly.
- Spoon the mixture into the tin and smooth the surface. Bake for 40 to 45 minutes until firm to the touch. Leave to cool for 10 minutes, then turn out on to a wire rack.
- To make the topping, sift the icing sugar into a small bowl and mix with the lime juice to form a soft, but not too runny, icing. Stir in the finely grated lime zest.
- Drizzle the icing over the cake, letting it run down the sides.

Chocolate marshmallow cake

SERVES 6

INGREDIENTS:

75g/3oz butter (plus extra for greasing)
225g/8oz caster sugar
½ teaspoon vanilla essence
2 eggs (beaten lightly)
75g/3oz dark chocolate (broken into pieces)
150ml/¼pt buttermilk
175g/6oz self-raising flour
½ teaspoon bicarbonate of soda
Pinch of salt

For the topping:
175g/6oz white marshmallows
1 tablespoon milk
2 egg whites
2 tablespoons caster sugar
50g/2oz milk chocolate (grated, to decorate)

- Preheat the oven to 160°C/325°F/Gas mark 3. Grease an 850ml/1½pt ovenproof pudding basin.
- Cream the butter, caster sugar and vanilla essence together until very pale and fluffy, then gradually beat in the eggs.
- Melt the dark chocolate in a heatproof bowl set over a pan of simmering water.
- When the chocolate has melted, gradually stir in the buttermilk, until well combined. Remove the pan from the heat and cool slightly.
- Sift the flour, bicarbonate of soda and salt into a separate bowl.
- Add the chocolate mixture and the flour alternately to the creamed mixture, a little at a time. Spoon into the basin and smooth the surface. Bake in the oven for about 50 minutes. Turn out on to a wire rack to cool.
- To make the topping, put the marshmallows and milk in a small saucepan and heat very gently until the marshmallows have melted. Remove the pan from the heat and leave to cool.
- Whisk the egg whites until soft peaks form, then add the sugar and continue whisking until stiff peaks form. Fold the egg white into the cooled marshmallow mixture and set aside for 10 minutes.
- When the cake is cool, cover the top and sides with the marshmallow topping.
- Sprinkle with the grated milk chocolate and serve.

Cinnamon apple gâteau

SERVES 8

INGREDIENTS:

Butter for greasing
3 eggs
100g/4oz caster sugar
75g/3oz plain flour
1 teaspoon ground cinnamon

For the filling and topping:
4 large dessert apples

50ml/2fl oz clear honey
1 tablespoon water
75g/3oz sultanas
½ teaspoon ground cinnamon
350g/12oz soft cheese
50ml/2fl oz fromage frais
2 teaspoons lemon juice

- Preheat the oven to 190°C/375°F/Gas mark 5. Grease and line a 23cm/9in sandwich cake tin.
- Place the eggs and caster sugar in a bowl and beat with a hand-held electric whisk until thick and mousse-like.
- Sift the flour and cinnamon over the egg mixture and fold in with a large spoon.
- Pour into the prepared tin and bake for 25 to 30 minutes or until the cake springs back when lightly pressed. Turn the cake on to a wire rack to cool.
- To make the filling, peel, core and slice 3 apples and put them in a saucepan.
- Add half of the honey and all of the water. Cover and cook over a gentle heat for about 10 minutes. Add the sultanas and cinnamon, stir well, replace the lid and leave to cool.
- Put the soft cheese in a bowl with the remaining honey, the fromage frais and half the lemon juice. Beat until the mixture is smooth.
- Halve the cake horizontally, place the bottom half on a board and drizzle with any liquid from the apples. Spread with two-thirds of the cheese mixture, then top with the apple filling.
- Fit the other half of the cake on top. Swirl the remaining cheese mixture over the top of the sponge. Core and slice the remaining apple, sprinkle with lemon juice and use to decorate the edge of the cake.

Rhubarb cake

SERVES 8-10

INGREDIENTS:

150g/5oz butter (softened, plus extra
for greasing)
350g/12oz caster sugar
200g/7oz flour
2 teaspoons baking powder
Pinch of salt

3 eggs (lightly beaten)
Grated zest and juice of 1 lemon
4 tablespoons milk
600g/1¼ lb rhubarb (cut into
2.5cm/1in pieces)
1 teaspoon ground cinnamon

- Preheat the oven to 190°C/375°F/Gas mark 5. Grease a 20cm/8in springform cake tin.
- Cream the butter with 150g/5oz sugar until the mixture is light and fluffy. Mix together the flour, baking powder and salt. Add the flour mixture to the butter alternately with the eggs. Beat in the lemon zest and juice and lastly the milk. Put the dough into the prepared cake tin and level the top.
- Mix the rhubarb with the cinnamon and the remaining sugar and spread on top of the dough. Bake in the oven for 40 to 45 minutes, or until the rhubarb is soft and the cake has shrunk slightly from the sides of the tin. Leave the cake to cool completely in the tin.

Chocolate cake

SERVES 10

INGREDIENTS:

100g/4oz butter (softened)
100g/4oz caster sugar
50g/2oz icing sugar
2 eggs (lightly beaten)
1 teaspoon vanilla essence
75g/3oz blackberry jam
150g/5oz self-raising flour (sifted)
50g/2oz cocoa powder
1 teaspoon bicarbonate of soda

225ml/8fl oz milk

For the chocolate butter cream:
50g/2oz dark chocolate (broken into
small pieces)
25g/1oz butter
3 teaspoons double cream
3 teaspoons icing sugar (sifted)

- Preheat the oven to 180°C/350°F/Gas mark 4. Lightly grease a 20cm/8in square cake tin and line with baking parchment.

- Cream the butter and sugars in a small bowl with an electric beater until light and fluffy. Add the eggs gradually, beating thoroughly after each addition. Beat in the vanilla and jam. Transfer to a large bowl. Combine the flour, cocoa and bicarbonate of soda. Using a wooden spoon, fold the flour mixture into the butter alternately with the milk. Stir until the mixture is just combined and almost smooth.
- Pour into the prepared tin and smooth the surface. Bake for 45 minutes. Leave in the tin for 15 minutes before turning on to a wire rack to cool completely.
- For the butter cream, stir the ingredients in a small pan over a low heat until smooth and glossy. Spread over the top of the cake with a flat-bladed knife.

Orange bundt cake

SERVES 8

INGREDIENTS:

225g/8oz butter (plus extra for greasing)
450g/1lb sugar
5 eggs
3 teaspoons baking powder
¼ teaspoon salt
700g/1½lb plain flour (sifted, plus extra for dusting)

175ml/6fl oz fresh orange juice
Grated zest of 1 orange

For the glaze:
225g/8oz butter (melted)
150g/5oz sugar
75ml/3fl oz bourbon whiskey

- Preheat the oven to 180°C/350°F/Gas mark 4. Grease a 20cm/8in tin with butter and dust with flour.
- Cream the butter until fluffy. Beat in the sugar until light. Beat in the eggs, one at a time.
- Sift the baking powder, salt and flour together and add to the creamed mix alternately with the orange juice. Add the grated orange zest. Pour into the prepared tin and bake for 1 hour.
- For the glaze, heat the butter and sugar until all the sugar is dissolved. Add the bourbon, then pour the glaze over the hot cake. Leave in the tin to cool.

Marbled cheesecake

SERVES 10

INGREDIENTS:

For the base:
225g/8oz toasted oat cereal
50g/2oz toasted hazelnuts (chopped)
50g/2oz butter
25g/1oz dark chocolate

For the filling:
350g/12oz full-fat soft cheese

100g/4oz caster sugar
200ml/7fl oz thick yogurt
300ml/½pt double cream
25g/1oz powdered gelatine
3 tablespoons water
175g/6oz dark chocolate (melted)
175g/6oz white chocolate (melted)

- Place the toasted oat cereal in a plastic bag and crush with a rolling pin. Pour the crushed cereal into a mixing bowl and stir in the hazelnuts.
- Melt the butter and chocolate together over a low heat and add to the cereal mixture, stirring until well coated.
- Using the bottom of a glass, press the mixture into the base and up the sides of a 20cm/8in springform tin.
- Beat together the cheese and sugar with a wooden spoon until smooth. Beat in the yogurt. Whip the cream until it just holds its shape and fold into the mixture.
- Sprinkle the gelatine over the water in a heatproof bowl and leave to go spongy. Place over a pan of hot water and stir until dissolved. Stir into the mixture.
- Divide the mixture in half and beat the dark chocolate into one half and the white chocolate into the other. Place alternate spoonfuls of each mixture on top of the cereal base. Swirl the filling together with the tip of a knife to give a marbled effect. Level the top with a spatula. Chill for at least 2 hours to set before serving.

Swiss roll

SERVES 8

INGREDIENTS:

Butter for greasing
75g/3oz self-raising flour
3 eggs (lightly beaten)

175g/6oz caster sugar
175g/6oz strawberry jam

- Preheat the oven to 190°C/375°F/Gas mark 5. Lightly grease a shallow 30 x

25cm/12 x 10in Swiss roll tin and line the base with baking parchment, extending over the two long sides.
- Sift the flour 3 times on to baking parchment.
- Beat the eggs with an electric beater in a small bowl for 5 minutes, or until thick and pale. Add 100g/4oz sugar gradually, beating constantly until the mixture is pale and glossy.
- Transfer to a large bowl. Using a metal spoon, quickly fold in the flour.
- Spread into the tin and smooth the surface. Bake for 10 to 12 minutes, or until lightly golden and springy to touch.
- Place a clean tea towel on a work surface, cover with baking parchment, then dust with the remaining caster sugar. When the cake is cooked, turn it out immediately on to the sugar.
- Using the tea towel as a guide, carefully roll the cake up from the short side, with the paper. Stand the rolled cake on a wire rack for 5 minutes, then carefully unroll and allow the cake to cool to room temperature. Spread with the jam and re-roll. Trim the ends with a knife and serve sliced.

Sweet pumpkin cake

SERVES 16

INGREDIENTS:

Butter, for greasing
550g/1lb 4oz pumpkin (cut into wedges)
250ml/9fl oz sunflower oil
275g/10oz muscovado sugar
3 large eggs

225g/8oz self-raising flour (plus extra for dusting)
1 teaspoon bicarbonate of soda
2 teaspoons ground ginger
Vanilla ice-cream, to serve

- Preheat the oven to 200°C/400°F/Gas mark 6. Grease a 23cm/9in cake tin generously with butter and dust with flour.
- Put the pumpkin on a baking tray and roast for 40 minutes until tender.
- Remove the pumpkin from the oven and allow to cool for 15 minutes. Reduce the oven temperature to 180°C/350°F/Gas mark 4.
- Spoon out 250g/9oz of the pumpkin flesh into a blender or food processor and blend to a purée.
- Put the oil and sugar in a freestanding mixer and whisk for 2 minutes, then whisk in the eggs, one at a time.
- Add the flour, bicarbonate of soda and ginger and fold in. Add the purée and stir.
- Pour into the prepared tin and bake for 40 to 45 minutes, until the cake is shrinking from the edges. Turn out and cool on a wire rack. Serve with vanilla ice-cream.

Tangerine & chocolate cheesecake

SERVES 12

INGREDIENTS:

For the base:
100g/4oz butter (plus extra for greasing)
225g/8oz chocolate digestive biscuits (crushed)

For the filling:
8 tangerines

25g/1oz powdered gelatine
450g/1lb Mascarpone cheese
4 eggs (separated)
175g/6oz caster sugar
300ml/¹/₂pt crème fraîche
3 tablespoons Grand Marnier

- Line a 25cm/10in springform cake tin with baking parchment and lightly grease.
- Melt the butter and mix in the biscuit crumbs. Press into the base of the tin and chill for 30 minutes.
- Finely grate the zest of 2 tangerines and set aside. Squeeze the juice from 4 tangerines into a small pan, sprinkle the gelatine over and leave to soak. Remove the flesh from the membranes of the remaining tangerines, then roughly chop.
- Place the Mascarpone, egg yolks, 100g/4oz caster sugar, crème fraîche and Grand Marnier in a bowl and beat until smooth.
- Heat the gelatine slowly until it has dissolved, cool slightly, then stir into the cheese mixture. Fold in the tangerine zest and the chopped tangerines.
- Whisk the egg whites until stiff, then whisk in the remaining caster sugar. Gently fold into the cheese mixture, pour into the tin, level the surface and chill for at least 2¹/₂ hours until set.

Bramble scones

SERVES 8

INGREDIENTS:

450g/1lb self-raising flour
¹/₂ teaspoon salt
2 teaspoons baking powder
75g/3oz butter (cubed)

75g/3oz caster sugar
225g/8oz frozen blackberries
200ml/7fl oz buttermilk
1 egg (beaten)

- Preheat the oven to 220°C/425°F/Gas mark 7.
- Sift the flour, salt and baking powder together in a large bowl. Rub in the butter until the mixture resembles breadcrumbs. Stir in the sugar and the frozen blackberries.
- Stir in the buttermilk to form a firm dough. Knead very lightly and roll out on a floured surface to 2.5cm/1in thick. Using a 6.5cm/2½in cutter, stamp into rounds, being careful not to cut through the blackberries. Knead and re-roll as necessary.
- Place the scones on a greased baking tray and brush the tops with beaten egg.
- Bake in the oven for about 10 minutes, or until well risen and golden brown.
- Serve while still hot.

Rose mousse gâteau

SERVES 16

INGREDIENTS:

For the sponge:
Butter for greasing
5 eggs (separated)
150g/5oz caster sugar
75g/3oz ground almonds
25g/1oz plain flour
1 tablespoon lemon juice

For the mousse:
4 tablespoons rosewater
2 tablespoons water
4 teaspoons powdered gelatine
600ml/1pt double cream
500g/1lb 2oz fresh custard

- Preheat the oven to 180°C/350°F/Gas mark 4. Grease a 25cm/10in loose-bottomed cake tin and line with baking parchment.
- To make the sponge, whisk together the egg yolks and sugar in a bowl until pale and thickened. Gently fold in the almonds, flour and lemon juice.
- Whisk the egg whites in a separate bowl until just peaking. Gently fold a spoonful into the egg yolk mixture, then fold in the remainder. Turn into the prepared tin and bake for 20 minutes until well risen and just firm. Leave to cool in the tin for 5 minutes, then turn out on to a wire rack and cool completely.
- Wash the tin and reline the base and sides with baking parchment. Carefully halve the sponge horizontally and place the bottom half back in the tin.
- To make the mousse, place the rosewater in a heatproof bowl with the water. Sprinkle the gelatine over and set aside for 5 minutes. Set the bowl of gelatine over a pan of simmering water and stir until dissolved.
- Whip the cream until it just holds its shape. Fold the cream and the custard together. Gradually pour the gelatine into the mixture, stirring well all the time.
- Carefully pour over the sponge in the tin, then level and place the other half of the sponge on top. Chill for several hours, until the mousse has set.

Orange truffle cake

SERVES 8

INGREDIENTS:

100g/4oz cooking chocolate
100g/4oz butter (plus extra for greasing)
2 tablespoons caster sugar
4 eggs (separated)
175g/6oz plain flour
½ teaspoon baking powder
Pinch of salt

For the filling:
225g/8oz cooking chocolate
225g/8oz butter
225g/8oz icing sugar
4 tablespoons orange juice
1 teaspoon orange zest
2 tablespoons orange liqueur

- Preheat the oven to 180°C/350°F/Gas mark 4. Grease a 20cm/8in springform cake tin.
- To make the cake, melt the chocolate in a heatproof bowl set over a pan of simmering water. Remove from the heat and allow to cool slightly.
- Beat the butter with 1 tablespoon sugar until creamy, then add the egg yolks a little at a time. Add the melted chocolate, then sift the flour and baking powder over and mix in.
- Beat the egg whites with the salt until stiff and then add the remaining sugar.
- Fold gently into the mixture and pour into the prepared tin. Bake for 40 minutes, then turn out on to a wire rack to cool.
- To make the truffle filling, melt the chocolate as before and leave to cool slightly. Cream the butter and sugar until pale and thick. Add half the orange juice and all the zest. Mix in the chocolate and beat until fluffy.
- Cut the cake in half horizontally and sprinkle the remaining orange juice and the liqueur on the cut side of the bottom half. Spread the lower layer with half of the truffle filling and place the other layer on top. Spread the rest of the truffle filling over the top. Chill for 2 hours before serving.

Date & apple muffins

SERVES 6–12

INGREDIENTS:

150g/5oz self-raising wholemeal flour
150g/5oz self-raising white flour
1 teaspoon ground cinnamon
1 teaspoon baking powder
25g/1oz margarine (softened)
75g/3oz muscovado sugar
250ml/9fl oz apple juice

2 tablespoons pear and apple spread
1 egg (lightly beaten)
1 dessert apple (peeled, cored
and diced)
75g/3oz chopped dates
1 tablespoon chopped pecan nuts

- Preheat the oven to 200°C/400°F/Gas mark 6. Arrange 12 paper cake cases in a 12-hole muffin tin.
- Put the wholemeal flour in a mixing bowl. Sift in the white flour with the cinnamon and baking powder. Rub in the margarine until the mixture resembles breadcrumbs, then stir in the muscovado sugar.
- Stir a little of the apple juice into the pear and apple spread until smooth. Mix in the remaining juice, then add to the flour mixture with the egg. Add the chopped apple with the dates. Mix quickly until just combined.
- Divide the mixture among the muffin cases. Sprinkle with the pecan nuts and bake for 20 to 25 minutes until golden brown and firm in the middle.
- Transfer to a wire rack and serve while still warm.

Polish orange Easter cake

SERVES 10

INGREDIENTS:

4 oranges
300g/11oz icing sugar
500g/1lb 2oz plain flour
1 teaspoon baking powder
150g/5oz caster sugar
150g/5oz butter (plus extra for
greasing)

2 egg yolks
75g/3oz sour cream
100g/4oz almonds (blanched
and chopped)

- Preheat the oven to 180°C/350°F/Gas mark 4. Grease a 20cm/8in round cake

→

←

tin and line with baking parchment.

- Prick each orange a few times with a fork, then place the oranges in a large pan, cover them with water and bring to the boil. Cook gently for about 5 minutes, or until they begin to soften. Remove and cool the oranges, then slice them and remove the pips.
- Dissolve the icing sugar in the orange-cooking water and boil this mixture for about 10 minutes to make a syrup. Poach the orange slices in the syrup for about 10 minutes, or until the zest is tender. Cool the slices in the syrup.
- Combine the flour, baking powder and caster sugar and rub in the butter to form a crumbly mixture. Add the egg yolks and the sour cream to make a soft and workable dough. Roll out the dough, put it in the prepared tin and bake in the oven for 1 hour or until the cake is lightly coloured.
- Turn the cake out of the tin and place it on a baking tray. Arrange a layer of poached orange slices over the top, draining them of their excess syrup. Sprinkle the almonds on top. Put the cake back in the oven for a few minutes to allow the oranges to dry.

Date & ginger cake

SERVES 8

INGREDIENTS:

1/2 teaspoon bicarbonate of soda
50ml/2fl oz milk
100g/4oz butter (plus extra for greasing)
100g/4oz muscovado sugar
2 large eggs (beaten)
150g/5oz golden syrup
150g/5oz treacle

100g/4oz stoned dates (roughly chopped)
50g/2oz stem ginger in syrup (roughly chopped)
225g/8oz plain flour (sifted)
1 1/2 teaspoon ground ginger
Pinch of salt

- Preheat the oven to 150°C/300°F/Gas mark 2. Grease a 23cm/9in square cake tin and line with baking parchment.
- Stir the bicarbonate of soda into the milk.
- Beat together the butter and sugar until pale and light. Slowly add the eggs and then stir in the syrup, treacle, milk, dates and stem ginger.
- Fold in the flour, ground ginger and salt. Pour into the tin and bake for 1 hour, or until a skewer inserted into the middle comes out clean. Leave in the tin for 1 hour, then turn out on to a wire rack to cool completely.

Polish honey cake

SERVES 8

INGREDIENTS:

500g/1lb 2oz honey
500g/1lb 2oz caster sugar
250g/9oz butter
900g/2lb self-raising flour
3 eggs
3 teaspoons bicarbonate of soda
(dissolved in 125ml/4fl oz milk)

½ teaspoon salt
1 teaspoon ground cinnamon
1 teaspoon ground ginger
1 teaspoon ground cardamom
25g/1oz pecan nuts (chopped)

Gradually heat the honey, sugar and butter together almost to boiling point. Allow to cool. Working the dough with your hands, gradually add the flour, eggs, bicarbonate of soda and milk, salt and spices. Add the pecan nuts. Shape the dough into a ball, put it in a bowl and cover with a tea towel. Leave in a cool place overnight to mature.
The next day, preheat the oven to 180°C/350°F/Gas mark 4.
Divide the dough into 3 parts, roll them out and place each piece in a 20cm/8in baking tin. Bake in the oven for 40 minutes or until the cakes are slightly browned and firm to the touch.

Steamed coffee sponge

SERVES 4

INGREDIENTS:

25g/1oz margarine (plus extra for greasing)
25g/1oz brown sugar
2 eggs
50g/2oz plain flour
¾ teaspoon baking powder
175ml/6fl oz milk
1 teaspoon coffee essence

For the sauce:
300ml/½ pt milk
1 tablespoon brown sugar
1 teaspoon cocoa powder
2 tablespoons cornflour
4 tablespoons cold water

Lightly grease a 600ml/1pt pudding basin.
Cream the margarine and sugar until light and fluffy. Then beat in the eggs.
Gradually stir in the flour and baking powder and then the milk and coffee

→

←

essence to make a smooth batter.

- Spoon the mixture into the prepared pudding basin and cover with a pleated piece of baking parchment and then a pleated piece of foil, securing around the bowl with a string. Place in a steamer or large pan and half fill with boiling water
- Cover and steam for 1 to 1¼ hours, or until cooked through.
- To make the sauce, put the milk, sugar and cocoa powder in a pan and heat, stirring constantly, until the sugar dissolves. Blend the cornflour with the water to make a smooth paste and stir into the pan. Bring to the boil, stirring constantly, until thickened. Cook over a gentle heat for 1 minute.
- Turn the pudding out on to a warm plate and spoon the sauce over the top.
- Serve immediately.

Slab cake

SERVES 8

INGREDIENTS:

350g/12oz sultanas
100g/4oz Morello cherries
150g/5oz candied orange and
lemon peel
100g/4oz chopped almonds
Grated zest of 1 orange
Grated zest of 1 lemon

500g/1lb 2oz butter (softened)
500g/1lb 2oz caster sugar
9 eggs
850g/1lb 14oz plain white flour
2 teaspoons baking powder
1 teaspoon milk

- Preheat the oven to 160°C/325°F/Gas mark 3. Line the base and sides of a rectangular 25 x 35cm/10 x 14in cake tin with baking parchment.
- Mix the fruit, peel and almonds with the grated orange and lemon zest.
- In another bowl cream the butter well, add the caster sugar and continue to beat until light and pale. Whisk the eggs and beat in bit by bit, adding a little flour if the mixture shows signs of curdling.
- Stir in the flour and baking powder and finally the mixture of fruit and almonds. If it appears too stiff, add a little milk. Pour into the tin and bake in the oven for 1½ to 1¾ hours. Cool in the tin.

Peach & hazelnut gâteau

SERVES 8

INGREDIENTS:

Butter or oil for greasing
175g/6oz caster sugar (plus extra
for dusting)
75g/3oz plain flour (sifted, plus extra
for dusting)
3 eggs

Grated zest and juice of 1 lemon
75g/3oz toasted hazelnuts (ground)
300ml/½pt water
700g/1½lb medium peaches
300ml/½pt whipping cream (whipped
to stiff peaks)

- Preheat the oven to 180°C/350°F/Gas mark 4. Grease a 23cm/9in round cake tin with butter or oil, then line the base with baking parchment. Dust with a little extra caster sugar and flour.
- Place the eggs, 100g/4oz sugar and all the lemon zest in a large deep bowl. Whisk vigorously until very thick and light. Fold the sifted flour lightly into the mixture with 50g/2oz hazelnuts. Spoon the mixture into the prepared tin and level the surface.
- Bake in the oven for about 35 minutes or until firm to the touch. Turn out and cool on a wire rack.
- Make a syrup from the water, remaining sugar and 2 tablespoons lemon juice.
- Reserve 2 peaches to decorate. Skin and slice the remaining peaches and poach for 5 to 10 minutes in the sugar syrup, until tender, then drain.
- Split the gâteau into 3 layers. Spread the bottom layer with half the whipped cream and half the peaches, top with the middle third of the gateau and repeat the cream, peaches and top cake layer. Refrigerate for at least 2 hours.
- At serving time, slice the reserved peaches and use to decorate the top of the gateau with the rest of the hazelnuts.

Hazelnut meringue cake

SERVES 10

INGREDIENTS:

5 egg whites
375g/13oz caster sugar
1 teaspoon ground mixed spice
200g/7oz hazelnuts (toasted and chopped)

75g/3oz white chocolate (in small pieces)
75g/3oz plain chocolate (in small pieces)
300ml/½pt double cream (lightly whipped)
Cocoa powder for dusting

→

←

- Preheat the oven to 140°C/275°F/Gas mark 1.
- Line two baking trays with baking parchment. Draw a 23cm/9in circle on one sheet, using a plate as a guide. On the other sheet draw an 18cm/7in circle. Turn each sheet of paper over.
- To make the meringue, whisk the egg whites in a large bowl until stiff but not dry.
- Gradually whisk in 250g/9oz of the sugar, a tablespoon at a time, whisking well after each addition until the meringue is stiff and very shiny. Whisk in the spice with the last tablespoon of sugar. Carefully fold in 100g/4oz hazelnuts, and the white and plain chocolate.
- Spoon the meringue on to the baking parchment circles, then spread neatly into rounds using the guidelines. Bake for 2 to 2½ hours until dry and the undersides are firm when tapped. Turn the oven off and leave the meringues to cool in the oven.
- Put the remaining hazelnuts in a small heavy-based pan with the remaining sugar. Heat over a gentle heat until the sugar melts. Continue cooking until the mixture caramelizes to form a rich golden brown colour, then pour on to a greased baking tray. Leave to cool and harden.
- Pour the caramel mixture into a polythene bag and crush with a rolling pin until it forms coarse praline.
- Spread the double cream evenly over the large meringue and cover with the small meringue round. Sprinkle with the praline and dust the top of the cake swith cocoa powder before serving.

Chocolate chip muffins

SERVES 4-6

INGREDIENTS:

100g/4oz soft margarine	5 tablespoons milk
225g/8oz caster sugar	275g/10oz plain flour
2 large eggs	1 teaspoon bicarbonate of soda
150ml/¼pt full-fat natural yogurt	175g/6oz dark chocolate chips

- Preheat the oven to 190°C/375°F/Gas mark 5. Line a 12-hole muffin tin with paper cases.
- Place the margarine and sugar in a mixing bowl and beat with a wooden spoon until light and fluffy. Beat in the eggs, yogurt and milk until combined.
- Sift the flour and bicarbonate of soda together and add to the mixture with the chocolate chips. Stir until just blended.
- Spoon the mixture into the paper cases and bake in the oven for 25 minutes.
- Leave to cool in the tin for 5 minutes, then turn out on to a wire rack to cool.

Macadamia nut cake with rum-flavoured butter cream

SERVES 8-10

INGREDIENTS:

50g/2oz butter (softened, plus extra for greasing)
100g/4oz unsalted macadamia nuts (finely chopped)
75g/3oz plain flour
½ teaspoon baking powder
4 egg whites
Pinch of salt
100g/4oz sugar

For the butter cream:
75g/3oz butter
100g/4oz icing sugar
4 tablespoons dark rum
75g/3oz unsalted macadamia nuts (crushed in a blender or food processor)

- Preheat the oven to 190°C/375°F/Gas mark 5. Butter a deep 20cm/8in round cake tin generously and line the base with baking parchment.
- Beat the butter into the chopped nuts until the mixture is very creamy. Sift the flour with the baking powder, then add the flour to the nut mixture.
- Beat the egg whites with the salt until they form soft peaks. Sprinkle on the sugar and continue beating until the meringue holds fairly stiff peaks. Stir one quarter of the meringue into the nut mixture to lighten it, then delicately fold in the rest. Turn the batter into the prepared tin and bake in the oven for 20 to 25 minutes, until the cake has risen nicely.
- Remove the tin to a wire cooling rack. After 10 minutes, run a knife around the inside edges, unmould the cake and remove the baking parchment.
- To make the butter cream, beat the butter, sugar and 2 tablespoons rum into the nuts.
- When the cake has cooled completely, slice it in half horizontally. Sprinkle the cut sides with the remaining rum, then spread one half with one third of the butter cream. Sandwich the other layer on top and spread the top and sides of the cake with the remaining butter cream.

Potato apple cake

SERVES 2

INGREDIENTS:

450g/1lb cooked potatoes (mashed)
100g/4oz plain white flour
½ teaspoon salt
1–2 Bramley apples (peeled, cored and sliced)

25g/1oz butter (plus extra for basting)
Sprinkling of caster sugar

- Mix together the potatoes, flour and salt. Roll the potato mixture into a round about 2cm/1in thick. Divide into 4 and put a couple of layers of apple on top of two of the sections, then sandwich the other two sections on top. Pinch around the edges to seal.
- Place a non-stick frying pan over a medium heat and melt the butter. Cook the cake on both sides for about 20 minutes, until the cake is brown on both sides.
- Remove the top sections and brush the apple with butter and sprinkle with sugar.
- Replace the tops and return to the pan until the butter has melted. Remove carefully to warm plates and serve immediately.

Lemon chocolate cake

SERVES 8

INGREDIENTS:

100g/4oz butter (plus extra for greasing)
225g/8oz brown sugar
Grated zest of 1 lemon
2 eggs
75g/3oz cooking chocolate (grated)
300g/11oz self-raising flour (sifted)

Pinch of salt
100g/4oz sour cream

For the topping:
2 tablespoons icing sugar
1 tablespoon grated lemon zest

- Preheat the oven to 180°C/350°F/Gas mark 5. Grease a 23 x 13cm/9 x 5in loaf tin.
- Cream the butter, sugar and lemon zest together. Add the eggs and beat well.
- Mix in the chocolate. Sift the flour and salt together and alternately with the sour cream and beat well.
- Place in the loaf tin and sprinkle with the icing sugar and lemon zest. Bake for 50 to 60 minutes until cooked.

Orange cake

SERVES 8

INGREDIENTS:

225g/8oz self-raising flour
50g/2oz custard powder
300g/11oz caster sugar
75g/3oz butter (chopped and softened,
plus extra for greasing)
3 eggs
2 teaspoons finely grated orange zest
225ml/8fl oz orange juice

For the orange butter cream:
75g/3oz icing sugar
100g/4oz butter (softened)
1 tablespoon orange juice
1 teaspoon finely grated orange zest

- Preheat the oven to 180°C/350°F/Gas mark 4. Lightly grease a 23cm/9in round cake tin and line the base with baking parchment.
- Sift the flour and custard powder into a large bowl and add the sugar, butter, eggs, orange zest and juice. Beat with an electric beater for 4 minutes or until the mixture is smooth.
- Spoon the mixture into the tin and smooth the surface. Bake for 50 minutes, or until a skewer comes out clean when inserted into the centre of the cake.
- Leave the cake in the tin for 5 minutes before turning out on to a wire rack to cool.
- For the orange butter cream, beat all the ingredients in a small bowl with an electric beater until smooth and creamy. Spread evenly over the cooled cake.

Pistachio cake

SERVES 8–10

INGREDIENTS:

50g/2oz butter (melted, plus extra for
greasing)
50g/2oz plain flour (sifted, plus extra
for dusting)
4 eggs
100g/4oz caster sugar
50g/2oz shelled pistachio nuts (grated)
50ml/2fl oz kirsch
50g/2oz ground rice (sifted)
Grated zest of ½ lemon

For the pistachio cream:
75g/3oz shelled pistachio nuts
(blanched)
75ml/3fl oz kirsch
1 egg, plus 2 egg yolks
75g/3oz caster sugar
1 teaspoon plain flour
Pinch of salt
225ml/8fl oz milk
50g/2oz butter

$\rightarrow$

←

- Preheat the oven to 180°C/350°F/Gas mark 4. Grease a 23cm/9in cake tin with butter and dust with flour.
- Place the eggs and sugar in a heatproof bowl set over a pan of simmering water. Never letting the mixture become more than warm, whisk over a very low heat for 10 to 15 minutes, until it is very thick and light and forms a ribbon.
- Mix the pistachio nuts with the kirsch and add this paste to the egg mixture with the flour, ground rice and grated lemon zest, working with a wooden spoon until everything is thoroughly blended. Finally stir in the melted butter.
- Pour the mixture into the prepared cake tin and bake in the oven for 25 to 30 minutes. Turn the cake on to a rack to cool.
- For the cream, pound the pistachio nuts, gradually adding the kirsch. When you obtain a thin paste, transfer it to a bowl.
- Beat the egg and yolks with the sugar until the mixture whitens, add the flour and salt, whisk for 1 minute more, and add the milk. Heat this custard until it comes to the boil, then pour on to the pistachio paste, stirring until the mixture cools slightly. Stir in 25g/1oz butter.
- Slice the cake horizontally into 3 layers. Spread each layer with a quarter of the pistachio cream and stack the layers. Spread a thin layer of the cream around the sides. Heat the remaining cream slightly and incorporate the remaining butter.
- Decorate the cake with this mixture using a piping bag.

Spiced date & walnut cake

SERVES 8

INGREDIENTS:

Butter for greasing
300g/11oz wholemeal self-raising flour
2 teaspoons mixed spice
150g/5oz dates (chopped)

50g/2oz walnuts (chopped)
4 tablespoons sunflower oil
100g/4oz dark muscovado sugar
300ml/½pt skimmed milk

- Preheat the oven to 180°C/350°F/Gas mark 4. Grease and line a 900g/2lb loaf tin with baking parchment.
- Sift together the flour and spice, adding back any bran from the sieve. Stir in the dates and walnuts.
- Mix the oil, sugar and milk, then stir evenly into the dry ingredients. Spoon into the prepared tin.
- Bake in the oven for 40 to 45 minutes, or until golden brown and firm. Turn out the cake, remove the lining paper and leave to cool on a wire rack.

Almond friands

SERVES 5

INGREDIENTS:

*150g/5oz butter (plus extra
for greasing)
75g/3oz flaked almonds
50g/2oz plain flour*

*175g/6oz icing sugar (plus extra
for dusting)
5 egg whites*

- Preheat the oven to 210°C/425°F/Gas mark 7. Lightly grease 10 x 125ml/4fl oz friand tins.
- Melt the butter in a small saucepan over a medium heat, then cook for 3 to 4 minutes, or until the butter turns deep golden. Strain to remove any residue. Remove from the heat and set aside to cool until just lukewarm.
- Place the flaked almonds in a blender or food processor and process until finely ground. Transfer to a bowl and sift the flour and icing sugar into the same bowl.
- Place the egg whites in a separate bowl and lightly whisk with a fork until just combined. Add the butter to the flour mixture along with the egg whites. Mix gently with a metal spoon until all the ingredients are well combined.
- Spoon some mixture into each friand tin to fill to three-quarters. Place the tins on a baking tray and bake in the centre of the oven for 10 minutes, then reduce the heat to 180°C/350°F/Gas mark 4 and bake for another 5 minutes. Remove and leave in the tins for 5 minutes before turning out on to a wire rack to cool completely. Dust with icing sugar before serving.

Coffee almond ice-cream cake

SERVES 8

INGREDIENTS:

*Vegetable oil for greasing
350g/12oz chocolate wafer crumbs
50g/2oz butter (melted)
350g/12oz coffee ice-cream*

*350g/12oz double cream
1 teaspoon vanilla essence
350g/12oz Amaretti biscuits (crushed)
100g/4oz slivered almonds (toasted)*

→

←

- Lightly oil a 20cm/8in springform tin.
- In a bowl, stir together the crumbs and butter with a fork until the mixture is well combined. Pat the mixture on to the base of the prepared tin and 2.5cm/1in up its sides. Freeze for 30 minutes or until firm.
- Spread the ice-cream evenly on the crust and return to the freezer for 30 minutes or until the ice-cream is firm.
- In a bowl, beat the cream with the vanilla essence using an electric mixer until it holds stiff peaks. Fold in the Amaretti biscuits thoroughly and spread over the ice-cream. Smooth the top of the cake, sprinkle with almonds and freeze for 30 to 45 minutes, or until the top is firm.

Upside-down cake

SERVES 6

INGREDIENTS:

425g/15oz canned unsweetened pineapple pieces (drained, with juice reserved)
4 teaspoons cornflour
50g/2oz brown sugar
50g/2oz margarine (plus extra for greasing)
125ml/4fl oz water
Grated zest of 1 lemon

For the sponge:
50ml/2fl oz sunflower oil
75g/3oz brown sugar
150ml/¼pt water
150g/5oz plain flour
2 teaspoons baking powder
1 teaspoon ground cinnamon

- Preheat the oven to 180°C/350°F/Gas mark 4. Grease a deep 18cm/7in cake tin.
- Mix the reserved juice from the pineapple with the cornflour until it forms a smooth paste. Put the paste in a saucepan with the sugar, margarine and water and stir over a low heat until the sugar has dissolved. Bring to the boil and simmer for 2 to 3 minutes, until thickened. Set aside to cool slightly.
- To make the sponge, place the oil, sugar and water in a saucepan. Heat gently until the sugar has dissolved – do not allow it to boil. Remove from the heat and leave to cool. Sift the flour, baking powder and cinnamon into a mixing bowl.
- Pour over the cooled sugar syrup and beat well to form a batter.
- Place the pineapple pieces and lemon zest on the base of the prepared tin and pour over 4 tablespoons pineapple syrup. Spoon the sponge batter on top.
- Bake in the oven for 35 to 40 minutes until set. Invert on to a plate, leave to stand for 5 minutes, then remove the tin. Serve with the remaining syrup.

Raspberry buns

SERVES 5

INGREDIENTS:

175g/6oz plain white flour
Pinch of salt
50g/2oz butter (plus extra for greasing)
50g/2oz caster sugar (plus extra
for dusting)

1 teaspoon baking powder
1 egg
2 teaspoons milk
1 tablespoon raspberry jam

- Preheat the oven to 200°C/400°F/Gas mark 6.
- Sieve the flour and salt into a bowl. Rub the butter into the flour, then add the sugar and baking powder. Whisk the egg and add the milk. Mix with the dry ingredients to form a stiffish dough. Divide the dough into 10 equal portions and roll into balls.
- Lay the balls of dough on a greased baking tray and make a hole in the top of each with your thumb. Fill with a small quantity of raspberry jam and pinch the dough together again.
- Flatten the buns slightly, brush with a little melted butter and dust with sugar.
- Bake in the oven for about 15 minutes. When the buns are ready they will crack on top and the jam will peep out.

Madeira cake

SERVES 8

INGREDIENTS:

175g/6oz butter (softened, plus extra
for greasing)
175g/6oz caster sugar
3 eggs (lightly beaten)
2 teaspoons finely grated orange zest

150g/5oz self-raising flour (sifted)
100g/4oz plain flour
2 tablespoons milk

- Preheat the oven to 160°C/325°F/Gas mark 3. Lightly grease a 20 x 10 x 7cm/8 x 4x 2½in loaf tin and line the base and sides with baking parchment.
- Cream the butter and sugar in a small bowl with an electric beater until light and fluffy. Add the eggs gradually, beating thoroughly after each addition. Add the zest and beat until combined. Transfer to a large bowl. Using a metal spoon, fold in both the flours and milk. Stir until smooth.

→

←
- Spoon into the loaf tin and smooth the surface. Bake for 50 minutes, or until a skewer comes out clean when inserted into the middle of the cake. Cool the cake in the tin for 10 minutes before turning out on to a wire rack to cool completely.

Pecan & raisin muffins

SERVES 6

INGREDIENTS:

Butter for greasing
350g/12oz plain flour
1 tablespoon baking powder
Pinch of salt
100g/4oz caster sugar
2 eggs

150ml/¼pt milk
50ml/2fl oz corn oil
¼ teaspoon vanilla essence
75g/3oz pecan nuts (roughly chopped)
75g/3oz raisins

- Preheat the oven to 190°C/375°F/Gas mark 5. Grease a 12-hole muffin tin.
- Sift the flour, baking powder and salt into a bowl. Mix in the sugar and make a well in the centre.
- Lightly beat the eggs with the milk, oil and vanilla essence and pour into the centre of the dry ingredients. Mix quickly to blend the flour with the liquid. Do not over mix – the mixture should look slightly lumpy. Lightly stir in the nuts and raisins.
- Divide the mixture equally in the muffin tin and bake for 25 minutes or until well risen, golden brown and cooked through. Leave in the tin to cool for a few minutes. Can be served hot or cold.

Fudge-mint torte

SERVES 10

INGREDIENTS:

275g/10oz cooking chocolate (broken into small pieces)
225g/8oz butter (chopped, plus extra for greasing)
350g/12oz demerara sugar
4 eggs
350g/12oz plain flour (sifted)

For the filling:
450ml/¾pt double cream
50ml/2fl oz Crème de Menthe liqueur
2 tablespoons icing sugar

- Preheat the oven to 180°C/350°F/Gas mark 4. Grease 3 x 20cm/8in round cake tins and line with baking parchment.
- In a small saucepan, combine the chocolate and butter. Stir over a very low heat just until melted and combined. Remove from the heat.
- Transfer the chocolate mixture to a large mixing bowl and beat in the demerara sugar. Beat in the eggs, one at a time, until combined, then beat in the flour until well blended. Divide the batter evenly into the tins.
- Bake in the oven for 25 minutes. Cool in the tins for 10 minutes, then turn out on to wire racks. Peel off the paper and allow to cool completely.
- In a medium-sized bowl, beat together the cream, Crème de Menthe and icing sugar until stiff. Stack and fill cake layers on a serving plate, using a third of the filling between each layer and on the top.

Chocolate tray bake

SERVES 15

INGREDIENTS:

225g/8oz soft margarine (plus extra for greasing)
350g/12oz self-raising flour (sifted)
3 tablespoons cocoa powder (sifted)
225g/8oz caster sugar
4 eggs (beaten)

4 tablespoons milk
50g/2oz milk chocolate chips
50g/2oz dark chocolate chips
50g/2oz white chocolate chips
Icing sugar for dusting

- Preheat the oven to 180°C/350°F/Gas mark 4. Grease a 33 x 23 x 5cm/13 x 9 x 2in cake tin with margarine.
- Place all of the ingredients except for the chocolate chips and the icing sugar in a large mixing bowl and beat together, using a wooden spoon, until smooth. Then stir in the chocolate chips.
- Spoon the mixture into the prepared cake tin and level the top. Bake in the oven for 30 to 40 minutes, until risen and springy to the touch. Leave to cool in the tin.
- Once cool, dust with icing sugar. Cut into squares to serve.

Rock cakes

SERVES 10

INGREDIENTS:

75g/3oz butter (cubed, plus extra
for greasing)
225g/8oz self-raising flour
100g/4oz caster sugar

75g/3oz mixed dried fruit
1/2 teaspoon ground ginger
1 egg
50ml/2fl oz milk

- Preheat the oven to 200°C/400°F/Gas mark 6. Grease 2 baking trays.
- Sift the flour into a large bowl and rub in the butter with your fingertips until the mixture resembles fine breadcrumbs. Stir in the sugar, fruit and ginger.
- Whisk the egg into the milk in a bowl, add the dry ingredients and mix to a stiff dough. Drop rough heaps of mixture, about 3 tablespoons at a time, on to the trays. Bake for 10 to 15 minutes, or until golden. Cool on a wire rack.

Chocolate date cake

SERVES 10

INGREDIENTS:

50g/2oz butter (plus extra for greasing)
3 tablespoons cocoa powder
50ml/2fl oz hot water
350g/12oz self-raising flour
Pinch of salt

175g/6oz caster sugar
1 egg (beaten)
125ml/4fl oz milk
225g/8oz dates (chopped)
100g/4oz walnuts (chopped)

- Preheat the oven to 180°C/350°F/Gas mark 4. Grease a 27.5 x 18cm/11 x 7in cake tin.
- In a medium-sized bowl, stir the cocoa powder into the hot water and mix until smooth. Add the butter and place the bowl over a pan of simmering water. Stir until the butter melts.
- Sift the flour and salt into a basin. Mix in the sugar. Add the cocoa mixture, beaten egg and milk and beat well with a wooden spoon until smooth and well mixed. Then stir in the dates.
- Place in a greased tin, sprinkle the walnuts on top and bake in the oven for 30 to 35 minutes. Turn out on to a wire rack to cool.

Madeleines

SERVES 6

INGREDIENTS:

175g/6oz butter (melted and cooled, plus extra for greasing)
100g/4oz plain flour (plus extra for dusting)

2 eggs
175g/6oz caster sugar
1 teaspoon finely grated orange zest
2 tablespoons icing sugar for dusting

- Preheat the oven to 180°C/350°F/Gas mark 4. Lightly grease 12 madeleine holes in a madeleine tin. Lightly dust the madeleine tin with flour and shake off any excess.
- Combine the eggs and sugar in a heatproof bowl. Place the bowl over a pan of simmering water and beat the mixture with a whisk or an electric beater until thick and pale yellow. Remove the bowl from the heat and continue to beat the mixture until cooled slightly and increased in volume.
- Sift the flour 3 times on to baking parchment. Add the flour, butter and orange zest to the bowl and fold in quickly and lightly with a metal spoon until just combined. Spoon the mixture carefully into the madeleine holes.
- Bake for 10 to 12 minutes, or until lightly golden. Carefully remove from the tin and place on a wire rack until cold. Dust with icing sugar before serving.
- Madeleines are best eaten on the day of baking.

Pastries

Baking heavenly classics such as Tarte tatin, Bakewell tart and Mississippi mud pie, as well as naughty culinary marvels such as Chocolate éclairs and Golden passion fruit tarts should be a delight with these easy-to-follow recipes. With so many different mouth-watering recipes here, you can pick the perfect recipe for breakfast, teatime and after-dinner.

Apple galettes

SERVES 8

INGREDIENTS:

225g/8oz plain flour
350g/12oz butter (chopped, plus extra
for greasing)

125ml/4fl oz chilled water
8 apples (peeled, cored and sliced)
175g/6oz caster sugar

- Place the flour and 225g/8oz butter in a bowl. Cut the butter into the flour with 2 knives until it resembles large crumbs. Gradually add the chilled water, stirring with a knife and pressing together, until a rough dough forms.
- Turn on to a lightly floured board and roll into a rectangle. The dough is crumbly and hard to manage at this point. Fold the dough and re-roll several times. Wrap the pastry in clingfilm and refrigerate for 30 minutes, then fold and re-roll a few more times. Wrap again in clingfilm and refrigerate for another 30 minutes.
- Preheat the oven to 190°C/375°F/Gas mark 5. Roll the pastry until 3mm/½in thick. Cut into 8 x 10cm/4in rounds. Arrange the apples in a spiral on the pastry.
- Sprinkle well with the caster sugar and dot with the remaining butter. Bake on greased baking trays for 20 to 30 minutes, until the pastry is crisp and golden.

Baklava

SERVES 8–10

INGREDIENTS:

100g/4oz butter (melted, plus extra for
greasing)
450g/1lb walnuts (finely chopped)
50g/2oz caster sugar
A pinch of ground cinnamon
275g/10oz filo pastry

For the syrup:
Juice of 1 lemon
150g/5oz sugar
½ teaspoon ground cinnamon

- Preheat the oven to 180°C/350°F/Gas mark 4. Lightly grease a 25cm/10in loose-bottomed cake tin.
- Mix the walnuts, sugar and cinnamon in a bowl.
- Unfold the filo pastry and cover with a damp tea towel to stop it drying out.
- Brush a piece of the filo with melted butter and fit it into the bottom of the tin with the buttered side down. Let the edges spill over and brush with butter.
- Repeat with 3 more buttered filo sheets, making sure that the whole tin is lined.

- Sprinkle with half of the nut mixture. Repeat with 4 more layers of buttered filo and scatter over the remaining nut mixture over them. Place 2 more layers of buttered filo on top, then fold the edges in and under.
- Cut the last 2 pieces of filo so they fit the tin, place on top and brush generously with butter. Bake for 40 minutes, then increase the temperature to 200°C/400°F/ Gas mark 6. Bake for a further 20 minutes, or until golden brown.
- To make the syrup, gently heat the lemon juice, sugar and cinnamon until the sugar has dissolved and the syrup has reduced slightly. Pour over the cooked baklava and leave to cool in the tin for 1 to 2 hours. Cut into wedges and serve.

Filo rhubarb pie

SERVES 3

INGREDIENTS:

500g/1lb 2oz pink rhubarb
1 teaspoon mixed spice
Grated zest and juice of 1 orange

1 tablespoon granulated sugar
1 tablespoon low-fat spread
3 sheets filo pastry

- Preheat the oven to 200°C/400°F/Gas mark 6.
- Trim the leaves and ends from the rhubarb sticks and chop them in 2.5cm/1in pieces. Place them in a medium-sized mixing bowl.
- Add the mixed spice, orange zest and juice and sugar, and toss well to coat evenly. Tip the rhubarb into a 1.2 litre/2pt pie dish.
- Melt the spread and brush over the filo sheets. Crumple the filo loosely and place the pieces on top of the filling to cover.
- Place the dish on a baking tray and bake the pie for 20 minutes, until golden brown. Reduce the heat to 180°C/350°F/Gas mark 4 and bake for 10 to 15 minutes more until the rhubarb is tender. Serve warm.

Apple Betty

SERVES 4-6

INGREDIENTS:

5 cooking apples (peeled, cored and chopped)
100g/4oz butter
90g/3½oz demerara sugar

Grated zest of 1 lemon
¼ teaspoon ground cinnamon
Pinch of ground nutmeg
225g/8oz fresh breadcrumbs

→

←

- Preheat the oven to 180°C/350°F/Gas mark 4.
- Cook the apples with 15g/½oz butter, 15g/½oz demerara sugar, lemon zest, cinnamon and nutmeg for 10 to 15 minutes, until the apples are soft enough to beat to a purée.
- Melt the remaining butter in a frying pan over a low heat and add the breadcrumbs and the remaining demerara sugar. Toss everything until the crumbs are coated, and continue tossing while you fry the crumbs until golden brown.
- Spread one third of the crumbs in a 1.2 litre/2pt ovenproof dish and add half the apple purée in an even layer. Add another third of the crumbs and the remaining apple, then finish with a layer of crumbs. Bake for 20 minutes, or until crisp and golden on top.

Mississippi mud pie

SERVES 8

INGREDIENTS

225g/8oz plain flour (plus extra for dusting)
2 tablespoons cocoa powder
150g/5oz butter
25g/1oz caster sugar
2 tablespoons cold water
450ml/¾pt double cream (whipped)

For the filling:
175g/6oz butter
350g/12oz muscovado sugar
4 eggs (lightly beaten)
4 tablespoons cocoa powder (sifted)
150g/5oz dark chocolate
300ml/½pt single cream
1 teaspoon chocolate essence

- To make the pastry, sift the flour and cocoa powder into a mixing bowl. Rub in the butter until the mixture resembles fine breadcrumbs. Stir in the sugar and enough cold water to mix to a soft dough. Chill for 15 minutes.
- Preheat the oven to 190°C/375°F/Gas mark 5.
- Roll out the pastry dough on a lightly floured surface and use to line a greased 23cm/9in loose-bottomed flan tin. Line with aluminium foil and baking beans.
- Bake blind in the oven for 15 minutes. Remove the beans and foil and cook for a further 10 minutes, until crisp.
- To make the filling, beat the butter and sugar in a bowl and gradually beat in the eggs with the cocoa powder. Melt the dark chocolate in a heatproof bowl set over a pan of simmering water. Then beat the melted chocolate into the mixture in the other bowl with the single cream and the chocolate essence.
- Pour the mixture into the cooked pastry case and bake at 170°C/325°F/Gas mark 3 for 45 minutes or until the filling is set.
- Leave to cool completely then transfer to a serving plate. Cover with the whipped cream and leave to chill.

Vanilla cream tarts

SERVES 6

INGREDIENTS:

For the dough:
200g/7oz butter (plus extra for greasing)
400g/14oz plain flour
½ teaspoon bicarbonate of soda
100g/4oz caster sugar
1 egg, plus 4 egg yolks (2 hard-boiled and finely crumbled)

For the filling:
3 egg yolks
150g/5oz caster sugar
125ml/4fl oz double cream
½ vanilla pod (split lengthways, seeds scraped out)

- Preheat the oven to 180°C/350°F/Gas mark 4.
- To make the dough, cut the butter into the flour, then add the remaining ingredients and knead briefly but thoroughly. Wrap or cover the dough to prevent drying and allow to rest, refrigerated, for at least 1 hour.
- For the filling, put the egg yolks in a saucepan and stir in the sugar, cream and vanilla pod. Cook over a low heat, stirring continuously with a wooden spoon, until the mixture thickens. Remove from the heat and put the saucepan in a shallow pan of cold water to stop the cooking. Cool the custard, stirring occasionally.
- Roll out the dough and line buttered tartlet moulds with it. Fill the cases with the custard and cover with rounds of the dough. Crimp the edges together to seal and bake the tartlets for 30 minutes or until lightly browned. Cool before unmoulding.

Jalousie

SERVES 4–6

INGREDIENTS:

25g/1oz butter (plus extra for greasing)
50g/2oz brown sugar
450g/1lb apples (peeled, cored and cubed)
1 teaspoon grated lemon zest
1 tablespoon lemon juice

¼ teaspoon nutmeg
¼ teaspoon cinnamon
25g/1oz sultanas
350g/12oz puff pastry
1 egg (lightly beaten, to glaze)

→

←

- Preheat the oven to 220°C/425°F/Gas mark 7. Lightly grease a baking tray and line with baking parchment.
- Melt the butter and sugar in a frying pan. Add the apples, lemon zest and lemon juice. Cook over a medium heat for 10 minutes, stirring occasionally, until the apples are cooked and the mixture is dark and syrupy. Stir in the nutmeg, cinnamon and sultanas. Cool completely.
- Cut the block of puff pastry in half. On a lightly floured surface, roll out one half of the pastry to a 24 x 18cm/10 x 7in rectangle. Spread the fruit mixture on to the pastry, leaving a 2.5cm/1in border. Brush the edges lightly with the beaten egg.
- Roll the second half of the pastry on a lightly floured surface to a 25 x 18cm/10 x 7in rectangle. Using a sharp knife, cut slashes in the pastry across its width, leaving a 2cm/³⁄₄in border around the edge. Place over the fruit and press the edges together. Glaze the top with egg. Bake for 25 to 30 minutes, or until puffed and golden.

Frangipane tart

SERVES 10

INGREDIENTS

For the pastry:
100g/4oz caster sugar
50g/2oz ground almonds
100g/4oz plain flour
75g/3oz butter (cut into small dice)
1 large egg
1 egg yolk
Grated zest of 1 small lemon
2 teaspoons water
Pinch of salt

For the filling:
50g/2oz butter
50g/2oz caster sugar
50g/2oz ground almonds
50g/2oz white breadcrumbs
1 large egg
3 drops almond essence
4 tablespoons raspberry jam

- To make the pastry, put the sugar, almonds and flour into a blender or food processor and blend at full speed for a few seconds. Add the butter and work again until just blended. The mixture should resemble fine breadcrumbs.
- Add the egg and egg yolk, the lemon zest, water and salt. Work again until the pastry balls. Wrap in clingfilm and refrigerate for 2 hours.
- Preheat the oven to 190°C/375°F/Gas mark 5.
- Roll the chilled pastry out and use to line a 20cm/8in loose-bottomed tart tin. If it breaks it can be repaired by pressing with your fingers. Make the shell as even as possible, with a double thickness round the edges and pushed right up to the top as it will shrink as it bakes. Be careful to press into the bottom edges to

eliminate air between the tin and the pastry.
- To make the filling, put the butter, sugar, almonds and breadcrumbs into the blender and work briefly to mix. With the machine running on full speed, add the egg and almond essence until combined to a smooth paste.
- Put the shell on a baking tray, prick the base with a fork and line with aluminium foil. Fill with baking beans and bake blind for 10 minutes.
- Remove the foil and beans and leave to cool slightly, then fill the base with a layer of raspberry jam. Cover this with the almond paste. Scrape the surface smooth and level.
- Return to the oven and bake for 25 to 30 minutes, until risen and lightly browned.

French apple tartlets

SERVES 8

INGREDIENTS:

For the pastry:
225g/8oz plain flour
150g/5oz butter
25g/1oz caster sugar
1 egg yolk
1 tablespoon cold water

For the filling:
900g/2lb cooking apples (peeled, cored and sliced)
50g/2oz caster sugar

15g/½oz butter
Grated zest of ½ lemon
1 tablespoon lemon juice

For the topping:
3 small green dessert apples (peeled, cored and thinly sliced)
1 tablespoon lemon juice
25g/1oz granulated sugar
Icing sugar for dusting

- Preheat the oven to 190°C/375°F/Gas mark 5.
- Sift the flour into a bowl and rub in the butter until the mixture resembles fine breadcrumbs. Stir in the sugar, egg yolk and water and mix to form a dough. Knead lightly until smooth. Divide into 8 portions. Roll out each portion on a lightly floured surface and use to line 8 x 10cm/4in diameter, loose-bottomed, fluted flan tins. Press the pastry firmly into the flutes, trim the top edges and prick the bases well with a fork. Chill for 30 minutes.
- To make the filling, put the cooking apples in a saucepan with the sugar, butter, lemon zest and juice. Cover and cook gently for 10 minutes until tender. Beat to form a smooth purée. Leave to cool.
- Put the shell on a baking tray, prick the base with a fork and line with aluminium foil. Fill with baking beans and bake blind for 10 to 15 minutes. Remove the baking beans and baking parchment and cook for a further 5 to 10 minutes or until cooked through. Cool on a wire rack while still in the tins.

→

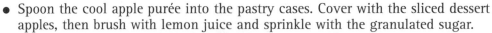

- Spoon the cool apple purée into the pastry cases. Cover with the sliced dessert apples, then brush with lemon juice and sprinkle with the granulated sugar.
- Put the tartlets on a baking sheet and bake at 190°C/375°F/Gas mark 5 for 20 to 25 minutes until the apple is golden brown. Leave to cool before removing from the tins and serve dusted with icing sugar.

Golden passion fruit tart

SERVES 8

INGREDIENTS:

8 large passion fruit
225g/8oz plain flour
50g/2oz icing sugar
Grated zest of 1 orange

150g/5oz butter (diced)
5 large eggs
150g/5oz caster sugar
200ml/7fl oz double cream

- Halve the passion fruit, scoop out the flesh and put to one side.
- To make the pastry, put the flour, icing sugar and the orange zest in a blender or food processor with the butter. Blend until the mixture resembles fine crumbs.
- Lightly beat 1 egg and add all but 1 tablespoon to the pastry mixture. Pulse until the mixture comes together in a ball. Wrap in clingfilm. Chill for 30 minutes.
- Preheat the oven to 200°C/400°F/Gas mark 6.
- Put the shell on a baking tray, prick the base with a fork and line with aluminium foil. Fill with baking beans and bake blind for 10 minutes. Remove foil and beans and cook for a further 2 minutes.
- Wipe out the blender, add the passion fruit pulp and the caster sugar, then blend for 1 minute or until the flesh comes away from the seeds. With the machine running, add the remaining 4 eggs and the double cream, then strain through a fine sieve. Fill the tart case with the passion fruit mixture and bake at 140°C/275°F/Gas mark 1 for 1 hour, or until the filling has just set in the middle.
- Set aside to cool, then chill for 2 hours. Serve with whipped cream.

Hot plum batter

SERVES 4

INGREDIENTS:

Vegetable oil for greasing
450g/1lb red plums (quartered
and stoned)
200ml/7fl oz skimmed milk
4 tablespoons skimmed milk powder

1 tablespoon muscovado sugar
1 teaspoon vanilla essence
75g/3oz self-raising flour
2 egg whites
Icing sugar to sprinkle

- Preheat the oven to 220°C/425°F/Gas mark 7. Lightly oil a wide, shallow ovenproof dish and add the plums.
- Pour the milk, milk powder, sugar, vanilla essence, flour and egg whites into a food processor. Process until smooth.
- Pour the batter over the plums. Bake for 25 to 30 minutes, or until well risen and golden. Sprinkle with icing sugar and serve immediately.

Strawberry apple tart

SERVES 4-6

INGREDIENTS:

150g/5oz self-raising flour
50g/2oz rolled oats
50g/2oz margarine
2 Bramley cooking apples (peeled,
cored and sliced)

200g/7oz strawberries (halved)
50g/2oz caster sugar
1 tablespoon cornflour

- Preheat the oven to 200°C/400°F/Gas mark 6.
- Mix together the flour and oats in a large bowl and rub in the margarine evenly. Stir in just enough cold water to bind the mixture to form a firm dough. Knead lightly until smooth.
- Roll out the pastry and use to line a 23cm/9in loose-bottomed flan tin. Trim the edges, prick the base and line with aluminium foil and baking beans. Bake the pastry case for 10 minutes, remove the foil and beans and bake for 10 to 15 minutes or until golden brown.
- Place the apples in a pan with the strawberries, sugar and cornflour. Cover and cook gently, stirring, until the fruit is just tender. Spoon into the pastry case and serve warm.

Lime meringue tarts

SERVES 6

INGREDIENTS:

For the pastry:
75g/3oz butter (diced, plus extra for greasing)
100g/4oz plain flour (sifted, plus extra for dusting)
50g/2oz pistachio nuts
Pinch of salt
50g/2oz icing sugar
2 medium eggs

For the filling:
1 egg
3 egg yolks
Grated zest and juice of 5 limes
200g/7oz caster sugar
150ml/¼pt double cream

- Preheat the oven to 190°C/375°F/Gas mark 5.
- Grease and flour 6 tartlet tins measuring 8 x 2.5cm/3¼ x 1in.
- To make the pastry, process the pistachios in a blender or food processor for 30 seconds. Add the flour, salt and butter and pulse until the mixture resembles crumbs. Add the icing sugar and pulse to mix. Separate the eggs, put 1 egg white to one side for the meringue and discard the other. Add the yolks to the mixture and pulse until it just holds together.
- Turn the dough on to a lightly floured surface and knead gently to bring the mixture together. Roll out the pastry and use to line the tins, pressing well into the edges and trimming off any excess pastry. Cover with clingfilm and chill for 30 minutes.
- Put the tins on a baking sheet, line with aluminium foil and fill with baking beans. Bake for 10 minutes. Remove the foil and beans and bake for a further 10 to 12 minutes until just cooked. Remove from the oven.
- Meanwhile, to make the filling, put the egg and egg yolks into a small pan, add the lime zest and juice, 150g/5oz caster sugar and the cream. Cook over a medium heat for 5 minutes, stirring regularly, until the custard has thickened and is smooth. Pour into a large bowl and allow to cool.
- Lower the oven temperature to 180°C/350°F/Gas mark 4. Spoon the lime filling into the pastry cases.
- Put the reserved egg white into a bowl and whisk until it stands in stiff peaks.
- Add the remaining sugar a little at a time and continue to beat until the mixture is stiff and shiny. Put into a piping bag fitted with a round 1cm/½in nozzle and pipe around the edge of the tarts.
- Bake the tarts for 10 minutes or until the meringue is hard to the touch. Can be served hot or cold.

Maple macadamia pie

SERVES 6

INGREDIENTS:

For the shortcrust pastry:
150g/5oz plain flour
Pinch of salt
75g/3oz butter (cubed)
25ml/1fl oz iced water
100g/4oz macadamia nuts (chopped)

75g/3oz shredded coconut
3 eggs (lightly beaten)
50g/2oz granulated sugar
225ml/8fl oz maple syrup
¼ teaspoon salt
75g/3oz butter (melted and cooled)

To make the shortcrust, sift the flour and salt together into a large mixing bowl. Add the cubes of butter. Rub the butter and flour together with your fingertips until the mixture has a coarse texture. Stirring lightly with a knife, sprinkle water over the dough until it just begins to cohere. Gather the dough together into a ball, pressing it together with your hands. Wrap in clingfilm and chill for 30 minutes.

Preheat the oven to 200°C/400°F/Gas mark 6.

Roll out the dough and use to line a 20cm/8in pie plate. Arrange the macadamia nuts in one layer over the unbaked pie case, covering as much of the dough as you can. Sprinkle the shredded coconut over the nuts and refrigerate the pie case. Put the eggs in a large bowl, add the sugar, maple syrup, salt and butter. Mix well and pour into the pie case.

Bake in the oven for 15 minutes. Then lower the heat to 180°C/350°F/Gas mark 4 and bake for a further 20 to 25 minutes, until the filling is custard-like. This pie is best served lukewarm with whipped cream.

Plum, apple & banana scone pie

SERVES 4

INGREDIENTS:

450g/1lb plums (stoned and halved)
1 Bramley apple (peeled, cored and diced)
1 large banana (sliced)
150ml/5fl oz water

100g/4oz plain wholemeal flour
2 teaspoons baking powder
25g/1oz raisins
4 tablespoons low-fat natural yogurt

→

←
- Preheat the oven to 180°C/350°F/Gas mark 4.
- Mix the fruit in a saucepan. Pour in the water. Bring to simmering point and cook gently for 15 minutes or until the fruit is completely soft. Spoon the fruit mixture into a pie dish and level the surface.
- Mix the flour, baking powder and raisins in a bowl. Add the yogurt and mix to a very soft dough.
- Transfer the scone dough to a lightly floured surface and divide it into 6 to 8 portions, then pat into flattish scones.
- Cover the plum and apple mixture with the scones. Bake the pie for 40 minutes until the scones topping is cooked through. Serve the pie hot with natural yogurt, or leave it until cold.

Gooseberry meringue tart

SERVES 8

INGREDIENTS:

For the shortcrust pastry:
150g/5oz plain flour
Pinch of salt
75g/3oz butter (cubed)
25ml/1fl oz iced water

50g/2oz butter (cubed)
2 tablespoons breadcrumbs
25g/1oz caster sugar
1 egg white (lightly beaten with 1 teaspoon sugar)

For the filling:
750g/1½lb gooseberries (topped and tailed)
2 egg yolks (beaten)

For the meringue:
50g/2oz granulated sugar
2 egg whites (stiffly beaten)

- To make the shortcrust pastry, sift the flour and salt together into a large mixing bowl. Add the butter. Rub the butter and flour together with your fingertips until the mixture has a coarse texture. Stirring with a knife, sprinkle water over the dough until it just begins to cohere. Gather together into a ball, pressing it together with your hands. Wrap in clingfilm and chill for 30 minutes.
- Preheat the oven to 150°C/300°F/Gas mark 2.
- Place the gooseberries in an earthenware jar or ovenproof bowl, cover, and set in the oven for 30 minutes, or until quite soft. Then rub the gooseberries through a sieve into a bowl. Add the egg yolks, butter, breadcrumbs and sugar.
- Raise the oven temperature to 180°C/350°F/Gas mark 4.
- Line a 20cm/8in pie dish round the sides and rims with the dough, glazing the edges with the egg white and sugar mixture. Put in the gooseberries. Bake in the oven for about 45 minutes, or until the pastry is lightly browned.
- Prepare the meringue by beating the sugar into the egg whites. Cover the

gooseberries with the meringue and return to the oven to cook for 10 minutes before serving.

Plum cobbler

SERVES 6–8

INGREDIENTS:

700g/1½lb red plums
50g/2oz caster sugar
1 tablespoon water

For the topping:
100g/4oz self-raising flour
50g/2oz plain flour

50g/2oz caster sugar
100g/4oz butter (chopped, plus extra for greasing)
1 egg
125ml/4fl oz milk
Icing sugar for dusting

- Preheat the oven to 180°C/350°F/Gas mark 4. Lightly grease a 2.1 litre/3½pt ovenproof dish.
- Cut the plums into quarters, discarding the stones. Put the plums in a pan with the sugar and water. Stir over a low heat for 5 minutes, or until the sugar dissolves, and the fruit softens slightly. Spread the plum mixture into the prepared dish.
- Sift the flours into a bowl, add the sugar and stir. Rub in the butter with your fingertips until the mixture is fine and crumbly. Combine the egg and milk and whisk until smooth. Stir into the flour mixture.
- Place large spoonfuls of mixture on top of the plums. Bake for 30 to 40 minutes or until the top is golden and cooked through. Dust with icing sugar before serving.

Apricot tart

SERVES 6

INGREDIENTS:

For the puff pastry:
100g/4oz plain flour
2 teaspoons salt
100g/4oz butter

50ml/2fl oz water
500g/1lb 2oz apricots
50g/2oz caster sugar
50g/2oz candied lemon peel

→

←

- To make the puff pastry, sift the flour and salt into a bowl. Cut a quarter of the butter into small pieces and add them to the bowl. Rub the butter into the flour with your fingertips. Add just enough cold water to bind the ingredients and work them into a ball. Wrap in clingfilm and refrigerate for 30 minutes.
- Put the remaining butter between 2 sheets of baking parchment and, with a rolling pin, flatten it into a slab about 15cm/6in square and 1cm/½in thick.
- Chill in the refrigerator for about 30 minutes.
- Place the dough on a lightly floured board and roll it into a 30cm/12in square.
- Place the square of butter diagonally in the centre of the dough and fold the corners of the dough over the butter so they meet in the centre. Roll the dough into a rectangle 30 x 40cm/12 x 18in.
- Fold the dough in thirds and give it a quarter turn. Roll the dough again into a rectangle and fold into thirds. Wrap and chill the dough for about 30 minutes. Roll and turn the dough twice more, refrigerate and repeat, giving it 6 turns in all. After a final refrigeration, it is ready to use.
- Preheat the oven to 220°C/425°F/Gas mark 7.
- If the apricots are not quite ripe, plunge them into boiling water, return the water to the boil, then drain, halve and stone them.
- Line a 20cm/8in tart tin with the puff pastry dough, sprinkle 25g/1oz of the caster sugar over the base, then sprinkle on the lemon peel.
- Arrange the apricots in the case. Dust with the remaining sugar and bake in the oven for 15 minutes, then reduce the heat to 190°C/375°F/Gas mark 5 for 20 to 30 minutes or until the pastry is puffed and golden brown.

Almond & cherry flan

SERVES 6

INGREDIENTS:

225g/8oz plain flour
225g/8oz butter
2 eggs (separated)
3 tablespoons water
350g/12oz fresh ripe black cherries (stoned)
50g/2oz caster sugar

100g/4oz ground almonds
1 teaspoon almond essence
1 tablespoon almond flavoured liqueur
50g/2oz self-raising flour
½ teaspoon baking powder
25ml/1fl oz milk
25g/1oz flaked almonds

- Preheat the oven to 200°C/400°F/Gas mark 6.
- Place the plain flour in a large mixing bowl. Cut up and rub in 175g/6oz butter until the mixture resembles fine breadcrumbs. Bind to a firm dough with 1 egg yolk mixed with water.
- Roll out the pastry and use to line a 24cm/9½in flan dish. Place on a baking

tray, prick the base with a fork and line with aluminium foil. Fill with baking beans and bake blind for 15 to 20 minutes until set but not browned. Remove the beans and foil and allow to cool slightly.

- Scatter the cherries over the pastry. Cream the remaining butter and sugar well together and beat in the ground almonds, with the almond essence, almond liqueur and the remaining egg yolk. Fold in the self-raising flour and baking powder, sifted together, and lightly stir in the milk.
- Whisk the 2 egg whites until they are stiff and fold them into the creamed ingredients.
- Spread over the cherries in the flan case and scatter the flaked almonds on top.
- Bake in the oven at 180°C/350°F/Gas mark 4 for about 30 minutes. Serve warm with cream.

Chocolate pecan pie

SERVES 6

INGREDIENTS:

For the pastry:
275g/10oz plain flour (plus extra for dusting)
50g/2oz cocoa powder
100g/4oz icing sugar
Pinch of salt
200g/7oz butter (diced)
1 egg yolk

For the filling:
350g/12oz shelled pecan nuts
75g/3oz butter
175g/6oz demerara sugar
3 eggs
2 tablespoons double cream
2 tablespoons plain flour
75g/3oz dark chocolate
1 tablespoon icing sugar for dusting

- Preheat the oven to 180°C/350°F/Gas mark 4.
- To make the pastry, sift the flour, cocoa, sugar and salt into a mixing bowl and make a well in the centre. Put the butter and egg yolk in the well and knead together, then gradually mix in the dry ingredients. Knead lightly into a ball.
- Cover with clingfilm and chill in the refrigerator for 1 hour.
- Unwrap the dough and roll it out on a lightly floured surface. Use it to line a 25cm/10in non-stick springform pie tin and prick the base with a fork. Line the pastry case with aluminium foil and fill with baking beans. Bake in the oven for 15 minutes. Remove from the oven, discard the beans and foil, and allow to cool. Leave the oven on.
- Roughly chop 225g/8oz pecan nuts. Mix the butter with 50g/2oz demerara sugar. Beat in the eggs one at a time, then add the remaining demerara sugar and mix.
- Stir in the double cream, flour and chopped pecan nuts. Melt the chocolate in a heatproof bowl set over a pan of simmering water, then add to the mixture.

→

←

- Spoon the filling into the pastry case and smooth the surface. Cut the remaining pecan nuts in half and arrange over the pie.
- Bake in the oven for 30 minutes, then cover the top of the pie with aluminium foil to prevent it from burning and bake for a further 25 minutes. Remove the pie from the oven and let it cool slightly before removing from the tin and transferring to a wire rack to cool completely. Dust with the icing sugar.

Spiced fruit ring

SERVES 8

INGREDIENTS:

225g/8oz plain flour
2 teaspoon dried yeast
1/2 teaspoon salt
25g/1oz muscovado sugar
1 teaspoon finely grated lemon zest
25g/1oz butter (melted)
1 egg (beaten)
125ml/4fl oz hand-hot milk
25g/1oz caster sugar for glazing
2 tablespoons water
75g/3oz icing sugar (sifted)

For the filling:
75g/3oz glacé cherries (chopped)
25g/1oz sultanas
50g/2oz ready-to-eat dried apricots (chopped)
25g/1oz angelica (washed and chopped)
75g/3oz flaked almonds (chopped)
25g/1oz muscovado sugar
1 teaspoon ground cinnamon
1/2 teaspoon mixed spice

- Sift the flour into a bowl, stir in the yeast, salt, muscovado sugar and lemon zest, then stir in the melted butter, egg and enough milk to form a soft dough.
- Knead for 5 to 10 minutes, until smooth. Leave in a warm place to rise for 30 minutes, then knead and roll into a 30 x 40cm/12 x 18in rectangle.
- To make the filling, mix together the fruit, angelica and almonds. Reserve 3 tablespoons and mix the rest with the sugar and spices. Sprinkle over the dough and roll up from one long side.
- Place the roll on a greased baking sheet and curve into a circle. Dampen the ends and stick together. Snip halfway through at 2.5cm/1in intervals and turn each section slightly.
- Cover with oiled clingfilm and leave in a warm place for an hour, or until doubled in size.
- Preheat the oven to 200°C/400°F/Gas mark 6.
- Remove the clingfilm from the roll and bake for 25 minutes, or until golden.
- Dissolve the caster sugar in the water and bring to the boil. Brush over the ring, leave to dry, then repeat.
- Blend the icing sugar with a little water and drizzle over the top. Scatter with the reserved fruit and nuts and leave to set.

Spiced pear strudel

SERVES 8

INGREDIENTS

75g/3oz fresh white breadcrumbs
150g/5oz butter
50g/2oz brown sugar
50g/2oz sultanas
½ teaspoon mixed spice
½ teaspoon ground cinnamon

450g/1lb pears (peeled, cored
and sliced)
4 large sheets of filo pastry
50g/2oz blanched almonds (toasted
and chopped)
Icing sugar for dusting

- Preheat the oven to 190°C/375°F/Gas mark 5.
- Fry the breadcrumbs in 50g/2oz butter, stirring frequently until crisp and golden. Mix together the brown sugar, sultanas, mixed spice, cinnamon and pear slices.
- Melt the remaining butter. Brush a sheet of filo pastry with a little of the melted butter. Cover with a second sheet of the pastry and brush with a little more melted butter.
- Cover the pastry with half the fried crumbs, leaving a 5cm/2in border on all sides. Arrange half the pear mixture over the crumbs and sprinkle with half of the chopped almonds.
- Fold the edges over the filling and brush with a little melted butter. Roll up, like a Swiss roll, starting from a long side. Place the strudel on a lightly greased baking tray and brush with melted butter. Make a second strudel the same way using the remaining ingredients.
- Bake for 35 minutes until crisp and golden, covering with aluminium foil if necessary to prevent over-browning. Brush halfway through cooking with butter from the baking sheet. Can be served hot or cold.

Cherry pie

SERVES 6–8

INGREDIENTS:

150g/5oz plain flour
25g/1oz icing sugar
100g/4oz butter (cubed)
50g/2oz ground almonds

3 tablespoons chilled water
650g/1lb 7oz pitted Morello cherries
1 egg (lightly beaten)
Caster sugar for sprinkling

→

←

- Sift the flour and icing sugar into a bowl. Add the butter and rub in with just your fingertips until the mixture is fine and crumbly. Stir in the ground almonds, then add almost all the water and stir into the flour mixture with a flat-bladed knife until the mixture forms a dough, adding the remaining water if necessary.
- Turn the dough onto a lightly floured surface and gather together into a ball.
- Roll out on a sheet of baking parchment into a circle about 26cm/10¹/₂in in diameter.
- Flatten slightly, cover with clingfilm and refrigerate for 20 minutes. Spread the cherries into a 23cm/9in pie dish.
- Preheat the oven to 200°C/400°F/Gas mark 6.
- Cover the pie dish with the pastry and trim the overhanging edge. Brush the pastry top all over with beaten egg and sprinkle lightly with caster sugar. Place the pie dish on a baking tray and cook for 35 to 40 minutes or until golden brown. Serve warm with cream or ice-cream.

Fruit & nut torte

SERVES 8

INGREDIENTS

75g/3oz caster sugar
150ml/¹/₄pt water
450g/1lb lemon sponge
500g/1lb 2oz ricotta cheese
100g/4oz plain chocolate-coated almonds (finely chopped)
75g/3oz soft nougat (finely chopped)
50g/2oz candied peel (finely chopped)

Finely grated zest of 1 orange
Finely grated zest of 1 lemon
75g/3oz sultanas
2 tablespoons Amaretto or orange liqueur
175g/6oz flaked almonds (toasted)
Icing sugar for dusting

- Place the caster sugar in a large pan with the water. Heat gently, stirring occasionally, until the sugar has dissolved. Bring to the boil and boil rapidly without stirring for 10 minutes until syrupy. Leave to cool.
- Line a 24cm/9¹/₂in springform cake tin with aluminium foil. Cut the lemon sponge into very thin slices and use to line the base and sides of the tin.
- Beat the cheese in a bowl, then gradually add 150ml/¹/₄pt of the sugar syrup, stirring constantly.
- Stir in the almonds, nougat, candied peel, orange and lemon zests, sultanas and liqueur. Beat thoroughly, then spoon into the sponge-lined tin. Sprinkle with the toasted almonds. Cover with clingfilm and chill overnight.

Caramelized apple tarts

SERVES 6

INGREDIENTS:

50g/2oz butter (plus extra for greasing)
1 sheet pastry from a 375g/13oz pack
puff pastry
100g/4oz white marzipan (chilled and
coarsely grated)

4 Braeburn apples (quartered, cored
and sliced)
Juice of 1 large lemon
25g/1oz demerara sugar
½ teaspoon mixed spice

- Preheat the oven to 200°C/400°F/Gas mark 6. Grease the bases of 6 x 7.5cm/3in individual tartlet tins.
- Roll out the pastry sheet more thinly. Stamp out 6 x 12.5cm/5in rounds of pastry. Line the tins and prick the bases twice with a fork. Chill for 10 minutes.
- Line the pastry with aluminium foil and baking beans. Bake blind for 10 minutes. Remove the foil and beans, sprinkle in the marzipan and cook for a further 5 minutes.
- Heat the butter in a large non-stick frying pan. Add the apples, lemon juice, sugar and spice and cook over a high heat for 5 minutes, turning as needed until most of the lemon juice has evaporated and the apples are just tender. Pile into the warm pastry cases, then put back in the oven for 2 to 3 minutes. Serve with crème fraîche.

Pear cream pie

SERVES 8

INGREDIENTS:

For the shortcrust pastry:
300g/11oz plain flour
Pinch of salt
175g/6oz butter (cubed)
50ml/2fl oz iced water

For the filling:
700g1½lb pears (peeled, cored
and sliced)
100g/4oz sugar
500ml/18fl oz double cream
¼ teaspoon freshly ground pepper
1 egg yolk (lightly beaten)

- To make the shortcrust pastry, sift the flour and the salt together into a large mixing bowl. Add the cubes of butter. Rub the butter and flour together with your fingertips until the mixture has a coarse texture.

→

←

- Stirring lightly with a knife, sprinkle water over the dough until it just begins to cohere. Gather the dough together into a ball, pressing it together with your hands. Wrap in clingfilm and chill for 30 minutes.
- Preheat the oven to 180°C/350°F/Gas mark 4. Roll out the dough to a thickness of 3mm/⅛in and use two-thirds of it to line a 23cm/9in pie dish.
- Mix the pear slices with the sugar and cream and add the pepper. Fill the pie with this mixture and cover with the remaining dough. Glaze with the egg yolk and cut a small hole in the top so the steam can escape during cooking.
- Bake in the oven for about 50 minutes, or until the top is browned.

Custard tarts

SERVES 6

INGREDIENTS:

225g/8oz plain flour
50g/2oz rice flour
25g/1oz icing sugar
100g/4oz butter (cubed)
1 egg yolk
3 tablespoons iced water
1 egg white (lightly beaten)

For the custard filling:
3 eggs
350ml/12fl oz milk
50g/2oz caster sugar
1 teaspoon vanilla essence
½ teaspoon ground nutmeg

- Sift the flours and icing sugar into a large bowl and rub in the butter using your fingertips until the mixture resembles fine breadcrumbs.
- Make a well and add the egg yolk and almost all the water. Mix with a flat-bladed knife, using a cutting action, until the mixture comes together in small beads, adding more water if the dough is too dry.
- Gather together and roll out between two sheets of baking parchment. Divide the dough into 12 equal portions and roll each portion out to fit the base and sides of a 10cm/4in loose-bottomed fluted tart tin. Line 12 tins with pastry and refrigerate for 20 minutes.
- Preheat the oven to 180°C/350°F/Gas mark 4. Line each pastry with crumpled baking parchment and baking beans. Place on baking trays and cook for 10 minutes. Remove the paper and beans and bake for a further 10 minutes. Cool, then brush the base and sides of each pastry case with the egg white. Reduce the oven temperature to 150°C/300°F/Gas mark 2.
- For the filling, whisk the eggs and milk in a bowl to combine. Add the sugar gradually, whisking to dissolve completely. Stir in the vanilla essence. Strain into a jug, then pour into the pastry cases. Sprinkle with the nutmeg and bake for 25 minutes, or until the filling is just set. Serve at room temperature.

Tropical fruit filo clusters

SERVES 8

INGREDIENTS:

1 banana (sliced)
1 small mango (peeled, stoned
and diced)
Lemon juice for sprinkling
1 small cooking apple (coarsely grated)
6 fresh dates (stoned and chopped)
50g/2oz ready-to-eat dried pineapple
(chopped)

50g/2oz sultanas
50g/2oz demerara sugar
1 teaspoon ground mixed spice
8 sheets filo pastry
2 tablespoons sunflower oil
Icing sugar for dusting

- Preheat the oven to 200°C/400°F/Gas mark 6. Line a baking tray with non-stick baking parchment. In a medium-sized mixing bowl, toss the banana slices and diced mango in lemon juice.
- Add the apple, dates, pineapple, sultanas, sugar and spice to the bowl and mix.
- To make each cluster, cut each sheet of pastry in half crossways to make 2 squares. Lightly brush two squares of pastry with oil and place one on top of the other at a 45° angle, making an 8-pointed star.
- Spoon some fruit filling into the centre, gather the pastry up over the filling and secure with string. Place the cluster on the baking tray and lightly brush all over with oil.
- Repeat with the remaining pastry squares and filling to make a total of 8 fruit clusters. Bake for 25 to 30 minutes, until golden brown and crisp. Carefully snip and remove the string from each cluster and serve hot or cold, dusted with sifted icing sugar.

Glazed nectarine tart

SERVES 6

INGREDIENTS:

175g/6oz puff pastry
25g/1oz butter (melted)
575g/11/4lb nectarines (quartered,

stoned and sliced)
2 tablespoons apricot jam

- Preheat the oven to 230°C/450°F/Gas mark 8.
- Roll out the pastry thinly to a 28cm/11in round. Put on a non-stick baking sheet

→

← and prick well all over with a fork. Bake for 8 to 10 minutes, or until well browned and cooked through.

- Brush some of the melted butter over the pastry and arrange the fruit slices over, right to the edges of the pastry. Drizzle with the remaining butter and grill for 5 minutes or until the fruit is just tinged with colour. Cool slightly.
- Warm the apricot jam with a little water and brush over the fruit to glaze.

Cranberry & apple mince pies

SERVES 12–16

INGREDIENTS:

For the mincemeat:
450g/1lb Bramley apples (cored and chopped)
225g/8oz fresh cranberries
100g/4oz candied peel (finely chopped)
350g/12oz raisins
350g/12oz sultanas
350g/12oz currants
175g/6oz light muscovado sugar
175g/6oz dark muscovado sugar
1 tablespoon ground mixed spice
Pinch of ground nutmeg
Grated zest and juice of 2 medium oranges
150ml/¼pt Calvados

For the almond pastry:
225g/8oz plain flour (sifted, plus extra for dusting)
Large pinch of salt
50g/2oz ground almonds
75g/3oz icing sugar
175g/6oz butter (cubed)
2 medium egg yolks

For the shortbread topping:
75g/3oz butter (softened)
25g/1oz caster sugar (plus extra for dusting)
75g/3oz plain flour
50g/2oz ground almonds

- For the mincemeat, combine all the ingredients together in a large bowl. Put into 5 warm sterilized jars and seal. Leave for at least 24 hours.
- For the pastry, put the flour, salt, almonds and icing sugar in a blender or food processor and pulse for 30 seconds. Add the butter and blend until the mixture resembles fine breadcrumbs. Add the egg yolks and process until the mixture just comes together, adding a little extra water if necessary. Knead lightly on a floured surface to bring together, then wrap and chill for 1 hour.
- For the topping, beat the butter and sugar until light and fluffy, then mix in the flour and almonds. Bring together with your hands, then wrap and chill for 15 minutes. Line 48 patty tins with paper cases.
- On a floured surface, roll out the pastry to a thickness of 2mm/¹/₁₆in and, using

a 7.5cm/3in fluted pastry cutter, cut out rounds. Put in the paper cases, prick the bases with a fork and chill for 10 minutes. Fill each one with 1 tablespoon of mincemeat.

- Preheat the oven to 190°C/375°F/Gas mark 5. Roll the pastry trimmings to 2mm/¹⁄₁₆in thick. Using a 4 x 2.5cm/1¹⁄₂ x 1in holly cutter, cut two leaves for each pie. Sprinkle with sugar and bake for 12 to 15 minutes or until golden.
- Cool for 15 minutes, then put on a wire rack to cool completely.

Tarte tatin

SERVES 6

INGREDIENTS:

200g/7oz plain flour
175g/6oz butter (cubed)
2 tablespoons caster sugar
1 egg (lightly beaten)

2 drops vanilla essence
8 Granny Smith apples
100g/4oz caster sugar
1 tablespoon water

- Sift the flour into a bowl and rub in the butter, using your fingertips, until the mixture resembles fine breadcrumbs. Stir in the caster sugar, then make a well in the centre. Add the egg and vanilla essence and mix with a flat-bladed knife, using a cutting action, until the mixture comes together in beads. Gather the dough together, then turn out on to a lightly floured surface and shape into a disc. Wrap in clingfilm and refrigerate for at least 30 minutes, to firm.
- Peel and core the apples and cut each one into 8 slices. Place the sugar and water in a heavy-based 25cm/10in frying pan with a metal handle. Stir over a low heat for 1 minute, or until the sugar has dissolved. Increase the heat to medium and cook for 4 to 5 minutes, or until the caramel turns golden. Remove the pan from the heat.
- Place the apples slices in neat circles to cover the base of the frying pan. Return the pan to a low heat and cook for 10 to 12 minutes, until the apples are caramelized. Remove the pan from the heat and leave to cool for 10 minutes.
- Preheat the oven to 220°C/425°F/Gas mark 7. Roll the pastry out on a lightly floured surface to a circle 1cm/¹⁄₂in larger than the frying pan. Place the pastry over the apples to cover them completely, tucking it down firmly at the edges.
- Bake for 30 to 35 minutes, or until the pastry is cooked. Leave for 15 minutes before turning out on to a plate. Serve warm or cold.

Pumpkin pie

SERVES 8

INGREDIENTS:

450g/1lb pumpkin
2 eggs (lightly beaten)
150g/5oz demerara sugar
75ml/3fl oz cream
1 tablespoon sweet sherry
1 teaspoon ground cinnamon
½ teaspoon ground nutmeg
½ teaspoon ground ginger

For the pastry:
150g/5oz plain flour
100g/4oz butter (cubed, plus extra for greasing)
2 teaspoons caster sugar
75ml/3fl oz iced water
1 egg yolk (lightly beaten, to glaze)
1 tablespoon milk, to glaze

Ice-cream or whipped cream, to serve

- Lightly grease a 23cm/9in round pie plate.
- Chop the pumpkin for the filling into small chunks and steam or boil for 10 minutes, or until the pumpkin is just tender. Drain the pumpkin thoroughly, then mash and set aside to cool.
- For the pastry, sift the flour into a large bowl and rub in the butter, using your fingertips, until the mixture resembles fine breadcrumbs. Stir in the caster sugar.
- Make a well in the centre, add almost all the water and mix with a flat-bladed knife.
- Gather the dough together and roll out between 2 sheets of baking parchment until large enough to cover the base and side of the pie plate. Line the dish with pastry, trim away excess pastry and crimp the edges. Refrigerate the pastry-lined dish for about 20 minutes.
- Preheat the oven to 180°C/350°F/Gas mark 4. Cut enough baking parchment to cover the pastry-lined dish. Spread baking beans over the paper and bake for 10 minutes. Remove the paper and beans and return to the oven for a further 10 minutes, or until lightly golden.
- For the filling, whisk the eggs and demerara sugar in a large bowl. Add the cooled mashed pumpkin, cream, sherry, cinnamon, nutmeg and ginger to the bowl and stir to combine thoroughly. Pour the filling into the pastry shell, smooth the surface with the back of a spoon, then bake for 40 minutes, or until it is set.
- Serve with ice-cream or whipped cream.

Chestnut tart

SERVES 8

INGREDIENTS:

For the shortcrust pastry:
150g/5oz plain flour
Pinch of salt
75g/3oz butter (cubed)
25ml/1fl oz iced water

For the filling:
450g/1lb chestnuts (puréed)
100g/4oz caster sugar
150ml/5fl oz double cream
1 tablespoon orange juice
1 tablespoon sweet sherry
2 egg yolks (well beaten)
50g/2oz butter (cubed)

- To make the shortcrust, sift the flour and salt together into a large mixing bowl.
- Add the cubes of butter. Rub the butter and flour together with your fingertips until the mixture has a coarse texture.
- Stirring lightly with a knife, sprinkle water over the dough until it just begins to cohere. Gather the dough together into a ball, pressing it together with your hands. Wrap in clingfilm and chill for 30 minutes.
- Preheat the oven to 190°C/375°F/Gas mark 5.
- Roll the pastry so it is large enough to line a 25cm/10in pie tin. Line with aluminium foil and baking beans and bake blind in the oven for 15 minutes. Cool for 5 minutes and remove the foil and beans.
- Mix the chestnut purée with the sugar, cream, orange juice, sherry and egg yolks. Pour the mixture into the pastry case and dot the filling with the butter.
- Lower the oven temperature to 150°C/300°F/Gas mark 2 and bake the tart for 20 minutes or until just firm. Serve cold with whipped cream.

Cherry clafoutis

SERVES 6-8

INGREDIENTS:

25g/1oz butter (melted, plus extra for greasing)
400g/1lb fresh cherries
50g/2oz plain flour

75g/3oz caster sugar
4 eggs (lightly beaten)
250ml/9fl oz milk
Icing sugar for dusting

- Preheat the oven to 180°C/350°F/Gas mark 4.

→

←

- Brush a 23cm/9in glass or ceramic pie plate with melted butter.
- Pit the cherries and spread onto the pie plate in a single layer.
- Sift the flour into a bowl, add the sugar and make a well in the centre.
- Gradually add the combined eggs, milk and butter, whisking until smooth and free of lumps.
- Pour the batter over the cherries and bake for 30 to 35 minutes. Remove from the oven and dust generously with icing sugar. Serve immediately.

Tiny fruit tartlets

SERVES 8

INGREDIENTS:

For the pastry:
75g/3oz plain flour
25g/1oz caster sugar
50g/2oz butter (cubed)
1 egg yolk

For the crème pâtissière:
1 egg yolk

25g/1oz caster sugar
15g/1/2oz plain flour
150ml/5fl oz milk
15g/1/2oz butter
2 drops vanilla essence
A selection of fresh fruit – strawberries, raspberries & grapes

- To make the pastry, sift the flour on to a clean surface. Make a well in the centre and add the sugar, butter and egg yolk. Using the fingertips of one hand, pinch and work the sugar, butter and egg together until well blended. Gradually work in the flour, adding a little water if necessary to bind together. Knead lightly, then wrap and chill for about 1 hour.
- To make the crème pâtissière, put the egg yolk and sugar in a bowl and beat until smooth and creamy. Stir in the flour and mix well. Heat the milk until hot, but not boiling, and gradually stir into the egg mixture. Return the mixture to the pan and bring to the boil over a low heat, stirring all the time. Remove from the heat and beat in the butter and vanilla essence. Cover with damp baking parchment and leave to cool.
- Roll out the pastry fairly thinly on a lightly floured surface and use to line 24 x 5cm/2in small tartlet tins. Prick the bases with a fork and chill for 15 minutes before baking. Preheat the oven to 190°C/375°F/Gas mark 5.
- Bake the pastry cases for 6 to 8 minutes until golden brown and cooked through. Remove from the tins and leave to cool.
- Fill each tartlet with crème pâtissière and top each with fruit.

Pine kernel tartlets

SERVES 8

INGREDIENTS:

For the pastry:
250g/9oz plain flour
Pinch of salt
100g/4oz butter
100g/4oz icing sugar
1 large egg
2 large egg yolks

For the filling:
50g/2oz continental chocolate (broken into pieces)
50g/2oz butter

175g/6oz caster sugar (plus 2 tablespoons extra)
75g/3oz brown sugar
175ml/6fl oz milk
3½ tablespoons golden syrup
Finely grated zest of 2 large oranges
2 tablespoons freshly squeezed orange juice
1 teaspoon vanilla essence
3 large eggs (lightly beaten)
100g/4oz pine kernels

- To make the pastry, sift the flour and the into a bowl. Make a well in the centre and add the butter, icing sugar, whole egg and egg yolks. Using your fingertips, mix the ingredients in the well into a paste.
- Gradually incorporate the flour to make a soft dough. Quickly and lightly knead the dough. Shape into a ball, wrap in clingfilm and chill for at least 1 hour.
- Roll the pastry into 8 circles, each 15cm/6in across. Use to line 8 loose-bottomed 10cm/4in tartlet tins. Line each with aluminium foil and fill with baking beans. Chill for 10 minutes.
- Preheat the oven to 200°C/400°F/Gas mark 6.
- Bake for 5 minutes, remove the foil and beans and bake for a further 8 minutes.
- Leave to cool on a wire rack. Reduce the oven temperature to 180°C/350°F/Gas mark 4.
- Put the chocolate and butter in a saucepan and stir over a medium heat until blended.
- Stir in the remaining ingredients.
- Spoon the filling into the tartlet cases on a baking tray. Bake for 25 to 30 minutes or until the tops puff up and crack and feel set. Cover with baking parchment for the final 5 minutes if the pastry is browning too much. Transfer to a wire rack and leave to cool for at least 15 minutes before unmoulding. Serve warm or at room temperature.

Caramelized orange tart

SERVES 6-8

INGREDIENTS:

For the pastry:
*225g/8oz plain flour (plus extra for
dusting)*
Pinch of salt
2 tablespoons icing sugar
100g/4oz butter (cubed)
1 egg yolk (beaten)
2 tablespoons cold water

For the filling:
Juice of 1 lemon
Juice of 1 orange

Grated zest of 2 oranges
75g/3oz butter
225g/8oz granulated sugar
3 eggs (beaten)
75g/3oz ground almonds
2 tablespoons orange liqueur

To decorate:
100g/4oz caster sugar
300ml/¹/₂pt water
Pared zest of 1 orange (cut into slivers)

- To make the pastry, sift the flour with the salt and the icing sugar into a bowl. Add the butter and, using your fingertips, rub into the flour until the mixture resembles fine crumbs. Add the egg and the water and bring together to form a dough. Knead lightly, wrap in clingfilm and chill.
- To make the filling, put the lemon and orange juice, orange zest, butter, sugar and eggs in a heavy-based pan and heat gently, stirring continuously, until thickened. Stir in the almonds and orange liqueur and put to one side.
- Preheat the oven to 200°C/400°F/Gas mark 6.
- Roll out the pastry on a floured surface and use to line a 23cm/9in tart tin. Prick the base with a fork and chill for 10 minutes. Line the pastry case with aluminium foil and fill with baking beans. Bake blind for 15 minutes, then remove the foil and beans and bake for a further 5 minutes. Remove from the oven and reduce the temperature to 180°C/350°F/Gas mark 4.
- Pour the orange filling into the pastry case, put back in the oven and continue to bake for 20 minutes, until just firm. Leave to cool.
- Put 50g/2oz sugar in a pan with the water. Heat to dissolve the sugar and add the orange slivers. Simmer for 10 to 15 minutes until the liquid has reduced and the peel is tender. Drain.
- Preheat the grill. Sprinkle the rest of the sugar over the tart and flash under the grill to caramelize. Cool and spoon the peel around the edge.

Citrus tart

SERVES 12

INGREDIENTS:

For the pastry:
175g/6oz plain flour
75g/3oz butter (plus extra for greasing)
3 tablespoons caster sugar
3 egg yolks

For the filling:
Juice of 3 lemons

Finely grated zest of 1 lemon
Juice of 1 orange
2 eggs
1 egg yolk
350ml/12fl oz double cream
175g/6oz caster sugar

- To make the pastry, sift the flour into a mixing bowl, make a well in the centre and place the butter, sugar and egg yolks in it. Work with the fingertips of one hand until these are blended then gradually work in the flour. Continue mixing until the pastry forms a smooth ball. Wrap in clingfilm and chill for 30 minutes.
- Preheat the oven to 190°C/375°F/Gas mark 5. Grease a 28cm/11in flan dish.
- Roll out the pastry and use to line the tin. Prick the base of the pastry with a fork and line with aluminium foil. Fill with baking beans and bake blind for 15 to 20 minutes or until just brown. Cool and reduce the oven temperature to 160°C/325°F/Gas mark 3.
- To make the filling, place the lemon zest in a large bowl with the lemon and orange juice. Add the eggs and yolk, cream and sugar. Whisk the mixture together until the sugar has dissolved and the top is fluffy. Pour the filling into the pastry case and bake in the centre of the oven for 30 to 35 minutes or until the filling is set.

Chocolate meringue pie

SERVES 6

INGREDIENTS:

225g/8oz dark chocolate digestive
biscuits
25g/1oz butter (melted)

For the filling:
3 egg yolks
50g/2oz caster sugar
50g/2oz cornflour

600ml/1pt milk
100g/4oz dark chocolate

For the meringue:
2 egg whites
100g/4oz caster sugar
¼ teaspoon vanilla essence

- Preheat the oven to 160°C/325°F/Gas mark 3.
- Place the digestive biscuits in a plastic bag and crush with a rolling pin. Pour into a mixing bowl. Stir the butter into the biscuit crumbs until well mixed.
- Press the biscuit mixture firmly into the base and up the sides of a 23cm/9in flan tin or dish.
- To make the filling, beat the egg yolks, sugar and cornflour in a large bowl until they form a smooth paste, adding a little of the milk if necessary. Heat the milk until almost boiling, then slowly pour into the egg mixture, whisking well.
- Return the mixture to the saucepan and cook gently, whisking constantly, until it thickens. Remove from the heat. Melt the chocolate in a heatproof bowl set over a pan of simmering water. Then whisk the melted chocolate into the mixture in the saucepan. Pour the mixture into the digestive biscuit base.
- To make the meringue, whisk the egg whites in a large mixing bowl until standing in soft peaks. Gradually whisk in about two thirds of the sugar until the mixture is thick and glossy. Fold in the remaining sugar and the vanilla essence.
- Spread the meringue over the filling. Bake in the centre of the oven for 30 minutes. Serve warm.

Bakewell tart

SERVES 6

INGREDIENTS:

225g/8oz puff pastry
100g/4oz ground almonds
100g/4oz caster sugar
50g/2oz butter

3 eggs
¼ teaspoon almond essence
4 tablespoons strawberry jam

- Pre-heat the oven to 200°C/400°F/Gas mark 6.
- Roll out the pastry on a floured surface and use to line a 900ml/1½pt shallow dish.
- Beat the almonds with the sugar, butter, eggs and almond essence.
- Spread the pastry with an even layer of jam and pour in the filling.
- Bake for 30 minutes or until set.

Pear tart

SERVES 6

INGREDIENTS:

275g/10oz plain flour
Pinch of salt
100g/4oz caster sugar
100g/4oz butter (diced)
1 egg
1 egg yolk
Few drops of vanilla essence

2-3 teaspoons water
4 tablespoons apricot jam
50g/2oz Amaretti biscuits (crumbled)
900g/2lb pears (peeled and cored)
1 teaspoon ground cinnamon
75g/3oz raisins
50g/2oz demerara sugar

- Preheat the oven to 200°C/400°F/Gas mark 6.
- Sift the flour and salt into a mixing bowl, make a well in the centre and add the sugar, butter, egg, egg yolk, vanilla essence and most of the water.
- Using your fingers, gradually work the flour into the other ingredients to give a smooth dough, adding more water if necessary. Wrap in clingfilm and chill for 1 hour.
- Roll out three-quarters of the dough and use to line a shallow 25cm/10in cake tin. Spread the jam over the base and sprinkle with the biscuits.
  Slice the pears very thinly. Arrange over the biscuits in the pastry case. Sprinkle with cinnamon, raisins and demerara sugar.
  Roll out the remaining pastry and use cutters or a knife to trim into the shapes of your choice to decorate the top of the dish. Alternatively, use to make a lattice.
- Cook in the oven for 50 minutes, until golden and cooked through. Leave to cool, then serve warm or cold.

Sticky plum tart

SERVES 6

INGREDIENTS:

100g/4oz plain flour
1 teaspoon ground cinnamon
Pinch of salt
75g/3oz butter
1 egg yolk
1 tablespoon chilled water

450g/1lb plums (halved, stoned and diced)
25g/1oz caster sugar
3 tablespoons apricot jam
2 tablespoons water

- Sieve the flour into a blender or food processor, add the ground cinnamon, salt, butter and egg yolk. Process for 30 seconds or until evenly combined. Add the chilled water and process for a further 30 seconds. Knead together lightly and roll out to a circle approximately 25.5cm/10in in diameter. Put on a baking tray and chill for 10 to 15 minutes.
- Preheat the oven to 200°C/400°F/Gas mark 6.
- Prick the pastry all over with a fork. Bake for 20 to 25 minutes, or until golden brown.
- Arrange the plums over the cooked pastry and sprinkle with the sugar. Put back in the oven for 40 to 45 minutes or until the plums are tender.
- Melt the jam in a small saucepan with the water, bring to the boil and bubble for 1 minute. Brush or spoon over the warm tart.

Melon marmalade tart

SERVES 8

INGREDIENTS:

For the pastry:
150g/5oz plain flour
Pinch of salt
75g/3oz butter (cubed)
25ml/1fl oz iced water

For the filling:
900g/2lb cantaloupe melon (quartered, seeded, flesh diced)
200ml/7fl oz white wine
2 macaroons
50g/2oz caster sugar
1/2 teaspoon ground cinnamon

- To make the pastry, sift the flour and salt together into a large mixing bowl. Add the cubes of butter. Rub the butter and flour mixture together with your fingertips until the mixture has a coarse texture. Stirring lightly with a knife, sprinkle water over the dough until it just begins to cohere. Gather the dough together into a ball, pressing it together with your hands. Wrap in clingfilm and chill for 30 minutes.

- Preheat the oven to 190°C/375°F/Gas mark 5.
- Boil the melon with the wine, stirring often, until the mixture has reduced to a purée and thickened.
- Pound together the macaroons, sugar and cinnamon, and add the melon purée.
- Line a 20cm/8in tart tin with the pastry dough and pour in the melon mixture.
- Bake in the oven for 30 to 35 minutes, until the pastry is crisp and golden.

Tarte au Citron

SERVES 6-8

INGREDIENTS:

For the pastry:
100g/4oz plain flour
Pinch of salt
75g/3oz butter (softened, plus extra for greasing)
1 egg yolk
2 tablespoons icing sugar (sifted)

For the filling:
3 eggs
2 egg yolks
175g/6oz caster sugar
125ml/4fl oz single cream
175ml/6fl oz lemon juice
1½ tablespoons finely grated lemon zest
2 small lemons
150g/5oz granulated sugar
200ml/7fl oz water

- To make the pastry, sift the flour and salt into a large bowl. Make a well and add the butter, egg yolk and icing sugar. Work together the butter, yolk and sugar with your fingertips, then incorporate the flour. Bring together into a ball, adding water if the mixture is too dry. Cover with clingfilm and refrigerate for 20 minutes.

Preheat the oven to 200°C/400°F/Gas mark 6. Lightly grease a 20cm/8in loose-bottomed flan tin.

Roll out the pastry between 2 sheets of baking parchment until it is 3mm/⅛in thick, to fit the base and sides of the tin. Trim the edge and chill for 10 minutes. Line the pastry with aluminium foil, fill with baking beans and bake for 10 minutes. Remove the foil and beans and bake for another 6 to 8 minutes, or until the pastry looks dry all over. Cool the pastry and reduce the oven temperature to 150°C/300°F/Gas mark 2.

For the filling, whisk the eggs, yolks and caster sugar together, add the cream and juice and mix well. Strain into a jug and then add the lemon zest. Place the

→

←

flan tin on a baking tray on the middle shelf of the oven and carefully pour in the filling right up to the top. Bake for 40 minutes, or until it is just set.
- Slice the lemons very thinly. Combine the granulated sugar and the water in a small frying pan and stir over a low heat until the sugar has dissolved. Add the lemon slices and simmer over a low heat for 40 minutes, or until the peel is very tender. Lift out of the pan and drain on baking parchment. Cover the tart with the lemon slices and serve immediately.

Chocolate brandy torte

SERVES 12

INGREDIENTS:

For the base:
250g/9oz gingernut biscuits
75g/3oz dark chocolate
100g/4oz butter

For the filling:
225g/8oz dark chocolate (broken into pieces)

250g/9oz Mascarpone cheese
2 eggs (separated)
3 tablespoons brandy
300ml/10fl oz double cream
4 tablespoons caster sugar

- Crush the biscuits in a bag with a rolling pin. Melt the chocolate and butter together and pour over the biscuits in a mixing bowl. Mix well, then use to line the base and sides of a greased 23cm/9in loose-bottomed flan tin or springform tin. Leave to chill.
- For the filling, melt the chocolate in a bowl set over a pan of simmering water, then remove from the heat and beat in the Mascarpone cheese, egg yolks and brandy.
- Lightly whip the cream until just holding its shape and gently fold in the chocolate mixture.
- Whisk the egg whites in a bowl until standing in soft peaks. Add the caster sugar a little at a time and whisk until thick and glossy. Fold into the chocolate mixture, in 2 batches, until just mixed.
- Spoon the mixture into the prepared base and chill for at least 2 hours before serving.

Redcurrant filo baskets

SERVES 6

INGREDIENTS:

3 sheets filo pastry
1 tablespoon sunflower oil
175g/6oz redcurrants

250ml/9fl oz Greek yogurt
1 teaspoon icing sugar

- Preheat the oven to 200°C/400°F/Gas mark 6. Cut the sheets of filo pastry into 18 squares, measuring 10cm/4in.
- Brush each filo square very thinly with the oil, then arrange 3 squares in each hole of a 6-hole muffin tin, placing each one at a different angle so that they form star-shaped baskets. Bake for 6 to 8 minutes, until crisp and golden. Lift the baskets out carefully and leave them to cool on a wire rack.
- Set aside a few redcurrants for decoration and stir the rest into the Greek yogurt.
- Spoon this mixture into the filo baskets. Decorate with the reserved redcurrants and sprinkle them with the icing sugar to serve.

Puff pastry slices with whipped cream

SERVES 6

INGREDIENTS:

For the puff dough:
150g/5oz plain flour
1 teaspoon salt
150g/5oz butter
75ml/3fl oz water

For the pastry cream:
50g/2oz caster sugar

3 egg yolks
25g/1oz flour
Pinch of salt
225ml/8fl oz milk
2.5cm/1in piece of vanilla pod
75ml/3fl oz double cream
50g/2oz icing sugar

- To make the puff pastry, sift the flour and salt into a bowl. Cut a quarter of the butter into small pieces and add them to the bowl. Rub the butter into the flour with your fingertips. Add just enough cold water to bind the ingredients and work them into a ball. Wrap in clingfilm and refrigerate for 30 minutes.

→

←

- Put the remaining butter between 2 sheets of baking parchment and, with a rolling pin, flatten it into a slab about 15cm/6in square and 1cm/½in thick. Chill in the refrigerator for about 30 minutes.
- Preheat the oven to 220°C/425°F/Gas mark 7.
- Lightly flour the worktop and roll out the dough into a 20 x 45cm/8 x 18in rectangle. Using a sharp knife, cut the dough cleanly into 3 strips, measuring 15 x 20cm/6 x 8in.
- Brush a large baking tray with water, lay the strips on it and prick all over with a fork. Bake for 20 minutes.
- To make the pastry cream, mix the sugar and egg yolks together with a spoon, beating until the mixture is thick. Gradually work in the flour and season with the salt.
- Heat the milk with the vanilla pod to boiling point. Stirring constantly, pour the hot milk into the egg mixture in a thin stream. Turn the pastry cream mixture into a saucepan and, stirring vigorously, cook over a medium heat until the mixture comes to boiling point. Boil for about 2 minutes. Strain the pastry cream and allow it to cool, stirring occasionally to prevent a skin from forming.
- Combine the double cream and 15g/½oz icing sugar in a chilled bowl and beat with a small wire whisk for 5 minutes until the cream is thickened. Add the pastry cream to the whipped cream and fold the two together carefully with a wooden spoon or spatula.
- Spread half of the cream on one of the strips of pastry. Place the second pastry strip on top, spread with the rest of the cream, and cover with the last pastry strip.
- Sprinkle with the remaining icing sugar and serve.

Pears in pastry cases

SERVES 4

INGREDIENTS:

200g/7oz butter (cubed)
75ml/3fl oz white wine (warmed)
Pinch of salt
50g/2oz caster sugar
300g/11oz plain flour (plus extra for dusting)

1 teaspoon ground cinnamon
4 pears (peeled and cored, stems left attached)
1 egg yolk (beaten with 1 tablespoon water)
125ml/4fl oz double cream

- Add the butter, piece by piece, to the wine and beat the mixture with a whisk until it becomes creamy. Beat in the salt, 1 tablespoon sugar and all of the flour, spoonful by spoonful. Roll the resulting dough into a ball, cover with a tea towel and leave for 2 hours.
- Preheat the oven to 220°C/425°F/Gas mark 7.

- Mix the remaining sugar with the cinnamon. Roll the pears in this mixture. Roll out the dough to 5mm/¼in thick and cut it into 4 squares large enough to wrap around the pears. Wrap each pear in a case of dough, leaving the stems sticking out. Brush the pastries with the egg yolk.
- Put the pears on a floured baking tray. Bake in the oven for 25 minutes, or until the pastry is golden. Serve hot with cream.

Pain au chocolat

SERVES 6

INGREDIENTS:

450g/1lb strong plain flour
½ teaspoon salt
½ teaspoon dried yeast
25g/1oz lard
1 egg (beaten lightly)
225ml/8fl oz hand-hot water

175g/6oz butter (softened, plus extra for greasing)
Beaten egg (to seal and glaze)
100g/4oz dark chocolate (broken into 12 squares)

- Lightly grease a baking tray.
- Sift the flour and salt into a mixing bowl and stir in the yeast. Rub in the fat with your fingertips. Add the egg and enough of the water to form a soft dough. Knead the dough for about 10 minutes until elastic.
- Roll the dough out to form a rectangle measuring 38 x 20cm/15 x 8in. Divide the butter into 3 portions and dot one portion over two-thirds of the rectangle, leaving a small border around the edge.
- Fold the rectangle into 3 by first folding the plain third of the dough over and then the other third. Seal the edges of the dough by pressing with a rolling pin.
- Give the dough a quarter turn. Re-roll and fold again, without butter, then wrap the dough and chill for 30 minutes.
- Repeat the buttering and folding outlined above twice more, chilling the dough each time. Re-roll and fold twice more without butter. Chill for a final 30 minutes.
- Roll the dough to a rectangle measuring 45 x 30cm/18 x 12in, trim and halve lengthways. Cut each half into 6 rectangles and brush with beaten egg. Place a chocolate square at the end of each rectangle and roll up to form a sausage.
- Press the ends together and place, seam side up, on the baking tray. Cover and leave to rise for 40 minutes in a warm place.
- Preheat the oven to 220°C/425°F/Gas mark 7.
- Brush the pastries with egg and bake for 20 to 25 minutes, until golden. Cool on a wire rack. Can be served warm or cold.

Chocolate éclairs

SERVES 9

INGREDIENTS

100g/4oz butter (plus extra for greasing)
225ml/8fl oz water
100g/4oz plain flour (sifted)

4 eggs (lightly beaten)
300ml/½pt double cream (whipped)
150g/5oz dark chocolate (broken into pieces)

- Preheat the oven to 210°C/425°F/Gas mark 7. Grease 2 baking trays.
- Combine the butter and water in a large heavy-based saucepan. Stir over a medium heat until the butter melts. Increase the heat, bring to the boil, then remove from the heat.
- Add the flour to the saucepan all at once and quickly beat into the buttery water with a wooden spoon. Return to the heat and continue beating until the mixture leaves the sides of the pan and forms a ball. Transfer to a large bowl and cool slightly.
- Beat the mixture to release any remaining heat. Gradually add the egg, about 3 teaspoonfuls at a time. Beat well after each addition until all the egg has been added and the mixture is glossy.
- Spoon the mixture into a piping bag fitted with a 1.5cm/⁵⁄₈in plain nozzle.
- Sprinkle the baking trays lightly with water. Pipe 15cm/6in lengths on to the trays, leaving room for them to expand. Bake for 10 to 15 minutes. Reduce the heat to 180°C/350°F/Gas mark 4 and bake for a further 15 minutes. Cool on a wire rack.
- Split each éclair and remove any uncooked dough. Fill with cream.
- Melt the chocolate in a bowl set over a saucepan of simmering water. Spread the melted chocolate over each éclair.

Apple turnovers

SERVES 6

INGREDIENTS:

Butter for greasing
500g/1lb 2oz puff pastry
1 egg white (lightly beaten)
Caster sugar for dusting

For the filling:
200g/7oz stewed apple
25g/1oz caster sugar
50g/2oz raisins (chopped)
25g/1oz walnuts (chopped)

- Preheat the oven to 210°C/425°F/Gas mark 7. Lightly grease a baking tray.
- Roll the pastry on a lightly floured surface to 45 x 35cm/18 x 14in. Cut out 12 rounds measuring 10cm/4in.
- For the apple filling, mix together the apple, sugar, raisins and walnuts in a mixing bowl.
- Divide the filling among the pastry rounds, then brush the edges with water.
- Fold in half and pinch firmly together to seal. Brush the tops with egg white and dust with caster sugar. Make 2 small slits in the top of each turnover. Bake for 15 minutes, then lower the heat to 190°C/375°F/Gas mark 5 and bake for a further 10 minutes. Serve warm.

Banana empanadas

SERVES 4

INGREDIENTS:

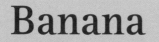

2 bananas (diced)	8 sheets filo pastry (halved
2 teaspoons sugar	lengthways)
Juice of ½ lemon	Vegetable oil for brushing
200g/7oz dark chocolate (broken into	Icing sugar for dusting
small pieces)	Ground cinnamon for dusting

- Preheat the oven to 190°C/375°F/Gas mark 5.
- Place the bananas in a mixing bowl with the sugar and lemon juice and stir well to combine. Add the chocolate.
- Working one at a time, lay a sheet of filo in front of you and brush with oil.
- Place a couple of teaspoonfuls of the banana mixture in one corner of the pastry, then fold over into a triangle shape to enclose the filling. Continue to fold in a triangular shape until all the pastry is completely wrapped around the filling.
- Make the remaining empanadas the same way. Brush all with a little more oil and dust with sugar and cinnamon to taste.
- Place on a baking tray and bake in the oven for about 15 minutes. Remove from the oven and serve hot.

Peaches in filo pastry

SERVES 6

INGREDIENTS:

150g/5oz Amaretti biscuits
100g/4oz ricotta cheese
2 teaspoons demerara sugar
1½ tablespoons Amaretto

6 peaches
450g/1lb filo pastry (large sheets)
100g/4oz butter (melted)
100g/4oz flaked almonds

- Preheat the oven to 180°C/350°F/Gas mark 4.
- Place the biscuits in a polythene bag and crush coarsely with a rolling pin. Mix together the ricotta, 75g/3oz crushed biscuits, the demerara sugar and Amaretto to form a fairly stiff paste.
- Carefully cut each peach in half and remove the stone. Replace the stone with a spoonful of the ricotta mixture and sandwich the halves back together again.
- Open out the pastry and, slicing through all the squares at once, cut into 20cm/8in squares. You will need 18 squares in total. Keep the filo covered with a damp tea towel while you work.
- For each peach use 3 of the filo squares. Working with one peach at a time, butter each square of pastry and lay on top of each other at different angles, so you have a 12-pointed star.
- Spoon one sixth of the remaining Amaretti crumbs into the middle of the filo.
- Put a whole peach on top of the crumbs, stalk-side down.
- Gather up the sides of the pastry and pinch together at the top, securing with string. Repeat with the remaining 5 peaches.
- Place the peaches on a greased baking tray. Brush each parcel with any remaining butter and sprinkle with flaked almonds. Bake for 30 to 40 minutes.

Sly cakes

SERVES 8

INGREDIENTS:

450g/1lb puff pastry
2 cooking apples (peeled, cored and diced)
50g/2oz butter (plus extra for greasing)
50g/2oz muscovado sugar

225g/8oz sultanas
50g/2oz mixed peel
2 teaspoons ground allspice
1 egg yolk (beaten)
Icing sugar for dusting

- Preheat the oven to 200°C/400°F/Gas mark 6.
- Roll out the puff pastry to a thickness of 1cm/½in, then trim and cut into 2 equal rectangles. Put one on a lightly greased non-stick baking tray.
- Fry the apples in the butter. When golden and starting to soften, add the muscovado sugar and toss to coat. Remove from the heat and stir in the sultanas, mixed peel and allspice.
- Spread the mixture on to the pastry rectangle on the baking tray. Put the other rectangle on top and press down lightly. Divide into 16 squares with a sharp knife, pressing nearly all the way through, and brush the tops with egg yolk.
- Bake for 15 to 20 minutes. Transfer to a wire rack to cool. Finish by dusting with icing sugar.

Cherry turnover

SERVES 8

INGREDIENTS:

450g/1lb shortcrust pastry
450g/1lb stoned sour cherries

Double cream, to serve

- Preheat the oven to 180°C/350°F/Gas mark 4.
- Roll out the pastry and place in it a greased 20cm/8in pie dish, allowing the sides of the pastryto hang over the edge. Fill the lined dish with the cherries. Fold the edges of the dough over the filling, sealing them where they meet in the centre.
- Prick the pastry top with a fork.
- Bake for 30 minutes, or until the pastry is lightly browned. Serve with cream.

Mango dumplings

SERVES 4

INGREDIENTS:

2 teaspoons baking powder
1 tablespoon caster sugar
150ml/¼pt water
150ml/¼pt milk
400g/14oz plain flour

1 small mango
100g/4oz canned lychees (drained)
1 tablespoon ground almonds
4 tablespoons orange juice

→

←

- To make the dough, place the baking powder and caster sugar in a large mixing bowl.
- Mix the water and milk together and then stir this mixture into the baking powder and sugar mixture until well combined. Gradually stir in the flour to make a soft dough. Set the dough aside in a warm place for about 1 hour.
- To make the filling, peel the mango and cut the flesh from the stone. Roughly chop the mango flesh, reserving half for the sauce.
- Chop the lychees and add to half of the chopped mango, together with the ground almonds. Leave to stand for 20 minutes.
- To make the sauce, blend the reserved mango and the orange juice in a blender or food processor until smooth. Using the back of a spoon, press the mixture through a sieve to make a smooth sauce.
- Divide the dough into 16 equal pieces. Roll each piece out on a lightly floured surface into 7.5cm/3in rounds.
- Spoon a little of the mango and lychee filling on to the centre of each round and fold the dough over the filling to make semi-circles. Pinch the edges together to seal firmly.
- Place the dumplings on a heatproof plate in a steamer, cover and steam for about 20 to 25 minutes or until cooked through.
- Remove the dumplings from the steamer and serve warm with the mango sauce.

Pear upside-down tart

SERVES 10

INGREDIENTS:

For the shortcrust pastry:
150g/5oz plain flour
Pinch of salt
75g/3oz butter (cubed)
25ml/1fl oz iced water

For the filling:
7 slightly under-ripe dessert pears
(halved, cored and peeled)
100g/4oz sugar
½ teaspoon ground cinnamon
600ml/1pt red wine

- To make the pastry, sift the flour and salt together into a large mixing bowl. Add the cubes of butter. Rub the butter and flour together with your fingertips until the mixture has a coarse texture.
- Stirring lightly with a knife, sprinkle water over the dough until it just begins to cohere. Gather the dough together into a ball, pressing it together with your hands. Wrap in clingfilm and chill for 30 minutes.
- Preheat the oven to 200°C/400°F/Gas mark 6.
- Arrange the pear halves in a deep 25cm/10in frying pan. Split the halves if necessary so the whole base is covered. Sprinkle the sugar and cinnamon over

the pears, then pour the red wine over. Bring to the boil and simmer, covered, for 1 hour. Drain all of the liquid into a saucepan, being careful not to displace the pears. Reduce the cooking liquid over a high heat, stirring occasionally, until only about 125ml/4fl oz remains. Dribble the remaining liquid evenly over the pears.

- Roll out a round of dough to the exact dimensions of the pan. Prick the dough 4 or 5 times with a knife tip and lay the dough gently over the pears. Bake for about 40 minutes or until golden and crisp. Turn out on to a plate to cool slightly, then serve.

Cream cheese & honey pie

SERVES 8

INGREDIENTS:

For the shortcrust pastry:
150g/5oz plain flour
Pinch of salt
75g/3oz butter (cubed)
25ml/1fl oz iced water

For the filling:
175g/6oz cream cheese

150ml/¹/₄pt milk
4 tablespoons sugar
1 teaspoon grated lemon zest
1 teaspoon ground cinnamon
4 teaspoon honey
2 eggs (lightly beaten)

- To make the shortcrust pastry, sift the flour and salt together into a large mixing bowl. Add the cubes of butter. Rub the butter and flour together with your fingertips until the mixture has a coarse texture.
- Stirring lightly with a knife, sprinkle water over the dough until it just begins to cohere. Gather the dough together into a ball, pressing it together with your hands. Wrap in clingfilm and chill for 30 minutes.
- Preheat the oven to 190°C/375°F/Gas mark 5.
- Spread the ball of dough into a 20cm/8in pie tin, patting it into place with your fingers.
- To make the filling, beat the cream cheese until smooth. Add the milk gradually, then stir in the sugar, lemon zest, cinnamon, honey and beaten eggs.
- Pour this filling mixture into the pastry case, stand the pie tin on a baking tray and cook in the centre of the oven for about 45 minutes, until the filling is set.

Puddings

From traditional fruit crumbles, Sticky toffee pudding and
Bread & butter pudding, all served with lashings of creamy
custard, to Italian imports such as Tiramisu and Zabaglione,
these scrumptuous recipes will leave you full and satisfied
but your taste buds will always be wanting more.

Grape & almond layer

SERVES 4

INGREDIENTS:

300ml/¹/₂pt fromage frais
300ml/¹/₂pt Greek set yogurt
25g/1oz icing sugar (sifted)
2 tablespoons crème de cassis

450g/1lb red grapes (deseeded)
175g/6oz Amaretti biscuits
2 passion fruit

- Mix together the fromage frais and yogurt in a bowl and lightly fold in the icing sugar and crème de cassis with a large metal spoon until lightly blended.
- Using a small knife, remove any seeds from the grapes if necessary. Rinse lightly and pat dry on kitchen paper.
- Place the grapes in a bowl. Place the Amaretti biscuits in a polythene bag and crush roughly with a rolling pin. Cut the passion fruit in half, scoop out the seeds with a teaspoon and reserve.
- Divide the yogurt mixture between 4 tall glasses, then layer alternately with grapes, crushed biscuits and most of the passion fruit seeds. Top with the yogurt mixture and the remaining passion fruit seeds. Chill for 1 hour and serve.

Fruited rice ring

SERVES 4

INGREDIENTS:

75g/3oz short-grain rice
900ml/1¹/₂pt milk
1 cinnamon stick
175g/6oz dried fruit salad

175ml/6fl oz orange juice
50g/2oz caster sugar
Finely grated zest of 1 small orange
Sunflower oil for greasing

- Place the rice, milk and cinnamon stick in a large pan and bring to the boil.
- Cover and simmer, stirring occasionally, for about 1¹/₂ hours until no free liquid remains.
- Meanwhile, place the fruit salad and orange juice in a pan and bring to the boil.
- Cover and simmer very gently for about 1 hour, until tender.
- Remove the cinnamon stick from the rice and stir in the sugar and orange zest.
- Tip the fruit into the base of a lightly oiled 1.5 litre/2¹/₂pt ring mould. Spoon the rice over, smoothing down firmly. Chill for 1 hour before serving.

Plum Charlotte

SERVES 4

INGREDIENTS:

450g/1lb plums (halved and stoned)
1 tablespoon water
*1 tablespoon caster sugar (plus extra
for sprinkling)*

4 slices white bread
25g/1oz butter

- Preheat the oven to 190°C/375°F/Gas mark 5.
- Put the plums in a saucepan with the water and stew until tender. Add the sugar.
- Spread the bread with the butter and use 2 of the slices to line a 20cm/8in ovenproof serving dish. Top with the plums.
- Cut the remaining bread into thin strips and arrange in a lattice on top of the plums. Sprinkle with caster sugar and bake in the oven for 30 to 40 minutes, until golden brown.

Mexican lemon rice pudding

SERVES 4

INGREDIENTS:

75g/3oz raisins
100g/4oz short-grain rice
250ml/9fl oz water
500ml/18fl oz milk
225g/8oz granulated sugar

¼ teaspoon salt
1 cinnamon stick
1 egg yolk (well beaten)
1 tablespoon butter (softened)

- Put the raisins in a small bowl. Cover with warm water and set aside to soak.
- Put the rice in a saucepan together with the water. Bring slowly to the boil, then lower the heat. Cover the pan and simmer gently for about 20 minutes or until all the water has been absorbed.
  Add the milk, sugar, salt and cinnamon stick. Cook, stirring, over a very low heat until all the milk has been absorbed. Do not cover the pan.
  Discard the cinnamon stick. Drain the raisins well and add to the pan with the egg yolk and butter, stirring constantly until the butter has been absorbed and the pudding is creamy.
- Cook the pudding for a few minutes more. Place on a serving dish and leave to cool.

Date, chocolate & walnut pudding

SERVES 4

INGREDIENTS:

Butter for greasing
25g/1oz chopped walnuts
25g/1oz chopped dates
1 egg (separated)
1 teaspoon vanilla essence

25g/1oz caster sugar
1 egg white
25g/1oz wholemeal flour
1 tablespoon cocoa powder
25ml/1fl oz milk

- Preheat the oven to 180°C/350°F/Gas mark 4. Grease a 1.2 litre/2pt pudding basin and place a small circle of baking parchment in the base. Spoon in the walnuts and dates.
- Place the egg yolk in a heatproof bowl. Add the vanilla essence and the sugar.
- Place the bowl over a pan of simmering water and whisk to thicken. Remove from the heat.
- Sift the flour and cocoa into the mixture and fold in. Stir in the milk. Whisk the egg whites and fold them in.
- Spoon the mixture into the prepared basin and bake for 40 to 45 minutes, or until the pudding has risen well and is firm to the touch.

Strawberry & apple crumble

SERVES 4

INGREDIENTS:

450g/1lb cooking apples (peeled, cored and sliced)
150g/5oz strawberries (halved)
25g/1oz granulated sugar
½ teaspoon ground cinnamon
25ml/1fl oz orange juice

For the crumble:
50g/2oz wholemeal flour
50g/2oz porridge oats
25g/1oz butter (softened)

Custard, to serve

- Preheat the oven to 180°C/350°F/Gas mark 4.
- Toss together the apples, strawberries, sugar, cinnamon and orange juice. Tip into a 1.2 litre/2pt ovenproof dish.

- To make the crumble, combine the flour and oats in bowl and mix in the butter with a fork.
- Sprinkle the crumble mixture evenly over the fruit and bake in the oven for 40 to 45 minutes, until golden brown.
- Serve warm with custard.

Pear & ginger crumble

SERVES 4

INGREDIENTS:

4 pears (peeled, cored and sliced)　　*50g/2oz butter*
25ml/1fl oz apple juice　　　　　　　*1 teaspoon granulated sugar (plus*
100g/4oz plain flour　　　　　　　　　*extra for sprinkling)*
1 teaspoon ground ginger

- Preheat the oven to 190°C/375°F/Gas mark 5.
- Place the pears in a 1.2 litre/2pt ovenproof serving dish with the apple juice.
- Sift the flour and ginger into a bowl, then rub in the butter and stir in the sugar.
- Spoon this mixture over the pears and press down lightly. Sprinkle with a little extra sugar.
- Bake for 45 minutes until golden. Serve hot.

Queen of puddings

SERVES 4

INGREDIENTS:

50g/2oz dark chocolate (broken into　　*100g/4oz caster sugar*
small pieces)　　　　　　　　　　　　　*2 eggs (separated)*
500ml/18fl oz chocolate milk　　　　　*4 tablespoons black cherry jam*
100g/4oz fresh white breadcrumbs

- Preheat the oven to 180°C/350°F/Gas mark 4.
- Place the chocolate pieces into a saucepan with the chocolate milk. Heat gently, stirring until the chocolate melts. Bring almost to the boil, then remove the pan from the heat.
- Place the breadcrumbs in a large mixing bowl with 25g/1oz sugar. Pour in the chocolate mixture and mix well. Beat in the egg yolks. Spoon into a 1.2

→

← litre/2pt pie dish and bake in the oven for 25 to 30 minutes, until set and firm.
- Whisk the egg whites in a large bowl until standing in soft peaks. Gradually whisk in the remaining sugar and whisk until you have a thick meringue.
- Spread the jam over the baked chocolate base and pile the meringue on top.
- Return the pudding to the oven for about 15 minutes, then serve.

Glazed berry pudding

SERVES 8

INGREDIENTS:

Butter for greasing
4 eggs (separated)
50g/2oz caster sugar
25g/1oz plain flour
150ml/¼pt double cream

150ml/¼pt milk
1 teaspoon vanilla essence
225g/8oz icing sugar (plus extra for dusting)
450g/1lb mixed red berries

- Lightly grease 8 x 150ml/5fl oz ramekins.
- Combine the egg yolks in a bowl with the caster sugar and beat until pale, then stir in the flour.
- Bring the cream and milk to the boil in a small saucepan then pour into the yolk mixture, stirring. Return the mixture to the pan and cook over a gentle heat for 2 minutes, stirring all the time or until thick and smooth. Turn into a clean bowl, add the vanilla essence, cover and leave to cool.
- Put the egg whites and icing sugar in a large heatproof bowl over a pan of simmering water, whisk for 10 minutes until thick then remove from the heat and whisk until cool.
- Put 2 tablespoonfuls of the berries in the bottom of each ramekin. Fold the meringue into the custard and pile on top of the berries, then put back in the freezers for at least 7 hours.
- Preheat the oven to 220°C/425°F/Gas mark 7.
- Remove the ramekins from the freezer, place on a baking tray and dust thickly with icing sugar. Bake for 20 minutes and serve immediately.

Blackcurrant pudding

SERVES 4

INGREDIENTS:

225g/8oz blackcurrants
225g/8oz raspberries
150ml/¹/₄pt water

50g/2oz caster sugar
1¹/₂ tablespoons arrowroot
1 tablespoon crème de mûre

- Place the blackcurrants, raspberries, water and sugar in a pan. Cover the pan and cook over a low heat for 12 to 15 minutes, until the fruit is soft.
- Blend the arrowroot to a paste with a little water in a small bowl and stir into the hot fruit mixture. Bring the fruit mixture back to the boil, stirring all the time until thickened and smooth.
- Remove the pan from the heat and leave the fruit compote to cool slightly, then gently stir in the crème de mûre.
- Pour the compote into 4 glass serving bowls and leave to cool. Chill until required.

Gentlemen's pudding

SERVES 6

INGREDIENTS:

150g/5oz butter (plus extra
for greasing)
75g/3oz caster sugar
150g/5oz self-raising flour
3 large eggs (whisked)
4 tablespoons sieved raspberry jam

For the sauce:
2 egg yolks
1 tablespoon caster sugar
175ml/6fl oz dry sherry
2 tablespoons sieved raspberry jam

- Beat the butter with the sugar to a pale cream. Sift in half the flour, then add one of the eggs, and incorporate. Sift in the remaining flour and beat in, followed by the remaining eggs to achieve a smooth batter. Add the jam and stir.
- Pour into a buttered 1 litre/1¹/₂pt pudding basin. Cover with a cloth and steam for 1¹/₂ hours.
- To make the sauce, whisk the egg yolks with the sugar in a heatproof bowl set over a pan of simmering water. As they thicken, add the sherry and sieved jam and cook for a few minutes, stirring constantly.
- Serve the sauce hot with the pudding.

Pear & blackberry crumble

SERVES 6

INGREDIENTS:

450g/1lb pears (peeled, cored and cut into chunks)
Juice of 1 lemon
225g/8oz caster sugar
1 teaspoon ground mixed spice

450g/1lb blackberries
100g/4oz butter (chopped, plus extra for greasing)
225g/8oz plain flour
75g/3oz ground almonds

- Preheat the oven to 200°C/400°F/Gas mark 6. Grease a 1.8 litre/3¼pt shallow dish.
- Put the pear pieces in a bowl, add the lemon juice and toss well.
- Add 100g/4oz sugar to the sliced pears, along with the ground mixed spice, then add in the blackberries and toss thoroughly to coat with sugar and spice. Tip the mixture into the prepared greased dish.
- Put the butter, flour, almonds and the remaining sugar into a blender or food processor and pulse until the mixture begins to look like breadcrumbs.
- Scatter the crumble topping evenly over the fruit, then bake for 35 to 45 minutes until the crumble is golden.

Sticky toffee pudding

SERVES 4

INGREDIENTS:

100g/4oz butter (plus extra for greasing)
50g/2oz caster sugar
2 tablespoons water
150ml/¼pt double cream

100g/4oz muscovado sugar
4 eggs (separated)
150g/5oz plain flour
1½ teaspoons baking powder

- Preheat the oven to 180°C/350°F/Gas mark 4. Grease 4 moulds, measuring 300ml/10fl oz.
- In a pan, dissolve the caster sugar in the water over a low heat. Warm the double cream in another pan. When the sugar has dissolved, turn up the heat under that pan and boil until golden brown. Remove from the heat and add the hot cream, stirring. Pour equally between the moulds.
- With an electric whisk, cream the butter and muscovado sugar until off-white and then whisk in the egg yolks, one at a time.

- In a glass bowl, whisk the egg whites to soft peaks and reserve.
- Sift the flour and baking powder into a bowl, then whisk into the butter cream. Then fold the egg whites into the mixture.
- Spoon into the moulds and cover the tops with buttered rounds of baking parchment. Put into a roasting tin and pour hot water from the kettle to come half-way up the moulds. Bake for 40 to 50 minutes.

Ginger upside-down pudding

SERVES 4-6

INGREDIENTS:

Sunflower oil for brushing
1 tablespoon brown sugar
4 peaches (halved and stoned)
8 walnut halves
150g/5oz wholemeal flour
½ teaspoon bicarbonate of soda

1½ teaspoons ground ginger
1 teaspoon ground cinnamon
100g/4oz molasses sugar
1 egg
125ml/4fl oz milk
50ml/2fl oz sunflower oil

- Preheat the oven to 180°/350°F/Gas mark 4. Brush the base and side of a 23cm/9in round springform cake tin with oil. Sprinkle the brown sugar over the base of the tin.
- Arrange the peaches cut-side down in the tin with walnut halves in place of stones.
- For the base, sift together the flour, bicarbonate of soda, ginger and cinnamon, then stir in the sugar. Beat together the egg, milk and oil, then mix into the dry ingredients until smooth.
- Pour the mixture evenly over the peaches and bake for 35 to 40 minutes, until firm to the touch. Turn out on to a serving plate. Serve hot.

Sticky marmalade pudding

SERVES 8

INGREDIENTS:

175g/6oz butter
175g/6oz muscovado sugar
300g/11oz marmalade
2 seedless oranges (peeled, all pith removed and sliced thinly into rounds)

2 large eggs (beaten)
175g/6oz self-raising flour
1½ teaspoons ground ginger
50g/2oz root ginger (peeled and finely chopped)

→

←

- Preheat the oven to 180°C/375°F/Gas mark 4. Line the base of a 23cm/9in round tin, at least 5cm/2in deep, with non-stick baking parchment.
- Warm together 50g/2oz each of the butter and sugar and half the marmalade.
- Spoon into the tin. Arrange the orange slices over the marmalade mixture.
- Beat together the remaining butter and sugar. Gradually beat in the eggs. Sift the flour and ground ginger and fold into the mixture with the remaining marmalade and the root ginger. Spread over the oranges.
- Stand the tin on a baking tray and bake for 1 hour 10 minutes or until just firm to the touch.
- Invert the pudding on to a serving plate and serve warm with custard.

Steamed berry pudding

SERVES 10-12

INGREDIENTS:

250g/9oz sultanas
150g/5oz currants
250g/9oz raisins
300g/11oz mixed dried fruit (chopped)
50g/2oz mixed peel
125ml/4fl oz brown ale
2 tablespoons rum
75ml/3fl oz orange juice
75ml/3fl oz lemon juice
1 teaspoon finely grated orange zest
1 teaspoon finely grated lemon zest

225g/8oz suet (grated)
225g/8oz brown sugar
3 eggs (lightly beaten)
200g/7oz fresh white breadcrumbs
75g/3oz self-raising flour
1 teaspoon mixed spice
¼ teaspoon grated nutmeg
100g/4oz blanched almonds (roughly chopped)
Pinch of salt
Butter for greasing

- Put the sultanas, currants and raisins, mixed dried fruit, mixed peel, brown ale, rum, orange and lemon juices and zests into a large bowl and stir together.
- Cover and leave overnight.
- Add the suet, brown sugar, eggs, breadcrumbs, flour, mixed spice, nutmeg, almonds and the salt to the bowl and mix well.
- Put a 2 litre/3½pt pudding basin on a trivet in a large saucepan with a lid and pour in enough water to come halfway up the side of the basin. Remove the basin and put the water on to boil.
- Brush the basin with melted butter and line the base with baking parchment. Fill with the pudding mixture, then cover with a round of buttered baking parchment and top with pleated aluminium foil, secured with string around the rim of the basin.
- Steam the pudding for 8 hours, topping up with boiling water when necessary.

Blackberry batter pudding

SERVES 8

INGREDIENTS:

350g/12oz blackberries
250g/9oz granulated sugar
3 tablespoons plain flour
Grated zest of 1 lemon
¼ teaspoon ground nutmeg

For the topping:
225g/8oz plain flour
225g/8oz granulated sugar
1 tablespoon baking powder
Pinch of salt
250ml/9fl oz milk
75g/3oz butter (melted)

- Preheat the oven to 180°C/350°F/Gas mark 4.
- In a large mixing bowl, combine the blackberries with 225g/8oz sugar.
- Add the flour and lemon zest. Using a large spoon, stir gently to blend. Transfer to a 2 litre/3½pt baking dish.
- To make the topping, sift the flour, sugar, baking powder and salt into a large bowl. Set aside. In a jug, combine the milk and butter. Gradually stir the milk mixture into the dry ingredients and stir until the batter is just smooth. Spoon the batter over the berries.
- Mix the remaining sugar with the nutmeg, then sprinkle the mixture over the pudding. Bake for about 50 minutes, until the topping is set. Serve hot.

Baked coconut rice pudding

SERVES 4-6

INGREDIENTS:

100g/4oz short-grain rice
600ml/1 pint coconut milk
300ml/½pt milk

50g/2oz caster sugar
1 teaspoon butter (plus extra
for greasing)

- Lightly grease a 1.2 litre/2pt shallow ovenproof dish.
- Mix the rice with the coconut milk, milk and sugar until all the ingredients are well blended.
- Pour the rice mixture into the prepared dish and dot the surface with a little butter. Bake in the oven for about 30 minutes.

Indian bread pudding

SERVES 6

INGREDIENTS:

6 medium slices white bread
75g/3oz ghee
150g/5oz granulated sugar
300ml/½pt water

3 green cardamoms (without husks)
600ml/1pt milk
175ml/6fl oz evaporated milk
½ teaspoon saffron strands

- Cut the bread slices into quarters. Heat the ghee in a large, heavy-based frying pan. Add the bread slices and fry, turning once, until golden brown.
- Place the fried bread in the base of a heatproof dish and set aside.
- To make a syrup, place the sugar, water and cardamom seeds in a saucepan and bring to the boil over a medium heat, stirring constantly, until the sugar has dissolved. Boil until the syrup thickens. Pour the syrup over the fried bread.
- Put the milk, evaporated milk and the saffron in a separate saucepan and bring to the boil over a low heat. Simmer until it has halved in volume. Pour the mixture over the syrup-coated bread.

Tapioca pudding

SERVES 6

INGREDIENTS:

50g/2oz tapioca
125ml/4fl oz cold milk
600ml/1pt hot milk
2 eggs (separated)

75g/3oz granulated sugar
Pinch of salt
1 teaspoon vanilla essence

- Soak the tapioca in the cold milk for 10 minutes, add the hot milk, and cook in a saucepan until transparent.
- Beat the egg yolks, sugar and salt together. Add the hot milk mixture gradually, stirring constantly. Continue to cook until it begins to thicken.
- Beat the egg whites stiff, flavour with vanilla essence, and fold in the hot mixture. Chill and serve.

Fresh fruit compote

SERVES 4

INGREDIENTS:

Grated zest and juice of 1 lemon
50g/2oz caster sugar
4 tablespoons elderflower cordial
300ml/¹/₂pt water
4 dessert apples (peeled, cored
and sliced)

225g/8oz blackberries
2 fresh figs (sliced)

For the topping:
150g/5oz thick natural yogurt
2 tablespoons clear honey

- Place the lemon zest and juice into a saucepan, together with the sugar, elderflower cordial and water. Set over a low heat and simmer, uncovered, for 10 minutes.
- Add the apples to the saucepan. Simmer gently for about 4 to 5 minutes, until just tender. Remove the pan from the heat and set aside to cool.
- When cold, transfer the apples and syrup to a serving bowl and add the blackberries. Add the figs and stir gently to mix. Cover and chill in the refrigerator until ready to serve.
- Spoon the yogurt into a small serving bowl and drizzle the honey over the top.
- Cover and chill before serving with the compote.

Chocolate fudge pudding

SERVES 6

INGREDIENTS:

For the pudding:
150g/5oz soft margarine
150g/5oz self-raising flour (sifted)
150g/5oz golden syrup
3 eggs
25g/1oz cocoa powder

For the chocolate fudge sauce:
100g/4oz dark chocolate
125ml/4fl oz condensed milk
125ml/4fl oz double cream

- Lightly grease a 1.2 litre/2pt pudding basin.
- Place all the pudding ingredients in a mixing bowl and beat until well combined and smooth. Spoon into the prepared basin and level the top. Cover with a disc of baking parchment and tie a pleated sheet of aluminium foil over the basin. Steam for 1¹/₂ to 2 hours, until the pudding is cooked and springy to the touch.

→

←

- To make the sauce, break the chocolate into small pieces and place in a small pan with the condensed milk. Heat gently, stirring until the chocolate melts. Remove the pan from the heat and stir in the double cream.
- To serve the pudding, turn it out on to a serving plate and pour over a little of the chocolate fudge sauce. Serve the remaining sauce separately.

Oat & fruit puddings

SERVES 4

INGREDIENTS:

Sunflower oil (for greasing)
100g/4oz rolled oats
50g/2oz butter (melted)
2 tablespoons chopped almonds
1 tablespoon clear honey

Pinch of ground cinnamon
2 pears (peeled, cored and finely chopped) 1 tablespoon marmalade

Custard or yogurt, to serve

- Preheat the oven to 200°C/400°F/Gas mark 6. Lightly oil the bases of 4 individual pudding bowls and line with a small circle of baking parchment.
- Mix together the oats, butter, almonds, honey and cinnamon in a small bowl.
- Using a spoon, spread two-thirds of the oat mixture over the base and around the sides of the pudding bowls.
- Toss together the pears and marmalade and spoon into the oat cases. Scatter the remaining oat mixture over to cover the pears and marmalade.
- Bake in the oven for 15 to 20 minutes, until golden and crisp. Leave for 5 minutes before removing the pudding bowls. Serve hot with custard or yogurt.

Fruity bread pudding

SERVES 4

INGREDIENTS:

75g/3oz mixed dried fruit
150ml/¼pt unsweetened apple juice
3-4 slices day-old white bread (cubed)
1 teaspoon mixed spice

1 large banana (sliced)
150ml/¼pt milk
1 tablespoon demerara sugar

- Preheat the oven to 200°C/400°F/Gas mark 6. Place the dried fruit in a small pan with the apple juice and bring to the boil.

- Remove the pan from the heat and stir in the bread cubes, mixed spice and banana. Spoon the mixture into a shallow 1.2 litre/2pt ovenproof dish and pour the milk over.
- Sprinkle with demerara sugar and bake for 25 to 30 minutes, until firm and golden brown. Serve hot or cold.

Chocolate & pear crumble

SERVES 4

INGREDIENTS:

4 pears (cored and sliced)
25ml/1fl oz apple juice
100g/4oz plain flour

15g/¹/₂oz cocoa powder
50g/2oz butter
2 teaspoons granulated sugar

- Preheat the oven to 190°C/375°F/Gas mark 5.
- Put the sliced pears in an ovenproof dish with the apple juice.
- Sift the flour and cocoa into a bowl. Add the butter and rub together with your fingertips. Stir in the sugar. Sprinkle over the pears and press down lightly.
- Bake for about 40 minutes, or until cooked through.

Treacle pudding

SERVES 6

INGREDIENTS:

50g/2oz butter (plus extra for greasing)
100g/4oz caster sugar
2 eggs
175g/6oz plain flour

2 teaspoons baking powder
Pinch of salt
2 tablespoons milk
4 tablespoons golden syrup

- Cream the butter and sugar in a bowl, then beat in the eggs, one at a time.
- Sift the flour, baking powder and salt together and fold into the mixture, adding just enough milk to give a dropping consistency.
- Butter a 1.2 litre/2pt pudding basin, then pour the syrup into the base. Spoon in the batter to fill the basin. Cover the top with a round of buttered baking parchment and secure pleated aluminium foil over that with string.
- Stand in a pan of simmering water with a lid on and steam for 1¹/₂ hours, topping up with boiling water when necessary.

Apricot & banana compote

SERVES 4

INGREDIENTS:

225g/8oz ready-to-eat dried apricots
300ml/½pt unsweetened orange juice
150ml/¼pt unsweetened apple juice

1 teaspoon ground ginger
3 bananas (sliced)

- Put the apricots in a saucepan with the fruit juices and ginger and stir. Cover, bring to the boil and then simmer gently for 10 minutes, stirring occasionally.
- Set aside to cool, leaving the lid on. Once cool, stir in the sliced bananas.
- Spoon the fruit and juices into a large serving dish. Serve immediately.

Summer pudding

SERVES 6

INGREDIENTS:

Butter for greasing
6–8 thin slices white bread (crusts removed)
175g/6oz caster sugar
300ml/½pt water

225g/8oz strawberries
500g/1lb 2oz raspberries
175g/6oz blackcurrants
175g/6oz blackberries

- Grease 6 x 150ml/5fl oz moulds with butter. Line the moulds with the bread, cutting it so it fits snugly with no gaps.
- Place the sugar in a saucepan with the water and heat gently, stirring frequently until dissolved, then bring to the boil and boil for 2 minutes.
- Reserve 6 large strawberries for decoration. Add the rest of the strawberries, halved if large, to the syrup with half the raspberries and all the rest of the currants and berries. Simmer gently for a few minutes, until it begins to soften.
- Spoon the currants and berries and some of the liquid into the moulds. Cover with more bread. Spoon a little juice around the sides of the mould, ensuring the bread is well soaked. Cover with a saucer and a heavy weight. Leave to cool, then chill overnight.
- Process the remaining raspberries in a blender or food processor and add enough of the liquid from the fruits to give a coating consistency.
- Turn on to serving plates and spoon the raspberry sauce over. Decorate with the reserved strawberries.

Zabaglione

SERVES 4

INGREDIENTS:

5 egg yolks
100g/4oz caster sugar

150ml/¼pt Marsala or sweet sherry

- Place the egg yolks in a large mixing bowl. Add the caster sugar to the egg yolks and whisk until the mixture is thick, very pale and doubled in volume.
- Place the bowl containing the egg yolk and sugar mixture over a saucepan of gently simmering water.
- Add the Marsala and continue whisking until the mixture becomes warm. This may take up to 10 minutes.
- Pour the mixture, which should be frothy and light, into 4 wine glasses.
- Serve warm.

Tiramisu

SERVES 6

INGREDIENTS:

500ml/18fl oz strong black coffee
(cooled)
50ml/2fl oz Marsala or coffee-
flavoured liqueur
2 eggs (separated)

50g/2oz caster sugar
225g/8oz Mascarpone cheese
225ml/8fl oz double cream
16 large sponge finger biscuits
2 tablespoons dark cocoa powder

- Combine the coffee and Marsala in a bowl and set aside.
- Beat the egg yolks and sugar in a bowl with an electric beater for 3 minutes, or until thick and pale. Add the Mascarpone cheese and mix until just combined.
- Transfer to a large bowl. Beat the cream in a separate bowl, with an electric beater, until soft peaks form, then fold into the Mascarpone mixture.
- Place the egg whites in a small bowl and beat with an electric beater until soft peaks form. Fold quickly and lightly into the cream mixture.
- Dip half of the biscuits into the coffee mixture, drain off any excess and arrange in the base of a 2.4 litre/4pt glass serving dish. Spread half the cream over the biscuits.
- Dip the remaining biscuits in the coffee mixture and repeat the layers. Smooth the surface and dust liberally with the cocoa powder. Refrigerate overnight.

Black Forest trifle

SERVES 6

INGREDIENTS:

6 thin slices chocolate Swiss roll
800g/1lb 12oz canned black cherries
in juice
2 tablespoons kirsch
1 tablespoon cornflour
25g/1oz caster sugar
450ml/³/₄pt milk

3 egg yolks
1 egg
75g/3oz dark chocolate (broken into
small pieces)
300ml/¹/₂pt double cream (whipped
lightly)
Maraschino cherries, to decorate

- Place the slices of chocolate Swiss roll in the bottom of a large glass serving bowl.
- Drain the black cherries, reserving 6 tablespoons of the juice. Place the cherries and the reserved juice on top of the Swiss roll slices. Sprinkle with the kirsch.
- In a heatproof bowl, mix the cornflour and caster sugar. Stir in enough of the milk to mix to a smooth paste. Beat in the egg yolks and the whole egg.
- Heat the remaining milk in a small saucepan until almost boiling, then gradually pour it on to the egg mixture, whisking well until it is combined.
- Place the bowl over a pan of hot water and cook over a low heat until the custard thickens, stirring. Add the chocolate and stir until melted.
- Pour the chocolate custard over the cherries and leave to cool. When cold, spread the cream over the custard. Chill thoroughly, decorate with the maraschino cherries and serve.

Raspberry &
Amaretti trifles

SERVES 12

INGREDIENTS:

650g/1lb 7oz cooking apples (peeled,
cored and sliced)
75g/3oz granulated sugar
75ml/3fl oz water
65g/1lb 7oz raspberries
Juice of 2 limes

50ml/2fl oz crème de framboise
25g/1oz icing sugar
24 boudoir biscuits (halved)
175g/6oz Amaretti biscuits (crushed)
600ml/1pt custard
450ml/³/₄pt double cream

- Put the apples, granulated sugar and water in a pan and bring to the boil. Cover and cook gently for 15 minutes or until soft. Beat with a wooden spoon until smooth. Leave to cool.
- Purée 450g/1lb of the raspberries with the lime juice and crème de framboise.
- Sieve the raspberry mixture and add the icing sugar. Spoon into 12 serving dishes, scatter over the rest of the whole raspberries.
- Divide the boudoir biscuits among the dishes and sprinkle the Amaretti biscuits over. Spoon the apple sauce over, followed by the custard. Whip the cream to form soft peaks and spoon it on to the trifles to finish.

Madeira cake trifle

SERVES 6

INGREDIENTS:

Butter (melted, for greasing)
500ml/18fl oz milk
1 vanilla pod (split lengthways)
4 egg yolks
100g/4oz caster sugar
25g/1oz plain flour

300g/11oz Madeira cake (cut into 1cm/½in slices)
75ml/3fl oz rum
25g/1oz milk chocolate (grated)
50g/2oz flaked almonds (toasted)

- Grease a 1.2 litre/2pt serving dish with melted butter.
- Place the milk and vanilla pod in a pan and slowly heat until bubbles appear around the edge of the pan. Whisk the egg yolks, sugar and flour together in a bowl until thick and pale.
- Discard the vanilla pod, whisk the warm milk slowly into the egg mixture and blend well. Return the custard mixture to a clean pan and stir over a medium heat until the custard boils and thickens.
- Line the base of the prepared dish with one third of the cake slices and brush well with the rum. Spread one third of the custard over the cake, top with a second third of the cake slices, brushed with rum, and more custard. Finish with final layers of cake slices, rum and custard. Cover and refrigerate for at least 4 hours. Sprinkle with chocolate and almonds before serving.

Blueberry trifle

SERVES 6

INGREDIENTS:

*350g/12oz Madeira cake (cut
into cubes)
175ml/6fl oz white wine
125ml/4fl oz elderflower cordial
3 tablespoons blueberry conserve*

*500g/1lb 2oz custard
250ml/9fl oz double cream
100g/4oz blueberries
1 tablespoon pistachio nuts (finely
chopped)*

- Put the cake into a 2.4 litre/4pt glass serving bowl. Mix the wine with 2 tablespoons cordial and pour over the cake.
- Dot the blueberry conserve over the cake, then pour the custard on top. Whip the cream into soft peaks, then fold in the remaining cordial and half the blueberries. Add to the trifle.
- Cover and chill overnight. Scatter with the nuts and remaining blueberries before serving.

Sherry trifle

SERVES 8

INGREDIENTS:

*1 Victoria sponge (halved)
3 tablespoons raspberry jam
3 tablespoons apricot jam
150ml/¼pt brandy
150ml/¼pt sweet sherry
600ml/1pt double cream*

For the custard:
*600ml/1pt milk
5 egg yolks
75g/3oz caster sugar
3 drops vanilla essence*

- Spread one half of the Victoria sponge with raspberry jam and the other with apricot jam. Cut each half into 4 and place into a dish in which they will just fit, alternating raspberry with apricot. Pour over the brandy and sweet sherry and leave to macerate for 2 hours.
- Make a custard by bringing the milk to the boil and pouring it over the egg yolks beaten with the caster sugar, whisking. Put the bowl over simmering water and whisk until thick. Stir in the vanilla essence and pour over the sponge.
- Refrigerate overnight.
- Whip the cream until stiff and spoon over the top.

Orange syllabub trifle

SERVES 3-4

INGREDIENTS:

For the orange syllabub:
Finely grated zest and juice of
1 orange
50g/2oz caster sugar
175g/6oz crème fraîche

225g/8oz thick natural yogurt

For the trifle:
4 trifle sponges
150ml/¼pt orange juice

- Put the zest and orange juice into a bowl with the sugar and leave to marinate for 1 hour. Strain the liquid into a clean bowl and add the crème fraîche gradually, beating until thick. Fold in the yogurt. Chill overnight.
- Cut the trifle sponges in half lengthways. Lay them in the bottom of a small serving dish, moisten with the orange juice, and finish with a layer of the syllabub. Chill for 2 to 3 hours before serving.

Chocolate charlotte

SERVES 8

INGREDIENTS:

22 boudoir biscuits
4 tablespoons orange-flavoured liqueur
250g/9oz dark chocolate (melted)

150ml/¼pt double cream
4 eggs (separated)
150g/5oz caster sugar

- Line the base of a charlotte mould or a deep 18cm/7in round cake tin with a piece of baking parchment.
- Place the boudoir biscuits on a tray and sprinkle with half of the orange-flavoured liqueur. Use to line the sides of the mould or tin, trimming if necessary to make a tight fit.
- Mix the chocolate with the double cream in a bowl and beat in the egg yolks.
- Whisk the egg whites in a large bowl until standing in stiff peaks, then gradually add the caster sugar, whisking until stiff and glossy. Carefully fold the egg whites into the chocolate mixture in 2 batches, taking care not to knock out the air. Pour into the centre of the mould and trim the biscuits so they are level with the chocolate mixture. Chill for at least 5 hours.

Pots au chocolat

SERVES 8

INGREDIENTS:

Butter for greasing
175ml/6fl oz double cream
½ vanilla pod (split lengthways)
150g/5oz dark chocolate (broken into small pieces)

75ml/3fl oz milk
2 egg yolks
50g/2oz caster sugar

- Lightly brush 8 x 75ml/3fl oz moulds or ramekins with butter and put them in a deep baking dish. Preheat the oven to 140°C/275°F/Gas mark 1.
- Heat the cream in a small pan with the vanilla pod until the cream is warm, then leave to infuse.
- Combine the chocolate and milk in a small pan. Stir constantly over a low heat until the chocolate has just melted.
- Place the egg yolks in a small bowl and slowly whisk in the sugar. Continue whisking until the sugar has dissolved and the mixture is light and creamy. Scrape the seeds out of the vanilla pod into the cream, and discard the empty pod. Add the vanilla cream and the melted chocolate mixture to the beaten egg yolks, and mix until well combined.
- Pour the mixture into the ramekins, filling approximately two-thirds full. Pour enough boiling water in to come halfway up the pots. Bake for 45 minutes, or until the chocolate pots have puffed up slightly and feel spongy. Remove from the baking dish and cool completely. Cover with clingfilm and refrigerate for 6 hours before serving.

Creamy puddings

SERVES 6

INGREDIENTS:

300ml/½pt double cream
250g/9oz ricotta cheese
50g/2oz caster sugar
100g/4oz white chocolate (broken into pieces)

350g/12oz mixed summer fruits (such as strawberries, blueberries & raspberries)
2 tablespoons Cointreau

- Whip the cream until soft peaks form. Fold in the ricotta cheese and half the sugar.

- Place the chocolate in a heatproof bowl set over a saucepan of simmering water. Stir until melted. Remove from the heat and leave to cool, stirring occasionally. Stir into the cheese mixture until well blended.
- Spoon the mixture into 6 individual pudding moulds and level the surface of each pudding with the back of a spoon. Place in the freezer and freeze for 8 hours, or overnight.
- Place the fruits and the remaining sugar in a pan and heat gently, stirring occasionally until the sugar has dissolved. Stir in the Cointreau.
- Dip the pudding moulds in hot water for 30 seconds and invert on to serving plates. Spoon the fruit compote over the puddings and serve immediately.

Rice pudding

SERVES 4

INGREDIENTS:

Sunflower oil (for greasing)
50g/2oz short-grain rice
50g/2oz granulated sugar
400ml/14fl oz evaporated milk

300ml/½pt milk
Pinch of freshly ground nutmeg
25g/1oz butter
Strawberry jam, to serve

- Preheat the oven to 150°C/300°F/Gas mark 2. Lightly oil a large ovenproof dish.
- Sprinkle the rice and the sugar into the prepared dish and mix.
- Bring the evaporated milk to the boil in a small pan, stirring occasionally. Stir both milks into the rice and mix well until the rice is coated thoroughly. Sprinkle the nutmeg over.
- Cover the dish with aluminium foil and bake in the oven to 30 minutes.
- Remove the pudding from the oven and stir well, breaking up any lumps. Cover with the same tin foil. Bake in the oven for a further 30 minutes. Remove from the oven and stir well again.
- Dot the pudding with butter and bake for a further 45 to 60 minutes, until the rice is tender and the skin browned.
- Divide the pudding into 4 individual serving bowls. Top with a large spoonful of jam and serve immediately.

Semolina

SERVES 4

INGREDIENTS:

100ml/3½fl oz pure ghee
3 whole cloves
3 whole cardamoms
125ml/4fl oz coarse semolina
½ teaspoon saffron

50g/2oz sultanas
150g/5oz caster sugar
300ml/½pt water
300ml/½pt milk

- Place the ghee in a saucepan and melt over a medium heat. Add the cloves and the whole cardamoms and reduce the heat, stirring to mix.
- Add the semolina to the mixture in the pan and stir-fry until it turns a slightly darker colour. Add the saffron, sultanas and the sugar to the semolina mixture, stirring to mix well.
- Pour in the water and milk and stir-fry the mixture constantly until the semolina has softened. Add a little more water if required.
- Remove the pan from the heat and transfer the semolina to a serving dish.

Bread & butter pudding

SERVES 6

INGREDIENTS:

60g/2oz butter (softened)
6 slices white bread
25g/1oz currants
25g/1oz sultanas
3 eggs

550ml/19fl oz milk
50g/2oz light muscovado sugar
Pinch of ground mixed spice

Single cream, to serve

- Lightly grease a 1.2 litre/2pt ovenproof dish with a little of the butter. Use the rest to spread evenly over the bread then cut each slice in half diagonally. Arrange the slices in the dish, each one slightly overlapping the last, and sprinkle the currants and sultanas over the top.
- Beat together the eggs, milk, sugar and mixed spice in a bowl and pour over the bread. Leave to soak for 30 minutes. Preheat the oven to 180°C/350°F/Gas mark 4.
- Bake the pudding in the oven for 45 to 55 minutes or until golden brown but still slightly moist in the centre. Serve with a drizzle of single cream.

Apple tapioca pudding

SERVES 6

INGREDIENTS:

75g/3oz tapioca
500ml/16fl oz water
Pinch of salt
450g/1lb apples (pared, quartered and cored)

2 teaspoons lemon juice
Grated zest of ¼ lemon
150g/5oz granulated sugar

- Soak the tapioca in the water for 1 hour. Put it into a saucepan, with the salt and 2 teaspoons sugar, to cook. Stir frequently and allow it to cook until transparent.
- While the tapioca is cooking, put the prepared apples into a pan, sprinkle the lemon juice, lemon zest and remaining sugar over, and heat gently. Pour the tapioca over the apples and heat long enough for the tapioca and apples to boil up together.

Chocolate rice pudding

SERVES 6

INGREDIENTS:

75g/3oz short-grain rice
300ml/½pt milk
50g/2oz caster sugar (plus 1 tablespoon extra)
3 egg yolks
300ml/½pt double cream

75g/3oz dark chocolate
50g/2oz butter
1 tablespoon brandy
300ml/½pt whipping cream (whipped until stiff)

- Boil the rice in unsalted water for 15 minutes, then drain.
- Put the rice into the milk with the 50g/2oz caster sugar, bring to the boil and simmer for a further 10 minutes.
- Remove from the heat and spoon a couple of tablespoonfuls of the mixture into a bowl with the egg yolks. Stir and return to the pan. Add the double cream, stir together, turn into a serving dish and chill for at least 1 hour.
- In a heatproof bowl set over a pan of simmering water, melt the dark chocolate with the butter, extra tablespoon of caster sugar and the brandy. Pour the mixture over the chilled rice pudding. Finish by piling whipped cream on top.

Soufflés, mousses, custards & pancakes

These egg-based recipes range from light, spongy bakes to richer brûlées and crème caramels. If you have a penchant for custard, try the Banana caramel custard or Thai coconut custard as an accompaniment or a main dish. Or if you are a pancake lover there are plenty of choices including Chinese chestnut pancakes and Exotic fruit pancakes. The mousses and soufflés are simply delicious as well.

Chocolate crêpes

SERVES 6

INGREDIENTS:

75g/3oz plain flour
1 tablespoon cocoa powder
1 teaspoon caster sugar
2 eggs (lightly beaten)
175ml/6fl oz milk
2 teaspoons dark rum
25g/1oz butter (melted, plus extra
  for brushing)

For the filling:
5 tablespoons double cream
225g/8oz dark chocolate
3 eggs (separated)
25g/1oz caster sugar

- Preheat the oven to 200°C/400°F/Gas mark 6.
- Sift the flour, cocoa and sugar into a bowl. Make a well in the centre, add the eggs and beat them in a little at a time. Add the milk, rum and butter and beat until smooth. Cover and set aside for 30 minutes.
- Brush an 18cm/7in crêpe pan with melted butter and set over a medium heat.
- Pour 3 tablespoons of the batter into the pan, swirling it to cover the base. Cook for 3 minutes, turning once, then slide on to a plate. Cook another 11 crêpes in the same way. Stack, interleaved with baking parchment.
- For the filling, put the cream and chocolate in a pan and melt gently, stirring. In a bowl, beat the egg yolks with half the sugar until creamy, beat in the chocolate cream and leave to cool. In a separate bowl, whisk the egg whites into soft peaks, add the rest of the sugar and beat until stiff. Stir a spoonful of the whites into the chocolate mixture, then fold in the remainder.
- Spread each crêpe with 1 tablespoon of the filling, then fold into quarters. Brush with melted butter, place on a buttered baking tray and bake in the oven for 20 minutes.

Chinese chestnut pancakes

SERVES 4

INGREDIENTS:

150g/5oz plain flour (plus extra
  for dusting)
100ml/3½fl oz boiling water
½ teaspoon vegetable oil

75g/3oz canned sweetened chestnut
  purée
1 tablespoon vegetable oil for frying
Caster sugar for dusting

- To make the pancakes, sift the flour and then pour in the boiling water, stirring as you pour. Mix in the oil and knead the mixture into a dough. Cover with a damp towel and leave to stand for 30 minutes.
- Knead the dough until smooth, then roll it out into a large sausage shape. Cut into 8 pieces and roll each piece into a ball. Flatten each piece, then press with a rolling pin into a 15cm/6in pancake.
- Heat an ungreased non-stick frying pan until hot, then reduce the heat to low and place the pancakes, one at a time, in the pan. Turn them when small brown spots appear on the underside.
- Spread about 1 tablespoon of the chestnut purée over each pancake, then roll it up.
- Heat the oil in a non-stick wok or frying pan. Add the rolls in batches and fry them briefly until golden brown, turning once. Dust with caster sugar and serve immediately.

Banana chocolate chip soufflés

SERVES 6

INGREDIENTS:

Butter for greasing
3 egg whites
75g/3oz granulated sugar

2 bananas
2½ tablespoons mini chocolate chips

- Preheat the oven to 230°C/450°F/Gas mark 8. Lightly grease 6 x 175ml/6fl oz ramekins.
- In a bowl, beat the egg whites with an electric mixer until they just hold soft peaks, then gradually beat in the sugar until the mixture holds stiff peaks.
- Thinly slice the bananas on to the mixture and gently fold in the chocolate chips.
- Arrange the ramekins on a baking tray and divide the mixture evenly among them. Run a knife around the sides of the ramekins and bake the soufflés in the middle of the oven for 15 minutes, or until golden brown.
- Serve immediately.

Frozen citrus soufflés

SERVES 4

INGREDIENTS:

1 tablespoon gelatine
100ml/3½fl oz very hot water (not boiling)
3 eggs (separated)
100g/4oz caster sugar
Freshly grated zest and juice of 1 lemon

Grated zest and juice of ½ lime
Grated zest and juice of ½ orange
150ml/¼pt double cream
100g/4oz fromage frais

- Tie a greaseproof paper collar around a 15cm/6in soufflé dish.
- Sprinkle the gelatine into the hot water, stirring well to disperse. Leave to stand for 2 to 3 minutes, stirring occasionally, to give a completely clear liquid. Leave to cool for 10 to 15 minutes.
- Meanwhile, whisk the egg yolks and sugar, using a hand-held electric mixer or wire whisk, until very pale and light in texture. Add the zest and juice from the fruits, mixing well. Stir in the cooled gelatine liquid, making sure that it is thoroughly mixed in.
- Put the cream in a large chilled bowl and whip until it holds its shape. Stir in the fromage frais to the cream, mixing it in gently. Fold the cream mixture into the citrus mixture using a large metal spoon.
- Using a clean whisk, beat the egg whites in a clean bowl until stiff and then gently fold them into the citrus mixture, using a metal spoon.
- Pour the mixture into the prepared dish. Transfer to the freezer and open-freeze for at least 2 hours. Remove from the freezer 10 minutes before serving.

Black cherry crêpes

SERVES 4

INGREDIENTS:

For the crêpe batter:
100g/4oz plain flour
1 egg
300ml/½pt milk

For the filling:
375g/13oz fresh black cherries
25g/1oz icing sugar
150g/5oz natural yogurt
2 tablespoons vegetable oil

- To make the crêpe batter, whisk together the flour, egg and milk until smooth.
- Cover and set aside for 30 minutes.
- For the filling, pit the cherries and halve or quarter them if they are large. Stir the icing sugar into the yogurt.
- Brush a 15cm/6in non-stick crêpe pan very lightly with oil and heat until hot.
- Whisk the batter well and thin it with a little milk if it is too thick. Pour one-eighth of the batter into the hot pan and swirl it around to cover the base. Cook for 1 to 2 minutes until golden underneath, then turn over and cook the other side.
- Turn the crêpe out of the pan and keep warm. Repeat with the remaining mixture until you have 8 crêpes, adding more oil as necessary.
- To serve, place a spoonful of sweetened yogurt in the centre of each crêpe and top with a spoonful of cherries. Fold the crêpe into quarters and serve warm.

Cherry pancakes

SERVES 4

INGREDIENTS:

400g/14oz canned stoned cherries
1/2 teaspoon almond essence
1/2 teaspoon mixed spice
25g/1oz cornflour

For the pancakes:
100g/4oz plain flour

Pinch of salt
2 tablespoons chopped fresh mint
1 egg
300ml/1/2pt milk
Sunflower oil for frying
Icing sugar for dusting

- Put the cherries and 300ml/1/2pt of the can juice in a pan with the almond essence and mixed spice. Stir in the cornflour and bring to the boil, stirring until thickened and clear. Set aside.
- To make the pancakes, sift the flour into a bowl with the salt. Add the mint and make a well in the centre. Gradually beat in the egg and milk to make a smooth batter.
- Heat 1 tablespoon of oil in a 18cm/7in frying pan and pour off the oil when hot.
- Add just enough batter to coat the base of the frying pan and cook for 1 to 2 minutes, or until the underside is cooked. Flip the pancake over and cook for 1 minute. Remove from the pan and keep warm. Heat another tablespoon of the oil in the pan and repeat to use up all the batter.
- Spoon the cherry filling on to a quarter of each pancake and fold the pancake into a cone shape.
- Dust with icing sugar and serve immediately.

Apple pancake stacks

SERVES 4

INGREDIENTS:

225g/8oz plain flour
1½ baking powder
50g/2oz caster sugar
1 egg
15g/½oz butter (melted, plus extra
for greasing)

300ml/½pt milk
1 dessert apple (peeled, cored
and grated)
50g/2oz dark chocolate chips

- Sift the flour and baking powder into a mixing bowl. Stir in the caster sugar.
- Make a well in the centre and add the egg and butter. Gradually whisk in the milk to form a smooth batter. Stir the apple in with the chocolate chips.
- Heat a heavy-based frying pan over a medium heat and grease it lightly. For each pancake, place 2 tablespoons of the batter on to the pan and spread to make a 7.5cm/3in round.
- Cook for a few minutes until you see bubbles appear on the surface of the pancake. Turn over and cook for a further 1 minute. Remove from the pan and keep warm. Repeat with the remaining batter to make about 12 pancakes. To serve, stack 2 or 3 pancakes on individual serving plates.

Lemon syrup pears with pancakes

SERVES 6

INGREDIENTS:

For the batter:
100g/4oz plain flour
75g/3oz self-raising flour
25g/1oz caster sugar
3 eggs (lightly beaten)
350ml/12fl oz milk
50g/2oz butter (melted)

For the lemon syrup pears:
175g/6oz caster sugar
2 tablespoons honey
350ml/12fl oz water
125ml/4fl oz lemon juice
5 firm pears (peeled, cored and cut
into wedges)
Zest of 1 lemon (cut into thin strips)
225g/8oz sour cream

- Sift the flours into a large bowl, add the sugar, make a well and whisk in the combined eggs, milk and butter. Beat until smooth, then set aside for 30 minutes.
- To make the lemon syrup pears, combine the sugar, honey and water in a pan, stirring over a low heat until the sugar dissolves. Add the lemon juice, bring to the boil, reduce the heat and simmer for 8 minutes. Skim any froth, add the pears and simmer for a further 5 minutes. Remove from the heat, stir in the lemon zest and leave to cool slightly.
- Heat a lightly greased 20cm/8in frying pan, then pour 50ml/2fl oz of the pancake batter into it and cook over a medium heat for 2 minutes on each side.
- Continue with the rest of the batter, greasing the pan when necessary. Stack the pancakes between greaseproof paper to prevent them sticking together.
- Strain 125ml/4fl oz of the lemon syrup and mix with the sour cream to make a sauce for the pancakes. Strain the pears to serve. Decorate with strips of lemon zest.

Exotic fruit pancakes

SERVES 4

INGREDIENTS:

For the batter:
100g/4oz plain flour
Pinch of salt
1 egg
1 egg yolk
300ml/½pt coconut milk
4 teaspoons sunflower oil (plus extra for frying)

For the filling:
1 banana (peeled and sliced)
1 papaya (peeled, sliced, with seeds discarded)
Juice of 1 lime
2 passion fruit
1 mango (peeled, stoned and sliced)
4 lychees (stoned and halved)
2 tablespoons honey

- Sift the flour and salt into a bowl. Make a well in the centre and add the egg, egg yolk and a little of the coconut milk. Gradually draw the flour into the egg mixture, beating well and slowly adding the remaining coconut milk to make a smooth batter. Stir in the oil. Cover and chill for 30 minutes.
- To make the fruit fillings, place the banana in a bowl with the papaya and the lime juice and mix well. Cut the passion fruit in half and scoop out the flesh and seeds into the fruit bowl. Stir in the mango, lychees and honey.
- Heat a little oil in a 15cm/6in frying pan. Pour in just enough of the pancake batter to cover the base of the pan and tilt so that it spreads thinly and evenly.
- Cook until the pancake is just set and the underside is lightly browned, then turn and cook the other side. Remove from the pan and keep warm. Repeat with the remaining batter to make a total of 8 pancakes.
- Place a little fruit filling in the centre of each pancake and then roll into a cone.

Crêpes Suzettes

SERVES 4

INGREDIENTS:

For the pancakes:
100g/4oz plain flour
Pinch of salt
2 eggs
300ml/½pt milk
25g/1oz butter (melted)
2 teaspoons vegetable oil
150ml/¼pt cold water
25g/1oz butter

For the sauce:
50g/2oz butter
25g/1oz caster sugar (sifted)
Finely grated zest and juice of 1 large orange
Finely grated zest of 1 large lemon
3 tablespoons Cointreau
2 tablespoons brandy

- To make the pancakes, place all the ingredients in a blender or food processor.
- Blend to a smooth batter. Or, sift the flour and salt into a bowl, add the eggs and about half the milk. Whisk to a thick paste. Whisk in the remaining milk and water for a smooth, pouring batter, then add the melted butter.
- Heat ½ teaspoon oil in a non-stick 18 cm/7in frying pan. Pour in 4 tablespoons batter and swirl around. Cook for 15 seconds until the edges brown. Turn the pancake over and cook until lightly browned.
- Repeat with the rest of the batter to make about 14 pancakes. Stack them on a plate between sheets of greaseproof paper. Rest the plate over a saucepan of simmering water to keep them warm.
- To make the sauce, place the butter, sugar, zests and juice in a frying pan and warm gently until the butter has melted. Add the pancakes and warm through gently, turning once.
- Pour in the Cointreau and brandy and swirl carefully over the heat to warm through gently. Once the alcohol is warm, flame the pancakes with a lighted match. Serve immediately.

Raspberry mousse

SERVES 4

INGREDIENTS:

1 tablespoon hot water
3 teaspoons gelatine
225g/8oz vanilla yogurt

400g/14oz fromage frais
4 egg whites
300g/11oz fresh raspberries (mashed)

Put the water in a small heatproof bowl, sprinkle the gelatine over the top and leave to go spongy. Bring a small pan of water to the boil, remove from the heat and place the bowl into the pan. The water should come halfway up the side of the bowl. Stir the gelatine until dissolved.

- In a large bowl, stir the vanilla yogurt and fromage frais together to combine, then add the cooled gelatine and mix well.
- Using an electric beater, beat the egg whites until stiff peaks form, then fold through the yogurt mixture until just combined. Fold the raspberries through the mixture. Chill for several hours before serving.

Cappuccino creams

SERVES 8

INGREDIENTS:

550g/1lb 4oz fromage frais
2 tablespoons finely ground espresso coffee

1 tablespoon icing sugar
175g/6oz dark chocolate (finely grated)

- Mix the fromage frais with the coffee and icing sugar. Then spoon half of the mixture into 8 individual ramekins or glass dishes.
- Sprinkle over most of the grated chocolate and top with the remaining fromage frais, sprinkling the last of the grated chocolate over the top.

Layered chocolate mousse

SERVES 8

INGREDIENTS:

3 eggs (separated)
1 teaspoon cornflour
4 tablespoons caster sugar
300ml/½pt milk
2 teaspoons gelatine

3 tablespoons hot water
300ml/½pt double cream
75g/3oz dark chocolate
75g/3oz white chocolate
75g/3oz milk chocolate

- Line a 450g/1lb loaf tin with baking parchment. Put each egg white in a separate bowl.
- Place the egg yolks, cornflour and sugar in a large heatpfoof bowl and whisk until well combined. Place the milk in a pan and heat gently, stirring, until

→

almost boiling. Pour the milk on to the egg yolk mixture, whisking.

- Set the bowl over a pan of gently simmering water and cook, stirring, until the mixture thickens enough to thinly coat the back of a wooden spoon.
- Sprinkle the gelatine over the water in a small heatproof bowl and leave to go spongy. Place over a pan of hot water and stir until dissolved. Stir into the hot egg yolk mixture. Leave to cool.
- Whip the cream until just holding its shape. Fold it into the egg custard, then divide the mixture into 3. Melt the 3 types of chocolate separately by placing each in a heatproof bowl over a pan of simmering water. Fold the dark chocolate into one egg custard portion. Whisk one egg white until standing in soft peaks and fold into the dark chocolate custard. Pour into the prepared loaf tin and level the top.
- Chill in the coldest part of the refrigerator until just set. Leave the remaining mixtures at room temperature.
- Fold the white chocolate into another portion of the egg custard. Whisk another egg white and fold in. Pour on top of the dark chocolate layer and chill quickly.
- Repeat with the remaining milk chocolate and egg white. Chill for at least 2 hours until set. To serve, carefully turn out on to a serving dish.

Crema catalana

SERVES 6

INGREDIENTS:

450ml/³/₄pt milk
200ml/7fl oz double cream
Grated zest of 1 lemon
1 teaspoon fennel seeds (crushed)

6 egg yolks
175g/6oz caster sugar
25g/1oz cornflour
¼ teaspoon ground cinnamon

- Put the milk, cream, zest and fennel seeds in a heavy-based pan. Heat to boiling point and set aside for 30 minutes to infuse.
- In a small bowl, beat together the egg yolks, 100g/4oz of the sugar and the cornflour until the mixture is light and fluffy.
- Strain the infused milk on to the egg yolk mixture, a little at a time, stirring constantly. Pour the mixture back into the clean pan. Cook over a low heat, stirring, for 6 to 8 minutes, until the cream just comes to the boil.
- Pour into 6 x 150ml/5fl oz ramekins. Cool and cover loosely with aluminium foil. Chill overnight to set. Place in the freezer for 30 minutes before grilling.
- Mix the remaining sugar with the cinnamon and sprinkle over each pot. Place under a hot grill until the sugar has caramelized.
- Allow to cool for 20 minutes.

Passion fruit crème caramel

SERVES 6

INGREDIENTS:

Butter for greasing
4 eggs
1 egg yolk
175g/6oz caster sugar

150ml/¼pt double cream
150ml/¼pt milk
6 passion fruit
3 tablepoons cold water

- Preheat the oven to 150°C/300°F/Gas mark 2. Grease 6 x 150ml/5fl oz moulds.
- Whisk together the eggs, yolk and 100g/4oz sugar. Add the cream and milk and mix well to make a custard. Strain into a large jug. Halve the passion fruits and scoop out their flesh to make 150ml/¼pt pulp. Add to the custard and mix together.
- Put the remaining sugar into a small pan and add the cold water. Heat gently, stirring from time to time to dissolve the sugar, then bring to the boil over a medium heat, cooking to a pale golden syrup. Reduce the heat a little and boil steadily for around 5 minutes until a dark brown caramel forms. Add 2 tablespoons of cold water. When the mixture stops spluttering, pour the caramel evenly between the moulds, then pour the custard on top.
- Put the moulds in a roasting tin and half-fill with boiling water. Cover the tin with aluminium foil and bake for 50 minutes until the custards are firm.
- Leave in the tin with water to cool, then remove and chill for at least 2 hours. Turn out the caramels to serve.

Tofu berry brûlée

SERVES 4

INGREDIENTS:

300g/11oz silken tofu
25g/1oz icing sugar
225g/8oz red berries (strawberries,

raspberries and redcurrants)
75g/3oz demerara sugar

- Mix the tofu and icing sugar in a blender and process until smooth.
- Stir in the fruits, then spoon into a 900ml/1½pt dish. Flatten the top.
- Sprinkle the top with enough demerara sugar to cover evenly. Place under a very hot grill until the sugar melts and caramelizes. Chill before serving.

Iced minted blackcurrant soufflés

SERVES 8

INGREDIENTS:

50g/2oz granulated sugar
125ml/4fl oz water
300g/11oz blackcurrants (topped and tailed)
4 egg whites

175g/6oz caster sugar
200ml/7fl oz whipping cream
200g/7oz natural yogurt
3 tablespoons Crème de Menthe

- Tie greaseproof paper collars around 8 x 125ml/4fl oz glass dishes or ramekins to come about 2.5cm/1in about the rims.
- Dissolve the granulated sugar in a saucepan in the water. Add the blackcurrants and simmer for 3 to 4 minutes, then pour into a blender or food processor. Work to a purée, then pour through a sieve into a bowl to remove the skins and seeds.
- Whisk the egg whites until stiff, then whisk in the caster sugar a little at a time to make a shiny meringue. Half whip the cream in a separate large bowl, then fold together with the blackcurrant purée, yogurt and Crème de Menthe. Fold in the meringue.
- Pour into the prepared dishes, level the surface and freeze for at least 4 hours before serving.

Crème caramel

SERVES 8

INGREDIENTS:

Butter for greasing
175g/6oz granulated sugar
50ml/2fl oz water
750ml/1¼pt milk

75g/3oz caster sugar
4 eggs
1 teaspoon vanilla essence

- Preheat the oven to 160°C/325°F/Gas mark 3. Brush 8 x 125ml/4fl oz ramekins or moulds with melted butter.
- Place the granulated sugar and water in a pan. Stir over a low heat until the sugar dissolves. Bring to the boil, reduce the heat and simmer until the mixture

turns golden and starts to caramelize. Remove from the heat immediately and pour enough hot caramel into each ramekin to cover the base.
- To make the custard, heat the milk in a pan over a low heat until almost boiling.
- Remove from the heat. Whisk together the caster sugar, eggs and vanilla essence for 2 minutes, then stir in the warm milk. Strain the mixture into a jug and pour into the ramekins.
- Place the ramekins in a baking dish and pour in enough boiling water to come halfway up the sides of the ramekins. Bake for 30 minutes, or until the custard is set. Allow to cool and refrigerate for at least 2 hours.

Mocha crème caramel

SERVES 6

INGREDIENTS:

150g/5oz granulated sugar
3 tablespoons water
350ml/12fl oz whipping cream
125ml/4fl oz milk
50g/2oz caster sugar

100g/4oz milk chocolate
2½ teaspoons instant coffee powder
3 egg yolks
1 egg

- Preheat the oven to 170°C/325°F/Gas mark 3. Place 6 x 125ml/4fl oz ramekins in a roasting pan.
- Stir the granulated sugar and water in a heavy-based small saucepan over a low heat until the sugar dissolves. Increase the heat to medium-high and bring the mixture to the boil. Boil without stirring for about 9 minutes, until the mixture turns a deep golden brown. Immediately divide the caramel among the ramekins.
- Bring the cream, milk and caster sugar to the boil in a heavy medium-sized saucepan, whisking until the sugar dissolves. Remove from the heat. Add the chocolate and stir until the chocolate melts and the mixture is smooth. Whisk in the coffee, yolks and egg. Divide the custard mixture evenly among the ramekins. Add enough hot water to a roasting tin to come halfway up sides of the ramekins.
- Bake until the custards are set around the edges and the centres move only slightly when the baking tin is shaken, about 30 minutes. Remove the custards from the water and cool completely. Refrigerate for at least 4 hours. Invert custards onto plates and serve.

Strawberry mousse

SERVES 2

INGREDIENTS:

200ml/7fl oz double cream
4 digestive biscuits

55g/2oz strawberries (sliced)
30g/1oz dark chocolate (grated)

- Oil the inside of 2 moulds and line the inside with clingfilm.
- Whisk up the cream so that it is thick and crumble in the digestives. Stir through the strawberries and chocolate.
- Fill the moulds with the mousse and chill for 10 minutes.
- Turn out onto a plate to serve.

Cold chocolate soufflé

SERVES 6

INGREDIENTS

100g/4oz dark chocolate
300ml/½pt milk
50g/2oz caster sugar
2 eggs (separated)

5 tablespoons water
15g/½oz gelatine
150ml/¼pt double cream

- Increase the depth of a soufflé dish by wrapping a collar of doubled greaseproof paper around the outside of the dish.
- Dissolve the dark chocolate in 150ml/¼pt of the milk over a very gentle heat in a pan. Add the rest of the milk and heat to just under boiling. Remove from the heat.
- Add the sugar to the yolks and beat until light and pale in colour. Pour the chocolate milk over this mixture and stir. Put back into the pan and heat gently, stirring constantly, until the mixture coats the back of a wooden spoon. Do not allow to boil. Strain into a large bowl. Allow to cool.
- Put the water into a saucepan. Add the gelatine and dissolve over a very gentle heat. Allow to cool a little and then stir it quickly into the cold chocolate custard.
- Whip the cream until stiff. Whisk the egg whites to form stiff peaks.
- Stand the custard bowl in a bowl of ice and stir the custard until it begins to set.
- Fold in the egg white and cream, working quickly and lightly.
- Pour the mixture into a soufflé dish and leave in the refrigerator to set.

Panna cotta

SERVES 6

INGREDIENTS:

Butter for greasing
750ml/1pt 4fl oz double cream
3 teaspoons gelatine

1 vanilla bean
75g/3oz caster sugar

- Lightly grease the insides of 6 x 150ml/5fl oz ramekins. Place 3 tablespoons double cream in a small bowl, sprinkle the gelatine in an even layer over the surface and leave to go spongy.
- Put the remaining cream in a pan with the vanilla bean and sugar. Heat gently, stirring until almost boiling. Remove from the heat and whisk the gelatine into the cream mixture until dissolved. Pour into the ramekins and chill for 2 hours.

Banana caramel custard

SERVES 10

INGREDIENTS:

300g/11oz granulated sugar
2 bananas (sliced)
8 eggs
600ml/1pt evaporated milk

2 teaspoons vanilla essence
½ teaspoon grated nutmeg
¼ teaspoon salt

- Fill a large deep roasting tin half full of hot water and place on an oven rack in the centre of the oven. Heat the oven to 180°C/350°F/Gas mark 4.
- In a small heavy-based saucepan, heat 100g/4oz sugar over a medium heat for about 5 minutes, swirling the pan occasionally until the sugar has melted and turns golden brown.
- Immediately pour the mixture into a 23 x 12cm/9 x 5in cake tin so the sugar covers the bottom of the tin completely.
- In a large bowl, beat the banana and the remaining sugar with an electric mixer on a high speed until completely liquefied with no lumps. Beat in the eggs.
- Add the evaporated milk, vanilla, nutmeg and salt. Beat with a mixer on a low speed or stir until just blended. Pour the mixture into the cake tin.
- Carefully place the cake tin in the centre of the pan of hot water. Bake for 1¼ hours. Remove the tin from the water and set on a wire rack to cool completely.
- When cooled, cover and refrigerate for at least 8 hours.

Iced honey & lemon mousse

SERVES 4

INGREDIENTS:

4½ large lemons
1 egg white

6 tablespoons clear honey

- Trim the stalk end from 4 of the lemons so they stand up. Cut off the tops and put to one side. Using a knife and a teaspoon, score around the insides of the lemons and scrape out the flesh. Put the flesh into a blender or food processor and blend until smooth, then strain into a jug. Put the hollowed lemon skins and tops on a small tray and freeze.
- Finely grate the zest of the half lemon and set aside. In a bowl, whisk the egg white until stiff peaks form. Gradually whisk in the honey until the mixture is thick and shiny. Slowly whisk in 75ml/3fl oz of the lemon juice and fold in the zest.
- Transfer to a freezer container and freeze for 2 hours, until frozen 2.5cm/1in from the sides of the container. Scrape into a bowl and beat until smooth. Cover with clingfilm and freeze until set.Spoon into a piping bag and pipe into the frozen lemon skins. Add the tops and freeze until ready to serve.

Apricot soufflé

SERVES 2

INGREDIENTS:

175ml/6fl oz double cream
2¼ teaspoons plain flour
50g/2oz caster sugar (plus extra for
dusting)
8 large fresh apricots (4 diced,
4 sliced)

1 teaspoon kirsch
3 eggs (separated)
1 pinch cream of tartar
1 teaspoon butter
Icing sugar for dusting

- Preheat the oven to 230°C/450°F/Gas mark 8.
- Combine the cream, flour, sugar and diced apricots in a large saucepan. Bring to a simmer over a medium heat and cook, whisking until thick, for 3 minutes.
- Remove from the heat, add the kirsch, then whisk in the egg yolks one at a time.
- Beat the egg whites in a mixing bowl until stiff.
- Butter a small soufflé dish, dust with sugar, and spread 50g/2oz of the apricot mixture on the bottom. Add about a third of the egg whites to the remaining

apricot mixture and gently fold together. Repeat, carefully folding in remaining egg whites in two batches. Spoon over the apricot mixture in the soufflé dish.
- Bake the soufflé for 12 to 15 minutes, until lightly browned on top. Dust generously with icing sugar and arrange sliced apricots on top. Serve immediately.

Thai coconut custard

SERVES 4

INGREDIENTS:

5 eggs
225ml/8fl oz coconut milk

225g/8oz granulated sugar

- Beat the eggs with the coconut milk and sugar until the mixture is frothy. Pour the liquid into small ramekins.
- Place in a steamer over boiling water, cover and cook for about 20 minutes or until the mixture has set.

Banana, maple & lime pancakes

SERVES 4

INGREDIENTS:

100g/4oz plain flour
1 egg white
250ml/9fl oz milk
4 tablespoons cold water
Oil for frying

For the filling:
4 bananas (sliced)
3 tablespoons maple syrup
2 tablespoons lime juice

- Make the pancake batter by beating together the flour, egg white, milk and water in a bowl until smooth.
- Heat the oil in a frying pan and pour in a little batter to coat the base. Swirl it around the pan to coat evenly. Cook the pancake until golden, then toss and coat the other side. Slide on to a plate and and prepare a further 7 pancakes.
- To make the filling, mix the bananas, syrup and lime juice in a pan and simmer gently for 1 minute. Spoon into the pancakes and fold into quarters.

Biscuits, slices & small treats

This section includes all the bite-sized sweets that are perfect for teatime or after-dinner treats. From rich brownies, flapjacks and biscuits to fruit slices, florentines and truffles, there is an array of flavours to choose from. Indulge yourself with favourites such as Chocolate fudge brownies, Cream horns or Viennese chocolate fingers.

Oatmeal cookies

SERVES 8

INGREDIENTS:

225g/8oz raisins
475g/1lb 1oz plain flour
1 teaspoon baking powder
1 teaspoon ground cinnamon
½ teaspoon salt

175g/6oz butter
225g/8oz granulated sugar
2 eggs
475g/1lb 1oz oatmeal

- Preheat the oven to 190°C/375°F/Gas mark 5. Lightly grease a baking tray.
- Place the raisins in a saucepan, cover with water and cook until tender. Cool in their liquid.
- Sift the flour and add the baking powder, cinnamon and salt.
- Cream the butter and sugar and add the eggs one at a time, beating well. Blend in the flour mixture. Add the oatmeal and fold in the raisins. Drop a teaspoonful at a time on to the baking tray.
- Bake for about 10 minutes or until barely brown. Cool and store in layers with waxed paper between the layers.

Cranberry biscotti

SERVES 10

INGREDIENTS:

500g/1lb 2oz plain flour
225g/8oz granulated sugar
½ teaspoon baking powder
½ teaspoon salt
75g/3oz butter (cubed)

2 eggs
1 teaspoon vanilla essence
225g/8oz pistachio nuts (coarsely chopped)
2 tablespoons dried cranberries

- Lightly grease a baking tray. In a large bowl combine the flour, sugar, baking powder and salt. With a pastry blender or 2 knives, cut the butter into the flour mixture until the mixture resembles coarse crumbs.
- Mix in the eggs, one at a time, until a stiff dough forms. Add the vanilla essence and stir in the pistachios and cranberries.
- On the baking tray, divide the dough in half and shape each half into a 30 x 5cm/12 x 2in log. Cover with clingfilm and refrigerate the logs for at least 30 minutes.

- Preheat the oven to 190°C/375°F/Gas mark 5. Remove the clingfilm from the logs and bake for 20 to 25 minutes or until the edges start to brown. Cool the logs on the baking tray for 10 minutes.
- Reduce the oven temperature to 170°C/325°F/Gas mark 3. Transfer the logs to a cutting board and cut crosswise diagonally into 1cm/½in thick slices. On the same baking tray, place the slices, cut sides down, in a single layer.
- Bake the slices for 20 to 25 minutes, turning once, until light golden brown on both sides. Cool completely on wire rack.

Anzac biscuits

SERVES 13

INGREDIENTS:

100g/4oz plain flour
150g/5oz granulated sugar
100g/4oz rolled oats
75g/3oz desiccated coconut

100g/4oz butter (cubed)
75g/3oz golden syrup
½ teaspoon bicarbonate of soda
1 tablespoon boiling water

- Preheat the oven to 180°C/350°F/Gas mark 4. Line 2 baking trays with baking parchment.
- Sift the flour into a large bowl. Add the sugar, oats and coconut and make a well in the centre.
- Put the butter and golden syrup together in a small saucepan and stir over a low heat until the butter has melted and the mixture is smooth. Remove from the heat.
- Dissolve the bicarbonate of soda in the water and add immediately to the butter mixture. It will foam up. Pour into the well in the dry ingredients and stir with a wooden spoon until mixed.
- Drop level tablespoons of mixture on to the trays, allowing room for spreading.
- Gently flatten each biscuit with your fingertips. Bake for 20 minutes, or until just browned. Leave on the tray to cool slightly before transferring to a wire rack to cool completely.

Dutch macaroons

SERVES 10

INGREDIENTS:

Rice paper
2 egg whites
225g/8oz caster sugar

175g/6oz ground almonds
225g/8oz dark chocolate

- Preheat the oven to 180°C/350°F/Gas mark 4. Cover 2 baking trays with rice paper.
- Whisk the egg whites in a large mixing bowl until stiff, then fold in the sugar and the almonds.
- Place the mixture in a large piping bag fitted with a 1cm/½in plain nozzle and pipe fingers, about 7.5cm/3in long, allowing space for the mixture to spread during cooking.
- Bake in the oven for 15 to 20 minutes, until golden. Transfer to a wire rack and leave to cool. Remove the excess rice paper from around the edges.
- Melt the chocolate in a heatproof bowl set over a pan of simmering water. Then dip the base of each biscuit into the chocolate. Place the macaroons on a sheet of baking parchment and allow to set.
- Pipe any remaining chocolate over the biscuits. Leave to set before serving.

Fruity roulade

SERVES 4

INGREDIENTS:

For the sponge:
3 eggs
75g/3oz caster sugar (plus extra
for sprinkling)
75g/3oz plain flour (sieved)

For the filling:
100g/4oz sour cream
100g/4oz Greek yogurt
25g/1oz caster sugar
1 tablespoon orange liqueur
Grated zest of 1 orange
100g/4oz strawberries (hulled and
cut into quarters)

- Preheat the oven to 220°C/425°F/Gas mark 7. Lightly oil and line a 33 x 23cm/13 x 9in Swiss roll tin with greaseproof paper.
- Using an electric whisk, whisk the eggs and sugar until the mixture is double in

volume. Fold in the flour with a metal spoon. Pour into the prepared tin and bake in the oven for 10 to 12 minutes, until well risen and golden.
- Place a sheet of greaseproof paper on a flat work surface and sprinkle with caster sugar. Turn the cooked sponge out on to the paper, discard the lining paper, trim the sponge and roll up, encasing the paper inside. Reserve until cool.
- To make the filling, mix together the sour cream, yogurt, sugar, liqueur and orange zest. Unroll the roulade and spread the mixture over it. Scatter the strawberries over the top, and roll up again. Cut into slices.

Coconut ice

SERVES 4-6

INGREDIENTS:

450g/1lb granulated sugar
150ml/¼pt milk

150g/5oz desiccated coconut

- Grease a 20 x 15cm/8 x 6in shallow tin.
- Place the sugar and milk in a large saucepan and heat gently, stirring until the sugar has dissolved. Bring to the boil, and boil steadily to 116°C/240°F, the soft ball stage.
- Remove immediately from the heat and stir in the coconut. Quickly pour the mixture into the greased tin. Leave to cool and mark into squares. Leave to set completely and cut into bite-size pieces.

Rosemary biscuits

SERVES 5

INGREDIENTS:

50g/2oz butter (softened)
50g/2oz caster sugar
Grated zest of 1 lemon
4 tablespoons lemon juice

1 egg (separated)
2 teaspoons finely chopped fresh rosemary
200g/7oz plain flour (sieved)

- Lightly grease 2 baking trays.
- In a large mixing bowl, cream together the butter and sugar until pale and fluffy.
- Add the lemon zest and juice, then the egg yolk and beat until they are thoroughly combined. Stir in the rosemary.

→

- Add the flour, mixing well until a soft dough is formed. Wrap and leave to chill for 30 minutes.
- Preheat the oven to 180°C/350°F/Gas mark 4.
- On a lightly floured surface, roll out the dough thinly and then stamp out 25 circles with a 6cm/2½in biscuit cutter. Arrange the dough circles on the prepared baking trays.
- In a bowl, lightly whisk the egg white. Gently brush the egg white over the surface of each biscuit.
- Bake in the oven for about 15 minutes. Transfer the biscuits to a wire rack and leave to cool before serving.

Peanut-frosted brownies

SERVES 8

INGREDIENTS:

225g/8oz plain flour
100g/4oz cocoa powder
½ teaspoon baking powder
Pinch of salt
100g/4oz butter (softened)
350g/12oz brown sugar
3 eggs
1 teaspoon vanilla essence

225g/8oz unsalted peanuts

For the peanut frosting:
50g/2oz butter
225g/8oz icing sugar (sifted)
2 tablespoons smooth peanut butter
1 tablespoon boiling water

- Preheat the oven to 180°C/350°F/Gas mark 4. Grease a 30 x 23cm/12 x 9in baking tin.
- Sift the flour, cocoa, baking powder and salt into a bowl. Cream the butter and sugar, then beat in the eggs and the vanilla essence. Stir in the dry ingredients and beat until smooth. Fold in 100g/4oz nuts.
- Spoon into the greased tin and bake for 30 minutes.
- For the peanut frosting, cream the butter and gradually mix in the icing sugar.
- Combine the peanut butter with the boiling water and stir into the mixture.
- When the brownies are cooked, spread with the frosting and decorate with the remaining nuts.

Marzipan cherries

SERVES 4

INGREDIENTS:

12 glacé cherries
2 tablespoons brandy

250g/9oz marzipan
100g/4oz dark chocolate

- Line a baking tray with baking parchment.
- Cut the cherries in half and place in a small bowl. Add the brandy and stir well to coat. Leave for at least 1 hour, stirring occasionally.
- Divide the marzipan into 24 pieces and roll each piece into a ball. Press half a cherry into the top of each marzipan ball.
- Break the chocolate into pieces, place in a heatproof bowl and set over a pan of simmering water. Stir until all the chocolate has melted.
- Dip each sweet into the melted chocolate using a cocktail stick, allowing the excess to drip back into the bowl. Place the chocolate-coated marzipan cherries on the baking tray and chill in the refrigerator until set.

Chocolate coconut squares

SERVES 9

INGREDIENTS:

225g/8oz dark chocolate
digestive biscuits
75g/3oz butter (plus extra for greasing)
175g/6oz canned evaporated milk
1 egg (beaten)

1 teaspoon vanilla essence
25g/1oz caster sugar
50g/2oz self-raising flour (sifted)
100g/4oz desiccated coconut
50g/2oz dark chocolate

- Preheat the oven to 190°C/375°F/Gas mark 5. Grease a shallow 20cm/8in square cake tin and line the base.
- Crush the biscuits in a polythene bag with a rolling pin. Melt the butter in a saucepan and stir in the crushed biscuits until well combined. Press the mixture into the base of the cake tin.
- Beat together the evaporated milk, egg, vanilla essence and sugar until smooth. Stir in the flour and coconut. Pour the mixture over the biscuit base and level the top.
- Bake in the oven for 30 minutes. Leave to cool in the cake tin for about 5 minutes, then cut into squares. Leave to cool completely in the tin.

→

←

- Carefully remove the squares from the tin and place them on a board. Melt the dark chocolate in a heatproof bowl set over a pan of simmering water. Drizzle it over the squares to decorate them. Leave the chocolate to set before serving.

Eccles cake

SERVES 10-15

INGREDIENTS:

150g/5oz currants
100g/4oz mixed peel
1 tablespoon brandy
25g/1oz granulated sugar (plus extra for sprinkling)

½ teaspoon ground cinnamon
450g/1lb puff pastry
1 egg white

- Preheat the oven to 210°C/425°F/Gas mark 7. Lightly grease 2 baking trays.
- Combine the currants, peel, brandy, sugar and cinnamon in a bowl.
- Divide the pastry into 3 and roll each piece out to a thickness of 3mm/⅛in.
- Using a 7.5cm/3in scone cutter, cut 9 circles from each sheet of pastry. Place 2 teaspoons of filling on each circle. Bring the edges of the rounds up together and pinch to seal. Turn seam-side down and roll out to 1cm/½in thick ovals.
- Place on the trays. Brush the tops with egg white and sprinkle with sugar. Make 3 slashes across the top of each cake. Bake for 15 to 20 minutes, or until golden.
- Serve warm.

Peanut butter cornets

SERVES 4

INGREDIENTS:

8 sugar ice-cream cones
100g/4oz milk chocolate (broken into small pieces)

4 tablespoons crunchy peanut butter
15g/½oz unsalted peanuts (finely chopped and toasted)

- Slice about 2.5cm/1in off the top of each cone and crush well.
- Place the chocolate and the peanut butter in a small saucepan and heat very gently until melted. Stir in the crushed cone tops.
- Pour or spoon the mixture into the cones, sprinkle with the peanuts, and leave to set.

Brandy snaps

SERVES 6

INGREDIENTS:

75g/3oz caster sugar
25g/1oz butter (plus extra for greasing)
1 tablespoon golden syrup

25g/1oz plain flour
2 teaspoons ground ginger

- Preheat the oven to 150°C/300°F/Gas mark 2. Lightly grease a baking tray.
- Beat the sugar with the butter and golden syrup until light and thick. Sift in the flour and ginger and stir together. Divide into 12 equal parts, then roll these into small balls. Place them on the baking tray and bake for 10 to 15 minutes, when the balls will have spread into dark brown biscuits.
- Allow to cool briefly and then lift them off, one at a time. At this point they will be pliable. Lay them one at a time around the handle of a wooden spoon to bend in half. They should set hard very quickly.

Yogurt flapjacks

SERVES 4

INGREDIENTS:

700g/1½lb vanilla yogurt
50g/2oz maple syrup
1 egg
350g/12oz pancake mix

450g/1lb chopped fresh fruit
(strawberries, grapes, blueberries,
peaches, etc)

- Combine 350g/12oz yogurt with the maple syrup and set aside.
- Combine the remaining yogurt with the egg and beat well. Add the pancake mix and blend to combine. Heat a greased frying pan over a medium heat. Spoon 50g/2oz of the batter on a hot pan and gently spread out. Cook until the edges are firm, flip and brown the opposite side. Repeat with the remaining batter.
- Serve warm with the chopped fruit and maple yogurt sauce.

Ginger parfait

SERVES 10

INGREDIENTS:

150g/5oz gingernut biscuits
15g/½oz butter (melted)
2 eggs

175g/6oz icing sugar
1 tablespoon ground ginger
500ml/18fl oz double cream

- Put the biscuits in a blender or food processor and blend briefly to make crumbs.
- Use some of the melted butter to grease a 900g/2lb loaf tin. Line the tin with clingfilm, then brush the clingfilm with the rest of the butter. Spoon about 3 tablespoons of the biscuit crumbs into the loaf tin and place in the freezer for at least an hour.
- Put the eggs, icing sugar and ginger in a bowl and whisk together for 5 to 10 minutes until the mixture is thick and mousse-like.
- Whisk the cream until soft peaks form, then fold into the egg mixture. Put 3 tablespoons of the biscuit crumbs to one side, then fold in the remainder. Pour the mixture into the prepared loaf tin and sprinkle with the reserved biscuit crumbs.
- Cover with clingfilm and freeze for at least 3 hours. Serve cut into 1cm/½in slices.

Chocolate & chestnut cream vacherin

SERVES 8

INGREDIENTS:

6 egg whites
350g/12oz caster sugar
75g/3oz hazelnuts (skinned, toasted and finely chopped)
175g/6oz plain chocolate (broken into pieces)

500g/1lb 2oz canned sweetened chestnut purée
300ml/½pt double cream

- Preheat the oven to 140°C/275°F/Gas mark 1. Line 3 baking trays with baking parchment and draw a 20cm/8in circle on each.
- Stiffly whisk the egg whites, then gradually whisk in the sugar a little at a time, whisking well until the meringue is smooth and shiny. Very lightly fold in the nuts.

- Spread the mixture over the marked circles. Bake for 1 to 1½ hours until dried out. Remove from the oven and allow to cool, then remove the lining paper.
- Melt the chocolate in a heatproof bowl set over a pan of simmering water. Soften the chestnut purée in a bowl and stir in the melted chocolate. Lightly whip the cream until stiff peaks form and fold in the chestnut mixture.
- Sandwich the meringues together with a little of the chestnut cream. Cover the top and sides with the remainder of the cream.

Cheesecake brownies

SERVES 10

INGREDIENTS:

For the crust:
150g/5oz plain sweet biscuit crumbs
75g/3oz finely chopped almonds
25g/1oz granulated sugar
50g/2oz butter (melted)

For the cheese topping:
250g/9oz cream cheese
25g/1oz butter (softened)
100g/4oz granulated sugar
½ teaspoon vanilla essence
2 eggs

2 tablespoons milk
15g/½oz plain flour

For the chocolate filling:
175g/6oz cooking chocolate
50g/2oz cream cheese
25g/1oz butter (softened)
150g/5oz granulated sugar
2 eggs
1 teaspoon vanilla essence
¼ teaspoon salt
100g/4oz plain flour (sifted)

- Preheat the oven to 180°C/350°F/Gas mark 4. Line a 23cm/9in square baking tin with aluminium foil.
- For the crust, combine the crumbs, almonds, sugar and butter, and mix well.
- Press the mixture evenly into the baking tin. Bake for 8 minutes, then remove from the oven and allow to cool completely, leaving the oven on.
- For the cheese topping, beat together the cream cheese, butter, sugar and vanilla essence until creamy. Add the eggs, milk and flour, and beat until light and smooth. Set aside.
- For the chocolate filling, melt the chocolate in a heatproof bowl set over a pan of simmering water, then leave to cool. Beat together the cream cheese and butter until smooth. Gradually beat in the sugar until well blended. Beat in the eggs, one at a time. Stir in the vanilla essence, salt and cooled chocolate. Fold in the flour.
- Spread the chocolate filling over the cooled crust. Pour the cheese topping slowly over the top of the chocolate filling, spreading evenly. Bake in the oven for about 50 minutes. Leave to cool completely before serving, cut into slices.

Fiesta slices

SERVES 6

INGREDIENTS:

100g/4oz blanched almonds
150g/5oz hazelnuts
100g/4oz granulated sugar
25g/1oz plain flour
1 teaspoon ground cinnamon
1 tablespoon honey
½ tablespoon lemon juice
50g/2oz mixed peel (finely chopped)

2 egg whites

For the icing:
100g/4oz drinking chocolate (sifted)
100g/4oz icing sugar (sifted)
1 tablespoon lemon juice
1 tablespoon water

- Preheat the oven to 180°C/350°F/Gas mark 4. Grease a baking tray.
- Grind the almonds. Roast the hazelnuts lightly, rub off the skin, then grind. Mix all the ingredients together except the egg whites.
- Whisk the egg whites until stiff then fold into the mixture. Shape the mixture into 4 rolls about 30cm/12in long and place on the baking tray. Bake in the oven for 15 to 20 minutes until light brown.
- To make the icing, combine all the icing ingredients together. Brush the icing on the slices while still hot. Cool, then cut into 2.5cm/1in lengths.

Butterscotch pear biscuits

SERVES 5-10

INGREDIENTS:

For the dough:
100g/4oz plain flour
A pinch of salt
25g/1oz hazelnuts (roasted and ground)
25g/1oz icing sugar
50g/2oz butter (diced)
1 egg yolk
2 tablespoons water

For the topping:
15g/½oz raisins
2 tablespoons water
1 tablespoon rum
450g/1lb pears (peeled, cored and finely sliced)
Juice of 1 lemon and pared zest
50g/2oz butter
50g/2oz demerara sugar
15g/½oz toasted chopped hazelnuts

- To make the dough, sift the flour and salt into the bowl of a blender or food processor, then add the hazelnuts and icing sugar. Add the butter and process until the mixture resembles fine breadcrumbs. Add the egg yolk and the water. Process to a smooth dough. Wrap in clingfilm and chill for 1 hour.
- Preheat the oven to 190°C/375°F/Gas mark 5. Grease a large shallow baking tray.
- Roll out the dough on a lightly floured surface to 3mm/⅛in thick. Using a fluted round pastry cutter, stamp out 1cm/½in rounds. Place slightly apart on the baking tray. Prick with a fork and chill for 15 minutes.
- Bake the biscuits for 8 to 10 minutes until golden. Cool on a wire rack.
- To make the topping, soak the raisins with the water mixed with the rum. Dip the pear slices in the lemon juice.
- Melt the butter and sugar in a large frying pan. Add the pear slices with the lemon zest and fry over a medium heat until the pear slices are soft and the butter and sugar are just starting to caramelize. Stir in the raisins, cook for 30 seconds and remove from the heat. Using a slotted spoon, remove the pears and raisins from the pan. Boil the syrup until it is thickened and coats the back of a spoon. Leave to cool.
- Top each biscuit with a little of the pear mixture and sprinkle with the chopped hazelnuts.

Orange & ginger soft cheese fudge

SERVES 6

INGREDIENTS:

350g/12oz dark chocolate (broken into pieces)
75g/3oz soft cheese

275g/10oz icing sugar (sifted)
1 satsuma (peeled and chopped)
50g/2oz crystallized ginger (chopped)

- Line a 10 x 8cm/4 x 3¾in baking tin with waxed paper.
- Place the chocolate in a small heatproof bowl over a pan of simmering water, and stir occasionally until melted.
- Gradually beat the melted chocolate into the soft cheese and add the icing sugar a little at a time.
- Stir the satsuma and ginger into the fudge and spoon into a the baking tin. Refrigerate until firm.
- Cut out shapes or squares of fudge. Keep refrigerated and eat within 7 days.

Apple brownies

SERVES 12

INGREDIENTS:

225g/8oz butter (softened)
400g/14oz granulated sugar
2 eggs (well beaten)
1 teaspoon vanilla essence
475g/1lb 1oz plain flour
1 teaspoon baking powder

1 teaspoon ground cinnamon
3/4 teaspoon salt
500g/1lb 2oz baking apples (peeled and chopped)
100g/4oz pecan nuts

- Preheat the oven to 180°C/350°F/Gas mark 4. Grease a 23cm/9in square baking tin.
- In a large mixing bowl, cream the butter, sugar, eggs and vanilla essence with an electric mixer.
- Combine the flour, baking powder, cinnamon and salt, then add to the butter mixture. Mix until the flour is moistened. Fold in the apples and pecan nuts.
- Spread the mixture into the baking tin and bake in the oven for 45 minutes.

Date flapjacks

SERVES 12

INGREDIENTS:

100g/4oz butter (plus extra for greasing)
4 tablespoons clear honey
175g/6oz rolled oats

1 tablespoon sesame seeds
100g/4oz chopped dates
1 teaspoon ground cinnamon

- Preheat the oven to 180°C/350°F/Gas mark 4. Grease a 20cm/8in square shallow baking tin.
- Melt the butter with the honey in a saucepan. Add the oats, sesame seeds, dates and cinnamon and mix thoroughly.
- Press the oat mixture into the baking tin and bake for about 25 minutes, or until golden. Cool on a wire rack.

Macadamia blondies

SERVES 12

INGREDIENTS:

*100g/4oz butter (cubed, plus extra
for greasing)*
*100g/4oz white chocolate (broken into
pieces)*
100g/4oz caster sugar

2 eggs (lightly beaten)
1 teaspoon vanilla essence
100g/4oz self-raising flour
*75g/3oz macadamia nuts (roughly
chopped)*

- Preheat the oven to 180°C/350°F/Gas mark 4. Lightly grease a 20cm/8in square tin and line with baking parchment, leaving the paper hanging over on 2 opposite sides.
- Place the butter and white chocolate in a heatproof bowl. Half fill a saucepan with water and bring to the boil. Remove from the heat. Place the bowl over the saucepan, making sure the bottom of the bowl does not sit in the water. Stir occasionally until the butter and chocolate have melted and are smooth.
- Add the caster sugar to the bowl and gradually stir in the eggs. Add the vanilla essence, fold in the flour and macadamia nuts, then pour into the prepared tin.
- Bake for 35 to 40 minutes. Leave to cool in the tin before lifting out and cutting into squares.

Truffles

SERVES 4-8

INGREDIENTS:

175g/6oz dark chocolate
2 tablespoons amaretto
25g/1oz butter

50g/2oz icing sugar
50g/2oz ground almonds
50g/2oz milk chocolate (grated)

- Melt the dark chocolate with the amaretto in a heatproof bowl set over a saucepan of simmering water, stirring until well combined. Add the butter and stir until it has melted.
- Stir in the icing sugar and the ground almonds.
- Leave the mixture in a cool place until firm enough to roll into 24 balls.
- Place the grated chocolate on a plate and roll the truffles in the chocolate to coat them.
- Place the truffles in paper cases and chill.

Raisin gingerbread

SERVES 8

INGREDIENTS:

150g/5oz granulated sugar
150ml/¹/₂pt molasses
150ml/¹/₂pt boiling water
25g/1oz butter
1 teaspoon bicarbonate of soda
75g/3oz raisins

50g/2oz pecan nuts (chopped)
1 egg (well beaten)
175g/6oz plain flour (sifted)
1 teaspoon ground cinnamon
1 teaspoon ground ginger
¹/₄ teaspoon ground cloves

- Preheat the oven to 180°C/350°F/Gas mark 4. Grease a 23cm/9in cake tin.
- Mix together the sugar, molasses and boiling water. While the mixture is still hot, stir in the butter and the bicarbonate of soda. Leave to cool. Add the raisins, pecan nuts and the egg.
- Sift together the flour and spices, and stir into the molasses mixture. Pour the mixture into the cake tin and bake for 35 to 40 minutes, or until an inserted skewer comes out clean.

Chocolate crunch biscuits

SERVES 6

INGREDIENTS:

100g/4oz milk chocolate (broken into pieces)

15g/¹/₂oz butter
50g/2oz praline (finely crushed)

- Grease a 15cm/6in shallow, square baking tin and line with waxed paper.
- Place the chocolate and butter in a small heatproof bowl over a pan of hot water and stir gently until melted.
- Remove the bowl from the pan and stir in the praline.
- Pour the mixture into the baking tin and leave to set.
- When set cut into biscuit-sized pieces and serve.

Viennese chocolate fingers

SERVES 9

INGREDIENTS:

100g/4oz butter (plus extra for greasing)
75g/3oz icing sugar

175g/6oz self-raising flour (sifted)
25g/1oz cornflour
200g/7oz dark chocolate

- Preheat the oven to 190°C/375°F/Gas mark 5. Lightly grease 2 baking trays.
- Beat the butter and sugar in a mixing bowl until light and fluffy. Gradually beat in the flour and cornflour.
- Melt 75g/3oz dark chocolate in a heatproof bowl set over a pan of simmering water. Then beat the chocolate into the biscuit dough.
- Place the mixture in a piping bag fitted with a large star nozzle and pipe fingers about 5cm/2in long on the baking trays, leaving room for spreading.
- Bake in the oven for 12 to 15 minutes.
- Leave to cool slightly on the baking trays, then transfer to a wire rack and leave to cool completely.
- Melt the remaining chocolate and dip one end of each biscuit in the chocolate, allowing the excess to drip back into the bowl.
- Place the biscuits on a sheet of baking parchment and leave to set before serving.

Walnut fancies

SERVES 10

INGREDIENTS:

75g/3oz cooking chocolate
75g/3oz butter
150g/5oz granulated sugar
1/2 teaspoon salt
2 eggs (slightly beaten)
1 1/2 teaspoons vanilla essence
100g/4oz plain flour (sifted)

For the walnut topping:
50g/2oz butter
50g/2oz granulated sugar
100g/4oz demerara sugar
2 tablespoons plain flour
2 eggs (slightly beaten)
1 1/2 teaspoons vanilla essence
350g/12oz broken walnut pieces

- Line a greased 23cm/9in square baking tin with baking parchment.
- Melt the chocolate with the butter in a large heatproof bowl over simmering

→

water. Remove from the heat and mix well. Mix in the sugar and salt. Stir in the eggs and vanilla essence, blending well. Fold in the flour until blended.
- Spread evenly into the baking tin. Chill until cold for about 2 hours.
- Preheat the oven to 180°C/350°F/Gas mark 4.
- About 10 minutes before baking, prepare the walnut topping by melting the butter in a heavy-based saucepan over a low heat. Stir in both sugars and cook, stirring constantly, for 1 minute. Remove from heat, stir in the flour and eggs, blending well.
- Return to the heat and cook for about 3 minutes, stirring until thick and light in colour. Remove from the heat and stir in the vanilla essence and walnuts, stirring well to coat the nuts evenly. Spoon over the chilled bottom layer, spreading to the edges.
- Bake for 40 to 45 minutes. Cool on a wire rack before cutting into slices.

Chocolate fudge brownies

SERVES 8

INGREDIENTS:

200g/7oz soft cheese
½ teaspoon vanilla essence
250g/9oz caster sugar
2 eggs
100g/4oz butter (plus extra for greasing)
25g/1oz cocoa powder
100g/4oz plain flour (sifted)

50g/2oz pecan nuts (chopped)

For the fudge icing:
50g/2oz butter
1 tablespoon milk
100g/4oz icing sugar
15g/½oz cocoa powder

- Preheat the oven to 180°C/350°F/Gas mark 4. Lightly grease a 20cm/8in shallow square cake tin and line the base with baking parchment.
- Beat together the cheese, vanilla essence and 25g/1oz caster sugar until smooth, then set aside.
- Beat the eggs and remaining caster sugar together until light and fluffy. Place the butter and cocoa powder in a small pan and heat gently, stirring until the butter melts and the mixture combines, then stir it into the egg mixture. Fold in the flour and nuts.
- Pour half of the cocoa mixture into the tin and level the top. Carefully spread the soft cheese mixture over it, then cover it with the remaining cocoa mixture.
- Bake in the oven for 40 to 45 minutes. Cool in the tin.
- To make the icing, melt the butter in the milk. Stir in the icing sugar and cocoa powder. Spread the icing over the brownies and decorate with pecan nuts. Leave the icing to set, then cut into squares to serve.

Traditional flapjacks

SERVES 12

INGREDIENTS:

25g/1oz golden syrup
50g/2oz caster sugar

75g/3oz butter
175g/6oz oats

- Preheat the oven to 170°C/325°F/Gas mark 3.
- Melt the syrup, sugar and butter together in a heavy-based pan. Remove from the heat. Stir in the oats and mix well. Press the mixture firmly into a shallow, greased tin and place in the oven for about 35 minutes. Leave to cool and then cut into generous portions while still warm.

Black & white chocolate brownies

SERVES 12

INGREDIENTS:

50g/2oz dark chocolate (broken
into pieces)
175g/6oz butter (cubed)
50g/2oz white chocolate (broken
into pieces)

4 eggs
275g/10oz demerara sugar
175g/6oz plain flour (sifted)
125ml/4fl oz sour cream

- Preheat the oven to 160°C/325°F/Gas mark 3. Line a 28 x 18cm/11 x 7in shallow baking tin with baking parchment.
- Melt the dark chocolate with 75g/3oz butter over a gentle heat then allow the mixture to cool slightly. Melt the white chocolate with the remaining butter and leave to cool.
- Beat the eggs with the sugar until light and fluffy and divide between 2 bowls.
- Stir the dark chocolate into one bowl and the white chocolate into the other.
- Carefully fold half the flour and then half the sour cream into each bowl.
- Place alternate spoonfuls of the mixture into the prepared tin and then lightly stir to give a marbled effect. Bake for 30 to 35 minutes until firm to the touch.
- Leave to cool before carefully turning out and cutting into squares.

Chocolate pretzels

SERVES 10

INGREDIENTS:

*100g/4oz butter (plus extra
for greasing)*
100g/4oz caster sugar
1 egg
225g/8oz plain flour
15g/½oz cocoa powder

To finish:
15g/½oz butter
100g/4oz dark chocolate
Icing sugar for dusting

- Preheat the oven to 190°C/375°F/Gas mark 5.
- Lightly grease a baking tray. Beat together the butter and sugar in a mixing bowl until light and fluffy. Beat in the egg.
- Sift together the flour and cocoa powder and gradually beat in to form a soft dough. Use your fingers to incorporate the last of the flour and bring the dough together. Chill for 15 minutes.
- Break small pieces from the dough and roll into thin sausage shapes about 10cm/4in long and 5mm/½in thick. Twist into pretzel shapes by making a circle, then twisting the ends through each other. Place the pretzels on the prepared baking tray, allowing room to expand.
- Bake in the oven for 8 to 12 minutes. Leave to cool slightly on the baking tray, then transfer to a wire rack to cool completely.
- Melt the butter and chocolate in a heatproof bowl set over a pan of gently simmering water, stirring to combine. Dip half of each pretzel in the chocolate and allow any excess to drip back into the bowl. Place on a sheet of baking parchment and leave to set. When set, dust the plain side of each pretzel with icing sugar.

Almond slices

SERVES 8

INGREDIENTS:

3 eggs
75g/3oz ground almonds
200g/7oz milk powder
200g/7oz granulated sugar

½ teaspoon saffron strands
100g/4oz butter
1 tablespoon flaked almonds

- Preheat the oven to 160°C/325°F/Gas mark 3. Grease a shallow 15cm/6in ovenproof dish.
- Beat the eggs together in a bowl and set aside.
- Place the ground almonds, milk powder, sugar and saffron in a large mixing bowl and stir well to mix.
- Melt the butter in a small saucepan. Pour the melted butter over the dry ingredients and mix well until thoroughly combined.
- Add the reserved beaten eggs to the mixture and mix well.
- Spread the mixture in the ovenproof dish and bake for 45 minutes. Cut into slices and decorate with flaked almonds. Serve hot or cold.

Berry almond slice

SERVES 15

INGREDIENTS:

1 sheet ready-rolled puff pastry
150g/5oz butter (plus extra
for greasing)
175g/6oz caster sugar
3 eggs (lightly beaten)
2 tablespoons grated lemon zest

100g/4oz ground almonds
25g/1oz plain flour
150g/5oz raspberries
150g/5oz blackberries
Icing sugar for dusting

- Preheat the oven to 200°C/400°F/Gas mark 6. Lightly grease a 23cm/9in square shallow tin and line with baking parchment, leaving the paper hanging over on 2 opposite sides.
- Place the pastry on a baking tray lined with baking parchment. Prick the pastry all over with a fork and bake for 15 minutes, or until golden. Ease into the tin, trimming the edges if necessary. Reduce the oven heat to 180°C/350°F/Gas mark 4.
- Cream the butter and sugar in a small bowl with an electric beater until light and fluffy. Gradually add the egg, beating after each addition, then the lemon zest.
- Fold in the almonds and flour, then spread the mixture over the pastry.
- Scatter the raspberries and blackberries on top and bake for 1 hour, or until lightly golden. Cut into pieces and dust with icing sugar to serve.

Easter nests

SERVES 4

INGREDIENTS:

1 egg white
75g/3oz caster sugar
25g/1oz cornflour (sifted)

50g/2oz dark chocolate (grated)
16 mini chocolate eggs

- Preheat the oven to 140°C/275°C/Gas mark 1. Line a baking tray with greaseproof paper.
- Whisk the egg white until stiff. Gradually whisk in half of the sugar and fold in the remainder with the cornflour and chocolate.
- Transfer the mixture to a piping bag with a large star nozzle and pipe 6.5cm/2½in nests on to the baking tray.
- Bake in the oven for 45 minutes. Leave to cool and fill with mini chocolate eggs.

Chocolate jam slices

SERVES 6

INGREDIENTS:

100g/4oz butter (plus extra for greasing)
50g/2oz cooking chocolate (broken into pieces)
2 eggs
175g/6oz granulated sugar

1 teaspoon vanilla essence
225g/8oz plain flour
½ teaspoon baking powder
Pinch of salt
50g/2oz raspberry jam
75g/3oz desiccated coconut

- Preheat the oven to 180°C/350°F/Gas mark 4. Grease a 20cm/8in square sandwich tin.
- Melt together the butter and chocolate in a saucepan over a very low heat, then leave to cool slightly.
- Beat the eggs until thick and foamy, then gradually beat in the sugar. Stir in the chocolate mixture and vanilla essence.
- Sift the flour, baking powder and salt together, then stir into the egg mixture.
- Turn into the sandwich tin and bake for 35 to 40 minutes.
- Cool in the tin, spread the jam over the top while still warm and sprinkle with the coconut. When cold, cut into slices.

Peanut butter slices

SERVES 8

INGREDIENTS:

100g/4oz crunchy peanut butter
200g/7oz butter (softened)
1 teaspoon vanilla essence
475g/1lb 1oz demerara sugar
3 eggs

225g/8oz plain flour
½ teaspoon salt
175g/6oz icing sugar (sifted)
2 teaspoons water

- Preheat the oven to 180°C/350°F/Gas mark 4. Grease a 23cm/9in square cake tin.
- Beat together the peanut butter, butter and vanilla essence. When well blended, add the sugar and beat until light and fluffy. Beat in the eggs, one at a time, then stir in the flour and salt, sifted together, until blended.
- Spread into the cake tin and bake for about 35 minutes. Remove from the oven and leave to cool slightly in the tin.
- Mix together the icing sugar and water. Drizzle over the mixture in the tin.
- When cold, cut into slices.

Highball cups

SERVES 5

INGREDIENTS:

100g/4oz plain chocolate (broken into pieces)
100g/4oz fudge

2 teaspoons whisky
2 teaspoons chopped stem ginger

- Melt the chocolate in a heatproof bowl set over a pan of simmering water. Then pour evenly between 10 small aluminium foil sweet cases. Tilt the cases to coat the entire inside. When set, remove the cases.
- Place the fudge in a small heatproof bowl over a pan of simmering water and stir until melted.
- Remove the bowl from the pan and stir in the whisky. Cool slightly.
- Divide the ginger between the chocolate cups and spoon some fudge into each one. Leave to set.

White chocolate Florentines

SERVES 12

INGREDIENTS:

200g/7oz butter
225g/8oz caster sugar
100g/4oz walnuts (chopped)
100g/4oz almonds (chopped)
50g/2oz sultanas (chopped)

25g/1oz glacé cherries
25g/1oz mixed candied peel (chopped finely)
2 tablespoons single cream
225g/8oz white chocolate

- Preheat the oven to 180°C/350°F/Gas mark 4. Line 4 baking trays with non-stick baking parchment.
- Melt the butter over a low heat and then add the sugar, stirring until it has dissolved. Boil the mixture for exactly 1 minute, then remove from the heat.
- Add the walnuts, almonds, sultanas, glacé cherries, candied peel and cream to the saucepan, stirring well to mix.
- Drop heaped teaspoonfuls of the mixture on to the baking trays, allowing plenty of room for them to spread while cooking. Bake in the oven for 10 minutes, or until golden brown.
- Remove the biscuits from the oven and neaten the edges with a knife while they are still warm. Leave to cool slightly, and then transfer them to a wire rack to cool completely.
- Melt the chocolate in a heatproof bowl set over a pan of gently simmering water. Spread the underside of the biscuits with chocolate and leave to set.

Chocolate & apricot squares

SERVES 6

INGREDIENTS:

100g/4oz butter (plus extra for greasing)
175g/6oz white chocolate (broken into small pieces)
4 eggs
100g/4oz caster sugar

200g/7oz plain flour (sifted)
1 teaspoon baking powder
Pinch of salt
100g/4oz ready-to-eat dried apricots (chopped)

- Preheat the oven to 180°C/350°F/Gas mark 4. Lightly grease a 23cm/9in square cake tin and line the base with a sheet of baking parchment.

- Melt the butter and chocolate in a heatproof bowl set over a saucepan of simmering water. Stir frequently with a wooden spoon until the mixture is smooth and glossy. Leave the mixture to cool slightly.
- Beat the eggs and caster sugar into the butter and chocolate mixture until well combined.
- Fold in the flour, baking powder, salt and apricots and mix together well.
- Pour the mixture into the tin and bake in the oven for 25 to 30 minutes. The centre of the cake may not be completely firm, but it will set as it cools. Leave in the tin to cool.
- When the cake is completely cold, turn it out and slice into squares or bars.

Vanilla slice

SERVES 9

INGREDIENTS:

450g/1lb puff pastry
250g/9oz caster sugar
75g/3oz cornflour
50g/2oz custard powder
1.2 litre/2pt double cream
50g/2oz butter (cubed, plus extra for greasing)
2 teaspoons vanilla essence

3 egg yolks

For the icing:
175g/6oz icing sugar
50g/2oz passion fruit pulp
15g/$\frac{1}{2}$oz butter (melted)

- Preheat the oven to 210°C/425°F/Gas mark 7. Grease 2 baking trays and line the base and sides of a shallow 23cm/9in square cake tin with aluminium foil, leaving the foil hanging over on 2 opposite sides.
- Divide the pastry in half, roll each piece to a 25cm/10in square about 3mm/$\frac{1}{8}$in thick and place each one on a baking tray. Prick all over with a fork and bake for 8 minutes. Trim each pastry sheet to a 23cm/9in square. Place one sheet top-side down in the cake tin.
- Combine the sugar, cornflour and custard powder in a saucepan. Gradually add the cream and stir until smooth. Place over a medium heat and stir constantly for 2 minutes, or until the mixture boils and thickens. Add the butter and vanilla essence and stir until smooth. Remove from the heat and whisk in the egg yolks until combined. Spread the custard over the pastry in the tin and cover with the remaining pastry, top-side down. Allow to cool.
- To mae the icing, blend all the ingredients in a mixing bowl.
- Lift the slice out, using the foil as handles, spread the icing over the top and leave it to set before carefully cutting into squares.

Honey & walnut nests

SERVES 4

INGREDIENTS:

Salt
225g/8oz angel hair pasta
100g/4oz butter
175g/6oz shelled pistachio nuts
(chopped)

100g/4oz granulated sugar
100g/4oz clear honey
150ml/¼pt water
2 teaspoons lemon juice

- Bring a large saucepan of lightly salted water to the boil. Add the angel hair pasta and cook for 8 to 10 minutes or until tender. Drain the pasta and return to the pan. Add the butter and toss to coat the pasta thoroughly. Set aside to cool.
- Preheat the oven to 180°C/350°F/Gas mark 4.
- Arrange 4 small flan or poaching rings on a baking tray. Divide the angel hair pasta into 8 equal quantities and spoon 4 of them into the rings and press down lightly. Top the pasta with half of the nuts, then add the remaining pasta. Bake in the oven for 45 minutes, until golden brown.
- Meanwhile, put the sugar, honey and water in a saucepan and bring to the boil over a low heat, stirring constantly until the sugar has dissolved completely.
- Simmer for 10 minutes, add the lemon juice and simmer for 5 minutes.
- Using a palette knife, carefully transfer the angel hair nests to a serving dish.
- Pour over the honey syrup, sprinkle the remaining nuts over and set aside to cool completely before serving.

Almond shortbread

SERVES 9

INGREDIENTS:

150g/5oz plain flour
75g/3oz ground almonds
175g/6oz butter (plus extra for greasing)
100g/4oz caster sugar (plus extra for dusting)

A few drops almond essence
1 egg white (lightly beaten)
50g/2oz flaked almonds

- Preheat the oven to 160°C/325°F/Gas mark 3. Lightly grease a 18 x 28cm/7 x 11in shallow baking tin.

- Combine the flour and ground almonds in a bowl. Cut the butter into small pieces and rub into the flour and almonds with your fingertips until the mixture resembles breadcrumbs.
- Stir in the sugar and almond essence, then squeeze the mixture together to form a dough. Place the dough in the prepared baking tin and spread to the edges by pressing it down with a metal spoon.
- Lightly brush the top of the dough with egg white and sprinkle the flaked almonds over. Bake for 30 to 35 minutes until lightly browned. Leave to cool in the tin, then cut into individual biscuits. Dust with sugar just before serving.

Spicy fruit biscuits

SERVES 10-12

INGREDIENTS:

175g/6oz butter (softened)
175g/6oz brown sugar
1 teaspoon vanilla essence
1 egg
250g/9oz plain flour (sifted)

1 teaspoon mixed spice
½ teaspoon ground ginger
1 teaspoon baking powder
100g/4oz mincemeat

- Cream the butter and sugar in a small bowl with an electric beater until light and fluffy. Add the vanilla essence and egg and beat until well combined. Transfer to a large bowl and add the sifted flour, mixed spice, ginger and baking powder.
- Using a knife, mix to a soft dough. Gather together, then divide the mixture into 2 portions.
- Roll one portion out on to a rectangle about 3mm/⅛in thick and trim the edges.
- Repeat with the other dough portion and refrigerate both until just firm.
- Preheat the oven to 180°C/350°F/Gas mark 4. Line 2 baking trays with baking parchment.
- Spread each dough rectangle with mincemeat, then roll up like a Swiss roll. Cut the rolls into slices about 1cm/½in thick. Place on the prepared trays, leaving space between each slice. Bake for 10 to 15 minutes, or until golden. Cool on the trays for 3 minutes before transferring to a wire rack to cool completely.

Coconut sweet

SERVES 6

INGREDIENTS:

75g/3oz butter
200g/7oz desiccated coconut

175ml/6fl oz condensed milk

- Place the butter in a heavy-based saucepan and melt over a low heat, stirring constantly. Add the desiccated coconut, stirring to mix. Stir in the condensed milk and mix continuously for 7 to 10 minutes.
- Remove the saucepan from the heat, set aside and leave the coconut mixture to cool slightly. Once cool enough to handle, shape the mixture into long blocks and cut into equal-sized rectangles. Leave to set for 1 hour, then serve.

Swiss biscuits

SERVES 6

INGREDIENTS:

100g/4oz butter (plus extra
for greasing)
50g/2oz granulated sugar
1 egg
1½ tablespoons orange juice
1 tablespoon grated orange zest

300g/11oz plain flour
⅛ teaspoon bicarbonate of soda
75g/3oz chopped walnuts
100g/4oz cooking chocolate (coarsely grated)

- Grease a medium-sized baking tray.
- Beat together the butter and sugar, add the egg and beat well. Beat in the orange juice and grated zest. Sift together the flour and bicarbonate of soda and beat into the creamed mixture.
- Stir in the walnuts and chocolate. Wrap the mixture in clingfilm and refrigerate until firm enough to handle.
- Shape into a roll about 2.5cm/1in diameter, wrap and chill again, until very firm.
- Preheat the oven to 180°C/350°F/Gas mark 4.
- Cut the roll into slices about 1cm/½in thick, place on the baking tray and bake for 10 to 12 minutes.

Date brownies

SERVES 8

INGREDIENTS:

225g/8oz stoned dates
100g/4oz granulated sugar
100g/4oz butter (plus extra
for greasing)
3 teaspoon grated lemon zest
175ml/6fl oz water

100g/4oz chocolate drops
2 eggs
300g/11oz plain flour
³/₄ teaspoon bicarbonate of soda
Pinch of salt
225g/8oz walnuts (coarsely chopped)

- Preheat the oven to 180°C/350°F/Gas mark 4. Grease a shallow 25 x 30cm/10 x 12in tin and line with greaseproof paper.
- Put the dates, sugar, butter and lemon zest into a saucepan, add 125ml/4fl oz water and cook gently, stirring frequently until the sugar has dissolved and the dates have softened. Remove from the heat and add the chocolate. Cool slightly, then add the eggs, one at a time, beating well after each.
- Sift together the flour, bicarbonate of soda and salt, then add alternately with 50ml/2fl oz water, beating until smooth. Turn into the prepared tin.
- Sprinkle the walnuts over the surface and bake for 25 to 30 minutes. Leave to cool in the tin, then cut into bars and serve.

Chocolate caramel squares

SERVES 8

INGREDIENTS:

100g/4oz butter (softened)
50g/2oz light muscovado sugar
100g/4oz plain flour (sifted)
50g/2oz rolled oats

For the caramel filling:
25g/1oz butter

25g/1oz light muscovado sugar
200g/7oz canned condensed milk

For the topping:
100g/4oz dark chocolate
25g/1oz white chocolate

- Preheat the oven to 180°C/350°F/Gas mark 4. Grease a 20cm/8in shallow square cake tin.
- Beat together the butter and sugar in a bowl until light and fluffy. Beat in the flour and the rolled oats.

→

←

- Press the mixture into the base of the cake tin. Bake for 25 minutes or until golden brown. Cool in the tin.
- Place the ingredients for the caramel filling in a pan and heat gently, stirring, until the sugar has dissolved and the ingredients combine. Gradually bring to the boil over a very low heat, then boil very gently for 3 to 4 minutes, stirring constantly until thickened. Pour the caramel filling over the biscuit base in the tin and leave to set.
- Melt the dark chocolate in a heatproof bowl set over a pan of simmering water.
- Then spread it over the caramel. Melt the white chocolate and pipe lines of white chocolate over the dark chocolate. Leave to set and cut into squares to serve.

Tollhouse cookies

SERVES 20

INGREDIENTS:

175g/6oz butter (softened)
100g/4oz demerara sugar
100g/4oz granulated sugar
2 eggs (lightly beaten)
1 teaspoon vanilla essence

275g/10oz plain flour
1 teaspoon bicarbonate of soda
300g/11oz dark chocolate chips
100g/4oz pecan nuts (roughly chopped)

- Preheat the oven to 190°C/375°F/Gas mark 5. Line 2 baking trays with baking parchment.
- Cream the butter and sugars in a bowl with an electric beater until light and fluffy.
- Gradually add the eggs, beating well after each addition. Stir in the vanilla, then the sifted flour and bicarbonate of soda until just combined. Mix in the chocolate chips and pecan nuts.
- Drop tablespoonfuls of the mixture onto the trays, leaving room for spreading.
- Bake the cookies for 8 to 10 minutes, or until lightly golden. Cool slightly on the trays before transferring to a wire rack to cool completely.

Cream horns

SERVES 8

INGREDIENTS:

350g/12oz puff pastry
1 egg (beaten with 2 tablespoons milk)
100g/4oz raspberry jam

150ml/¹/₄pt double cream (whipped with ¹/₄ teaspoon vanilla essence)
25g/1oz pistachio nuts (chopped)

- Roll out the pastry to 3mm/¹/₈in thick and cut it into strips measuring 1 x 30cm/¹/₂ x 12in. Moisten the strips with water and wind each one, overlapping slightly, round a cornet mould, from the pointed end upwards, keeping the moist surface on the outside. Allow the horns to stand for about 1 hour.
- Preheat the oven to 200°C/400°F/Gas mark 6.
- Place the horns on a greased baking tray, brush them with the egg, and bake for 15 to 20 minutes, until cooked through.
- Remove the moulds from the horns and return the pastries to the oven to dry for a few minutes. Leave to cool. When cool, place a little jam in each horn, pipe a rosette of whipped cream on top, and sprinkle with nuts.

Ice-creams, sorbets & cold desserts

This section is guaranteed to leave your mouth feeling refreshed and full of the flavours of spring and summer. It includes mouth-watering recipes ranging from Lychee & elderflower sorbet, Champagne granita and Mango sorbet to classic desserts such as Baked Alaska and Blackcurrant coulis.

Vanilla ice-cream

SERVES 6

INGREDIENTS:

600ml/1pt double cream
1 vanilla pod
Pared zest of 1 lemon

4 eggs (beaten)
2 egg yolks
175g/6oz caster sugar

- Place the cream in a heavy-based saucepan and heat gently, whisking.
- Add the vanilla pod, lemon zest, eggs and yolks to the pan and heat until the mixture nearly reaches boiling point.
- Reduce the heat and cook for 8 to 10 minutes, whisking the mixture continuously until thickened.
- Stir the sugar into the cream mixture, set aside and leave to cool.
- Strain the cream mixture through a sieve.
- Slit open the vanilla pod, scoop out the tiny black seeds and stir them into the cream.
- Pour the mixture into a shallow freezing container with a lid and freeze overnight until set.

Watermelon sorbet

SERVES 6

INGREDIENTS:

½ small watermelon
75g/3oz caster sugar

75ml/3fl oz unsweetened cranberry juice
2 tablespoons lemon juice

- Cut the watermelon into 6 equal-sized wedges. Scoop out the pink flesh, discarding the seeds but reserving the flesh and peel.
- Select a bowl that is about the same size as the melon. Line it with clingfilm.
- Arrange the melon peel in the bowl to re-form the shell. Place in the freezer.
- Mix the sugar and cranberry juice or water in a saucepan and stir over a low heat until the sugar dissolves. Bring to the boil, then lower the heat and simmer for 5 minutes. Leave the sugar syrup to cool.
- Put the melon flesh and lemon juice in a blender or food processor and process to a smooth purée. Stir in the sugar syrup and pour into a freezer-proof container.

- Freeze for 3½ hours, or until slushy.
- Tip the sorbet into a chilled bowl and whisk to break up the ice crystals. Return to the freezer for another 30 minutes, whisk again, then tip into the melon shell and freeze until solid.
- Carefully remove the sorbet–filled melon shell from the freezer and turn it upside down. Use a sharp knife to separate the segments, then quickly place them on individual plates and serve.

Marshmallow ice-cream

SERVES 4

INGREDIENTS:

75g/3oz dark chocolate (broken into pieces)
175g/6oz white marshmallows

150ml/¼pt milk
300ml/½pt double cream

- Put the chocolate and marshmallows into a pan and pour in the milk. Warm over a very low heat until the chocolate and marshmallows have melted. Remove from the heat and leave the mixture to cool completely.
- Whisk the cream until thick, then fold it into the cold chocolate mixture with a metal spoon. Pour into a 450g/1lb loaf tin and freeze for at least 2 hours.

Orange freeze

SERVES 4

INGREDIENTS:

4 large oranges

300g/11oz vanilla ice-cream

- Using a sharp knife, carefully cut a lid off each orange. Scoop out the flesh, discarding any pips and thick pith. Place the shells and lids in the freezer and chop the orange flesh, reserving the juice.
- Whisk together the orange juice, flesh and vanilla ice-cream until well blended.
- Cover and freeze for 24 hours, stirring occasionally.
- Place 2 large scoops of the ice-cream mixture into the frozen shells, so that it is over-flowing at the top. Place the lids on top and return to the freezer for 3 hours.

Atholl Brose ice-cream

SERVES 12

INGREDIENTS:

600ml/1pt milk
5 egg yolks
100g/4oz caster sugar
3 drops vanilla essence
50g/2oz medium oatmeal
50g/2oz granulated sugar

300ml/½pt double cream

For the sauce:
3 tablespoons clear honey
3 tablespoons whisky
450g/1lb fresh raspberries

- Bring the milk to the boil in a large pan. Whisk the egg yolks with the caster sugar in a heatproof bowl until pale and thick, then stir in the hot milk.
- Place the bowl over a pan of simmering water and stir for about 30 minutes, until the mixture thickens to coat the back of a wooden spoon. Leave to cool.
- Stir in the vanilla essence and freeze the mixture in its bowl for 1 hour.
- Meanwhile, mix the oatmeal and granulated sugar on a baking tray and toast under a hot grill, stirring frequently with a fork, until the sugar caramelizes.
- Break into large crumbs with a fork. Leave to cool, then chill.
- Whip the cream to soft peaks. Beat the partially frozen custard to loosen it slightly, stir in the oatmeal and fold in the cream. Return to the freezer for 1 hour.
- Beat the ice-cream again, transfer to a 1.5 litre/2½pt ring mould, slide it into a freezer bag and freeze until firm.
- Shortly before serving, heat the honey and whisky in a pan and stir until blended, then leave to cool.
- Remove the ice-cream from the freezer and invert on to a large serving plate.
- Remove the mould carefully. Heap raspberries in the centre of the ice-cream and drizzle the whisky sauce over the top over the top.

Blackcurrant coulis

SERVES 8

INGREDIENTS:

6 sheets of leaf gelatine
450ml/³/₄pt water
450g/1lb blackcurrants

225g/8oz caster sugar
150ml/¼pt ruby port
2 tablespoons crème de cassis

- In a small bowl, soak the gelatine in 75ml/3fl oz water, until soft. Place the blackcurrants, sugar and 300ml/½pt water in a large saucepan. Bring to the boil, lower the heat and simmer for 20 minutes.
- Strain, reserving the cooking liquid in a large jug. Put half the blackcurrants in a bowl and pour 4 tablespoons of the reserved cooking liquid over them. Set the bowl and jug aside.
- Squeeze the water out of the gelatine and place in a small saucepan with the port, crème de cassis and 75ml/3fl oz water. Heat gently to dissolve the gelatine but do not allow the mixture to boil. Stir the gelatine mixture into the jug of blackcurrant liquid until well mixed.
- Place 8 individual jelly moulds into a roasting tin. Fill with the port mixture.
- Chill for at least 6 hours until set. Tip the bowl of blackcurrants into a blender or food processor and purée until smooth.
- Turn each jelly out onto a serving plate and spoon the coulis around each jelly.
- Decorate with the remaining blackcurrants.

Mango sorbet

SERVES 8

INGREDIENTS:

175g/6oz granulated sugar
3 cardamom pods (split)
600ml/1pt cold water

2 ripe mangoes
3 egg whites

- Put the sugar and cardamom pods in a heavy-based saucepan, pour in the water and heat gently, stirring occasionally, until the sugar has dissolved. Increase the heat and bring to the boil, then boil for 7 minutes without stirring. Remove from the heat and leave to cool.
- Meanwhile, peel the mangoes and remove as much flesh as possible from the stones. Put the flesh in a blender or food processor and work to a purée, then pour into a shallow container.
- Strain the cooled syrup into the mango purée and stir well to mix. Freeze uncovered for 3 hours.
- Turn the mango mixture into a bowl and beat with a fork until broken up.
- Whisk the egg whites until stiff. Fold the egg whites into the mango mixture until evenly mixed, then return the mixture to the container. Cover and freeze overnight. Transfer to the refrigerator for 20 minutes before serving.

Peach & ginger pashka

SERVES 4

INGREDIENTS:

350g/12oz cottage cheese
2 ripe peaches (stoned and roughly chopped)
100g/4oz natural yogurt

2 pieces stem ginger in syrup (drained and chopped, plus reserve 2 tablespoons syrup from the jar)
½ teaspoon vanilla essence

- Drain the cottage cheese and rub it through a sieve into a bowl.
- In a bowl mix together the peaches, cottage cheese, yogurt, stem ginger and syrup and vanilla essence.
- Line a new, clean flower pot with a piece of cheesecloth. Tip in the cheese mixture, wrap the cloth over the top and weigh down. Leave over a bowl in a cool place to drain overnight. Unwrap, invert on to a plate and serve.

Cinnamon & nutmeg ice-cream

SERVES 8

INGREDIENTS:

½ teaspoon ground cinnamon
½ teaspoon ground nutmeg
50g/2oz caster sugar

150ml/¼pt double cream
250g/9oz mascarpone cheese
400ml/14fl oz custard

- Put the cinnamon, nutmeg, sugar and cream in a small pan. Bring slowly to the boil, then put to one side to cool.
- Put the Mascarpone in a large bowl and beat until smooth. Stir in the custard and the cooled spiced cream. Pour the mixture into a shallow freezer container and freeze for 2½ hours. Beat to break up the ice crystals and freeze for a further 2½ hours before serving.

Turkish delight ice-cream

SERVES 12

INGREDIENTS:

350g/12oz pink Turkish delight
5 tablespoons water
700ml/1pt 4fl oz fresh custard

300ml/¹/₂pt double cream
3 tablespoons rosewater

- Cut the Turkish delight into small pieces. Place in a pan with the water and cook over a low heat, stirring, until the mixture has almost melted. Stir into the custard.
- Lightly whip the cream until it forms soft peaks, then fold gently into the custard. Stir in the rosewater.
- Pour the mixture into a 1.2 litre/2pt loaf tin lined with clingfilm and freeze for at least 4 hours.

Orange granita

SERVES 6

INGREDIENTS:

4 large oranges
1 large lemon

150g/5oz granulated sugar
500ml/16fl oz water

- Thinly pare the orange and lemon zest and set aside for decoration. Cut the fruits in half and squeeze the juices into a jug. Set aside.
- Heat the sugar and water in a heavy-based saucepan, stirring, until the sugar dissolves. Bring to the boil, then boil without stirring until a syrup forms.
- Remove the syrup from the heat, add some of the orange and lemon zest and shake the pan. Cover and leave to cool.
- Strain the sugar syrup into a shallow freezer container and add the fruit juice. Stir well to mix, then freeze, uncovered, for about 4 hours, until slushy.
- Remove the half-frozen mixture from the freezer and mix with a fork, then return to the freezer and freeze again for at least 4 hours.
- To serve, turn into a bowl and leave to soften for about 10 minutes, then break up again and pile into long-stemmed glasses. Decorate with strips of orange and lemon zest.

Raspberry sorbet

SERVES 6-8

INGREDIENTS:

450g/1lb raspberries
400ml/14fl oz water

175g/6oz granulated sugar
50ml/2fl oz lemon juice

- Liquidize the raspberries in a blender or food processor, then strain.
- Boil 300ml/½pt water and the sugar for 5 minutes in a pan. Remove from the heat and allow to cool. Add the lemon juice, remaining water and the raspberries. Pour into a freezer container and freeze overnight.

Chocolate & Pernod creams

SERVES 4

INGREDIENTS:

50g/2oz dark chocolate (broken into pieces)
250ml/9fl oz milk
300ml/½pt double cream

25g/1oz caster sugar
1 tablespoon arrowroot (mixed with 2 tablespoons milk)
3 tablespoons Pernod

- Put the chocolate in a heatproof bowl set over a pan of barely simmering water. Stir over a low heat until melted. Remove the pan from the heat and cool slightly.
- Pour the milk and cream into a pan over a low heat and bring to just below boiling point, stirring occasionally. Remove the pan from the heat and set aside.
- Beat the sugar and the arrowroot mixture into the melted chocolate. Gradually stir in the hot milk and cream mixture, then stir in the Pernod. Set the bowl over a pan of barely simmering water and cook over a low heat for about 10 minutes, stirring constantly, until thick and smooth. Remove from the heat and set aside to cool.
- Pour the chocolate and Pernod mixture into 4 individual serving glasses. Cover with clingfilm and chill in the refrigerator for 2 hours before serving.

Ginger creams

SERVES 6

INGREDIENTS:

350g/12oz caster sugar
50ml/2fl oz water
1cm/½in fresh root ginger (peeled and grated)
375ml/13fl oz double cream

300ml/½pt milk
125ml/4fl oz ginger wine
3 eggs
4 egg yolks

- Preheat the oven to 150°C/300°F/Gas mark 2.
- Dissolve 225g/8oz caster sugar in the water over a low heat until clear.
- Bring to the boil and bubble for 5 to 6 minutes or until a golden caramel colour.
- Carefully swirl the caramel around the base and sides of 6 x 150ml/¼pt heatproof moulds, then put to one side.
- Whisk together the root ginger with the cream, milk and ginger wine. Pour into a small pan and warm over a gentle heat for 2 to 3 minutes. Whisk together the eggs, yolks and remaining caster sugar.
- Pour the flavoured milk slowly onto the whisked egg mixture, stirring constantly, then strain the mixture into a large jug.
- Pour the custard into the moulds and set them in a roasting tin. Add hot water to come halfway up the sides of the moulds. Bake for 1½ hours or until lightly set, then remove the moulds from the tin. When cool, cover with clingfilm and chill for at least 4 hours.

Citrus jelly

SERVES 4

INGREDIENTS:

3 oranges
1 lemon
1 lime

300ml/½pt water
75g/3oz caster sugar
1 tablespoon powdered gelatine

- With a sharp knife, cut all the peel and white pith from 1 orange and carefully remove the segments. Arrange the segments in the bottom of a 1.2 litre/2pt mould.
- Grate the zest from the lemon, lime and 1 orange. Place all the grated zest in a saucepan with the water and sugar. Heat gently until the sugar has dissolved. Remove from the heat.

→

←

- Squeeze the juice from the lemon, lime and 2 oranges and stir it into the pan.
- Strain the liquid into a measuring jug to remove the zest. You should have about 600ml/1pt: if necessary make up the amount with water. Sprinkle the gelatine over the mixture and stir until dissolved.
- Pour the jelly liquid over the orange segments in the bowl. Refrigerate until set.

Chocolate ice-cream sandwiches

SERVES 6

INGREDIENTS:

6 Amaretti biscuits
12 dark chocolate digestive biscuits

500ml/16fl oz vanilla ice-cream

- Put the Amaretti biscuits into a blender or food processor and process until they form coarse crumbs.
- Take one of the digestive biscuits and spread a 2.5cm/1in layer of ice-cream on its non-chocolate side. Place another biscuit on top, chocolate side uppermost.
- Squeeze the biscuits gently together and smooth the ice-cream around the edges.
- Repeat with the remaining biscuits and ice-cream.
- Roll the edges of the biscuit sandwiches in the crushed Amaretti biscuits to coat them, then place on a tray in the freezer. Freeze for at least 2 hours.

Raspberry & mint bavarois

SERVES 6

INGREDIENTS:

450g/1lb fresh raspberries
2 tablespoons icing sugar
2 tablespoons lemon juice
1 tablespoon finely chopped fresh mint

2 tablespoons powdered gelatine
75ml/3fl oz boiling water
300ml/½ pt custard
250ml/9fl oz Greek yogurt

- Reserve a few raspberries for decoration. Place the remaining raspberries in a blender or food processor. Add the icing sugar and lemon juice and process to a smooth purée.

- Press the purée through a sieve to remove the raspberry seeds. Pour it into a measuring jug and stir in the mint.
- Sprinkle 1 teaspoon gelatine over 2 tablespoons boiling water and stir until the gelatine has dissolved. Stir into 150ml/¼pt of the fruit purée.
- Pour this jelly into a 1.2 litre/2pt mould and chill in the refrigerator until the jelly has set completely.
- Mix the custard and yogurt in a bowl and stir in the remaining fruit purée.
- Dissolve the rest of the gelatine in the remaining boiling water and stir in quickly.
- Pour the raspberry custard into the mould and chill it until it has set completely.
- To serve, turn out on to a serving plate and decorate with the reserved raspberries.

Mixed berry sorbet

SERVES 6

INGREDIENTS:

225g/8oz strawberries
180ml/6½fl oz water
225g/8oz redcurrants

100g/4oz caster sugar
150ml/¼pt sparkling white wine
2 egg whites

- Hull the strawberries and remove the stalks from the redcurrants, then place all the berries in a saucepan with 2 tablespoons water. Cook for about 10 minutes until soft. Press the berries through a sieve to form a purée.
- Dissolve the sugar in the remaining water over a low heat and boil gently for 10 minutes. Leave to cool for 1 hour.
- Stir the wine and fruit purée into the cooled syrup. Pour into a shallow freezer container and freeze for 3 hours.
- Transfer the frozen mixture to a chilled basin and break up with a fork. Whisk the egg whites until stiff and fold into the mixture. Return to the freezer for 3 hours. Transfer to the refrigerator 30 minutes before serving.

Strawberry frozen yogurt

SERVES 4

INGREDIENTS:

400g/14oz canned strawberries and syrup

500ml/16fl oz Greek yogurt
125ml/4fl oz single cream

→

←

- Place the strawberries and syrup in a blender or food processor and blend to a smooth purée. Add the yogurt and cream and continue to process until a uniform colour is achieved.
- Pour into a shallow freezer container, cover with clingfilm and freeze until set.
- After 30 minutes, remove from the freezer and stir with a fork before returning.
- Repeat 1 hour later.

Chocolate praline bombe

SERVES 12-16

INGREDIENTS:

Oil for greasing
225g/8oz caster sugar
225g/8oz whole almonds (unblanched)
500g/1lb 2oz dark chocolate (broken into pieces)

75ml/3fl oz strong black coffee
150g/5oz butter (chopped)
2 tablespoons rum
750ml/1¼pt double cream

- To make the praline, brush a large baking tray with oil. Place the sugar and almonds into a heavy-based pan over a low heat without stirring, until the sugar has melted. Stir frequently until a good caramel colour has been reached and the almonds appear to be toasted. Turn the mixture immediately on to the baking tray and leave until quite cold and set. Break into pieces then pound to a fine powder between sheets of baking paper, or place in a blender or food processor and process until fine.
- Place the chocolate in a pan with the coffee over a low heat until melted.
- Remove from the heat and gradually stir in the butter until melted. Stir in the rum and leave in the refrigerator for several hours, until firm.
- Brush a 2.4 litre/4pt basin with oil. Stir the praline into the chocolate mixture.
- Whip the cream in the bowl until it holds its shape, then fold into the chocolate. Pour the mixture into the mould and leave in the refrigerator overnight.

Vanilla & caramel parfait

SERVES 4

INGREDIENTS:

100g/4oz butter
150g/5oz demerara sugar

175ml/6fl oz single cream
450g/1lb vanilla ice-cream

- Heat the butter in a heavy-based pan. Add the sugar and stir over a low heat, without boiling, until the sugar is dissolved. Increase the heat and simmer without boiling for 3 minutes, or until golden. Remove from the heat and allow to cool slightly.
- Layer caramel sauce with vanilla ice-cream into 4 tall glasses.

Key lime sorbet

SERVES 4

INGREDIENTS:

275g/10oz granulated sugar
600ml/1pt water
Grated zest of 1 lime

175ml/6fl oz fresh lime juice
25g/1oz icing sugar

- In a small heavy-based saucepan, dissolve the granulated sugar in the water, without stirring, over a medium heat. When the sugar has dissolved, boil the syrup for 5 to 6 minutes. Remove from the heat and leave to cool.
- Mix the cooled sugar syrup and lime zest in a bowl. Stir well. Add the lime juice and stir in the icing sugar.
- Freeze the mixture overnight in the freezer in a shallow container.

Baked Alaska

SERVES 6

INGREDIENTS:

900ml/1½pt round tub of vanilla
ice-cream
Victoria sponge

4 egg whites
75g/3oz caster sugar
1 tablespoon raspberry jam

- Freeze the ice-cream in the coldest section of the freezer and cut the sponge to match the top of the ice-cream tub, then freeze the sponge on a baking sheet overnight.
- Preheat the oven to 230°C/450°F/Gas mark 8.
- To make the meringue, whisk the egg whites with an electric mixer to form soft peaks.
- Increase the mixer speed and gradually add the sugar until the peaks are firm, but take care not to take it too far or the meringue will separate.

→

←

- Spread the sponge with the jam. Turn out the ice-cream to sit on top of the jam.
- Smooth the meringue all over it with a palette knife, taking it right down to the edge to seal the ice-cream in entirely, with no gaps.
- Bake for 4 to 5 minutes, until the meringue is just beginning to colour. Remove from the oven and serve immediately.

Chocolate rum pots

SERVES 6

INGREDIENTS:

225g/8oz dark chocolate
4 eggs (separated)
75g/3oz caster sugar

50ml/2fl oz dark rum
75ml/3fl oz double cream

- Melt the chocolate in a heatproof bowl set over a pan of simmering water and leave to cool slightly.
- Whisk the egg yolks with the caster sugar in a bowl until pale and fluffy, using an electric whisk or balloon whisk.
- Drizzle the chocolate into the mixture and fold in, together with the rum and the double cream.
- Whisk the egg whites in a separate bowl until standing in soft peaks. Fold the egg whites into the chocolate mixture in 2 batches. Divide the mixture between 6 ramekins and chill for at least 2 hours.

Strawberry & raspberry parfait

SERVES 6

INGREDIENTS:

75g/3oz strawberry-flavoured jelly crystals
450ml/³⁄₄pt boiling water
250g/9oz strawberries (hulled and chopped)

500g/1lb 2oz vanilla ice-cream
100g/4oz raspberries

- Stir the strawberry crystals in the boiling water until the crystals have dissolved, then refrigerate until set.
- Process 100g/4oz of the strawberries in a blender or food processor for 30 seconds to make a purée.
- Layer the jelly, ice-cream, remaining strawberries, raspberries and purée in six parfait glasses and serve immediately.

Tuscan pudding

SERVES 4

INGREDIENTS:

15g/1/2oz butter
75g/3oz mixed dried fruit
250g/9oz ricotta cheese
3 egg yolks

50g/2oz caster sugar
1 teaspoon ground cinnamon
Grated zest of 1 orange

- Preheat the oven to 180°C/350°F/Gas mark 4. Lightly grease 4 mini pudding basins or ramekin dishes with the butter.
- Put the dried fruit in a bowl and cover with warm water. Leave to soak for 10 minutes.
- Beat the ricotta cheese with the egg yolks in a bowl. Stir in the caster sugar, cinnamon and orange zest and mix to combine.
- Drain the dried fruit in a sieve set over a bowl. Mix the drained fruit with the ricotta cheese mixture. Spoon the mixture into the basins or ramekins.
- Bake in the oven for 15 minutes. Leave to cool, then refrigerate overnight.

Tropical caramel cream

SERVES 6–8

INGREDIENTS:

2 bananas (cut into chunks)
1 pineapple (cored and cut into chunks)
1 Charentais melon (halved, seeded and cut into chunks)
2 passion fruit (halved, with flesh and pips scooped out)

2 tablespoons dark rum
5 tablespoons orange juice
300ml/1/2pt double cream
300g/11oz Greek yogurt
100g/4oz caster sugar
2 tablespoons water

→

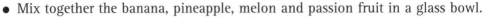

- Mix together the banana, pineapple, melon and passion fruit in a glass bowl.
- Sprinkle with the rum and the orange juice.
- Whip the cream until it forms stiff peaks and fold into the yogurt. Spread over the fruit mixture and chill.
- Place the sugar into a small pan with the water. Heat gently, stirring until the sugar has dissolved. Boil rapidly, without stirring, until the syrup turns a light caramel colour.
- Remove the pan from the heat and leave to stand for about 2 minutes. Drizzle the caramel into uneven shapes over a sheet of oiled aluminium foil. Leave to cool and harden for at least 30 minutes. Peel off the foil and stick the caramel shapes into the cream mixture just before serving.

Coconut cream moulds

SERVES 8

INGREDIENTS:

For the caramel:
100g/4oz granulated sugar
150ml/¹/₄pt water

For the custard:
300ml/¹/₂pt water

75g/3oz creamed coconut (chopped)
2 eggs
2 egg yolks
25g/1oz caster sugar
300ml/¹/₂pt single cream

- Preheat the oven to 150°C/300°F/Gas mark 2.
- To make the caramel, placed the sugar and water in a saucepan and heat gently to dissolve the sugar, then boil rapidly, without stirring, until the mixture turns a rich golden brown.
- Immediately remove the pan from the heat and dip the base into a bowl of cold water to stop it cooking further. Quickly pour the caramel evenly between 8 x 150ml/¹/₄pt ovenproof dishes, coating the base of each dish.
- To make the custard, place the water in the same saucepan, add the creamed coconut and heat, stirring constantly, until the coconut dissolves. Place the eggs, yolks and sugar in a bowl and beat well with a fork. Add the hot coconut milk and stir well to dissolve the sugar. Stir in the cream and strain the mixture into a jug.
- Arrange the caramel-lined dishes in a roasting tin and fill the tin with enough cold water to come halfway up the sides of the dishes. Pour the custard mixture into the dishes, cover with aluminium foil and cook for about 40 minutes, or until set.
- Remove the dishes, set aside to cool, and then chill overnight. To serve, invert on to serving plates.

Cinnamon ice-cream

SERVES 6

INGREDIENTS:

3 egg yolks
100g/4oz light muscovado sugar
2 cinnamon sticks (broken in half)

300ml/½pt milk
300ml/½pt double cream

- Whisk together the egg yolks and sugar until thick and pale. Slowly heat the cinnamon sticks in the milk until just boiling, then remove from the heat.
- Discard the cinnamon and stir the milk into the egg yolk mixture.
- Return the mixture to the pan and cook, stirring, over a low heat for about 15 minutes or until thickened.
- Remove from the heat, strain into a clean bowl and leave until cold. Stir occasionally to prevent a skin from forming.
- Stir the cream into the custard. Place the bowl in the freezer and leave for 2 to 3 hours, until the mixture is set 2.5cm/1in from the edges. Whisk the mixture to break down the large ice crystals, return to the freezer for a further 1 hour, then whisk again. Transfer to a freezer container and freeze until firm. Transfer to the refrigerator 30 minutes before serving.

Blueberry sundae

SERVES 4

INGREDIENTS:

800g/1¾lb fresh blueberries
2 tablespoons lemon juice
1 teaspoon vanilla essence
2 teaspoons cornflour

2 tablespoons water
350g/12oz granulated sugar
600ml/1pt vanilla yogurt

- Reserving a few blueberries for decoration, purée the blueberries in a blender or food processor. In a large saucepan, combine the blueberry purée with the lemon juice and vanilla essence. Cook over a medium heat for 5 minutes.
- Combine the cornflour and water and add to the fruit mixture, stirring constantly for about 3 minutes, until thickened. Remove from the heat and stir in the sugar.
- Using the back of a spoon, press the mixture through a sieve to remove the blueberry skins. Layer in tall glasses, alternating with the vanilla yogurt.
- Decorate with reserved blueberries.

Mango fool

SERVES 6

INGREDIENTS:

3 large mangoes
250ml/9fl oz custard

400ml/14fl oz double cream

- Peel and stone the mangoes and purée the flesh in a blender or food processor.
- Add the custard and blend to combine.
- Whip the cream until soft peaks form, then gently fold into the mango mixture until just combined.
- Pour the mixture into a serving dish or individual glasses. Refrigerate for at least 1 hour before serving.

Orange-blossom jelly

SERVES 4

INGREDIENTS:

75g/3oz caster sugar
150ml/¼pt water
25g/1oz powdered gelatine

600ml/1pt fresh orange juice
2 tablespoons orange-flower water

- Place the sugar and water into a small saucepan and heat gently to dissolve the sugar. Pour into a heatproof bowl and leave to cool.
- Sprinkle the gelatine over the surface of the syrup. Leave to stand until the gelatine has absorbed all the liquid.
- Gently melt the gelatine over a saucepan of simmering water until it becomes clear.
- Leave it to cool. When the gelatine is cold, mix it with the orange juice and orange-flower water.
- Pour into a jelly mould and chill in the refrigerator for at least 2 hours.

Brown bread ice-cream

SERVES 4

INGREDIENTS:

175g/6oz fresh wholemeal breadcrumbs
25g/1oz walnuts (finely chopped)
50g/2oz caster sugar

½ teaspoon finely grated orange zest
450ml/15fl oz natural yogurt
2 large egg whites

- Preheat the grill to medium. Mix the breadcrumbs, walnuts and sugar and spread over a sheet of aluminium foil in the grill pan.
- Grill, stirring frequently, for 5 minutes until crisp and evenly browned. Remove from the heat and leave to cool.
- When cool, transfer to a mixing bowl and mix in the orange zest and yogurt. In another bowl, whisk the egg whites until stiff. Gently fold into the breadcrumb mixture, using a metal spoon.
- Spoon the mixture into 4 ramekins, smooth over the tops and freeze for 1½ to 2 hours, until firm.

Mint-chocolate gelato

SERVES 4

INGREDIENTS:

6 eggs
150g/5oz caster sugar
300ml/½pt milk
150ml/¼pt double cream

Large handful fresh mint leaves (rinsed and dried)
50g/2oz dark chocolate (broken into small pieces)

- Put the eggs and sugar in a heatproof bowl that will sit over a saucepan with plenty of room underneath. Using an electric mixer, beat the eggs and sugar together until thick and creamy.
- Put the milk and cream in the saucepan and bring to a simmer, stirring. Pour on to the eggs, whisking constantly.
- Rinse the pan and put 2.5cm/1in water in the bottom. Place the bowl on top, making sure the base does not touch the water. Turn the heat to medium-high and stir the custard over the hot water until it is thick enough to coat the back of the spoon.
- Tear the mint leaves and stir them into the custard. Remove the custard from the heat. Leave to cool, then cover and infuse for at least 2 hours. Chill for 30 minutes.

→

←
- Strain the mixture through a small nylon sieve to remove the pieces of mint.
- Transfer to a freezer container and freeze for 2 hours, until frozen 2.5cm/1in from the sides.
- Scrape into a bowl and beat again until smooth. Stir in the chocolate pieces, smooth the top, cover with clingfilm and freeze until set. Transfer to the refrigerator 20 minutes before serving.

Chocolate & honey ice-cream

SERVES 8

INGREDIENTS:

500ml/18fl oz milk
150g/5oz dark chocolate (broken into pieces)
4 eggs (separated)

75g/3oz caster sugar
Pinch of salt
2 tablespoons clear honey

- Pour the milk into a pan, add the chocolate and stir over a medium heat for 3 to 5 minutes until melted. Remove the pan from the heat and set aside.
- In a bowl, whisk the egg yolks with all but 1 tablespoon of the sugar until pale and thickened. Gradually whisk in the milk mixture, a little at a time. Return the mixture to a clean pan and cook over a low heat, whisking constantly, until smooth and thickened. Remove from the heat and set aside to cool completely.
- Cover with clingfilm and chill in the refrigerator for 30 minutes.
- Whisk the egg whites with the salt until soft peaks form. Gradually whisk in the remaining sugar and continue whisking until stiff and glossy. Remove the chocolate mixture from the pan and transfer to a bowl. Then stir in the honey, then gently fold in the egg whites.
- Divide the mixture between 6 individual freezerproof moulds and place in the freezer for at least 4 hours. Transfer to the refrigerator 10 minutes before serving.

Coffee granita

SERVES 4

INGREDIENTS:

500ml/18fl oz water
100g/4oz granulated sugar

250ml/9fl oz very strong espresso coffee (cooled)

- Heat the water and sugar together gently until the sugar dissolves. Bring to the boil, stirring occasionally. Remove from the heat and allow to cool.
- Stir the coffee and sugar syrup together, place in a freezer container and freeze until solid.
- Shortly before serving, turn out of the freezer container and chop into chunks.
- Place in a blender or food processor and process until it forms small crystals.
- Spoon into tall glasses and serve.

Frozen cherry ripples

SERVES 8

INGREDIENTS:

100g/4oz dark chocolate (broken into pieces)
100g/4oz black cherries (pitted and chopped)
1 tablespoon caster sugar
1 tablespoon kirsch
1 tablespoon water

For the ice-cream:
250ml/9fl oz milk
1 vanilla pod (split)
3 egg yolks
50g/2oz caster sugar
200ml/7fl oz double cream

- Slowly melt the chocolate in a heatproof bowl over a pan of simmering water. Allow to melt slowly. Spread the chocolate round the insides of between 20 and 24 waxed mini paper cases. Leave in a cool place to set.
- Place the cherries in a pan with the sugar, kirsch and 1 tablespoon water. Cook over a low heat until the sugar dissolves. Turn up the heat and simmer for 5 minutes until the cherries are soft and the liquid syrupy. Place in a blender or food processor and liquidize until smooth. Cool and put in the freezer for 15 minutes.
- To make the ice-cream, place the milk and vanilla pod in a saucepan and bring to the boil. Whisk the egg yolks and sugar until thick and light. Stir in a little of the milk, then add the egg mixture to the pan. Cook, stirring, until the custard thickens. Cool and remove the vanilla pod.
- Pour into a freezer container and freeze until set 2.5cm/1in from the edge, then whisk to break down the large ice crystals and whisk in the cream. Freeze until just firm, then stir in the cherry mixture.
  Carefully peel the paper cases away from the set chocolate and place on a chilled tray. Spoon a little ice-cream into each. Freeze until firm.

Plum & cardamom fool

SERVES 4

INGREDIENTS:

*1kg/2¼lb dessert plums (stoned
and sliced)
100g/4oz caster sugar
4 cardamom pods (split, seeds removed
and crushed)*

*2 tablespoons fresh lemon juice
150ml/¼pt custard
200ml/7fl oz Greek yogurt*

- Remove 8 slices of plum for decoration and set aside. Put the remaining plums, sugar, cardamom seeds and lemon juice in a pan. Cover and bring to the boil, then simmer for 20 to 25 minutes or until plums are soft. Pour into a cold bowl and leave for 30 minutes.
- Lift the plums out of the bowl with a slotted spoon, reserving the juices. Purée in a blender or food processor and pour into a bowl. Boil the juices for 3 to 4 minutes, until reduced to 3 tablespoons, then stir into the plum purée with the custard and yogurt, until smooth. Spoon into 4 tumblers and chill for 2 hours.
- Decorate with reserved plum slices and serve.

Lemon curd ice-cream

SERVES 6

INGREDIENTS:

*6 eggs
100g/4oz butter
100g/4oz caster sugar*

*Juice and grated zest of 4 lemons
700ml/1¼pt thick plain yogurt*

- Put the eggs, butter, sugar and lemon juice and zest in a heavy-based pan and cook gently over a low heat, stirring, until the mixture coats the back of a spoon.
- Leave to cool slightly, then whisk in the yogurt. Place in a shallow freezer container and freeze until set, stirring occasionally to break up the ice crystals.
- Transfer to the refrigerator 20 minutes before serving.

Champagne granita

SERVES 4

INGREDIENTS:

100g/4oz granulated sugar
200ml/7fl oz water

400ml/14fl oz pink champagne

- Put the sugar and water in a heavy-based saucepan and heat gently, stirring occasionally, until the sugar has dissolved, then boil without stirring until a light sugar syrup is formed. Remove from the heat and allow to cool.
- Mix the champagne and the sugar syrup together, pour into a freezer container and freeze overnight.
- Flake into tall glasses to serve.

Lychee & elderflower sorbet

SERVES 4

INGREDIENTS:

175g/6oz caster sugar
400ml/14fl oz water
500g/1lb 2oz fresh lychees (peeled and stoned)

1 tablespoon undiluted
elderflower cordial

- Heat the sugar and water until the sugar has dissolved, then boil for 5 minutes and add the lychees. Lower the heat and simmer for 7 minutes. Remove from the heat and allow to cool.
- Purée the fruit and syrup. Place a sieve over a bowl and pour the purée into it.
- Press through with a spoon.
- Stir the elderflower cordial into the strained purée, then pour the mixture into a freezer container. Freeze for approximately 2 hours, until ice crystals start to form around the edge.
- Remove the sorbet from the freezer and process briefly in a blender or food processor to break up the crystals. Repeat this freezer/blender process twice more, then leave to freeze until firm.
- Transfer to the refrigerator 10 minutes before serving.

Chocolate banana sundae

SERVES 4

INGREDIENTS:

50g/2oz dark chocolate (broken into small pieces)
100g/4oz golden syrup
15g/½oz butter
1 tablespoon rum

150ml/¼pt double cream
12 scoops vanilla ice-cream
4 bananas (sliced)
75g/3oz flaked almonds (toasted)

- Place the chocolate in a heatproof bowl with the syrup and butter. Heat over a pan of simmering water until melted, stirring until well combined. Remove the bowl from the heat and stir in the rum.
- Whip the cream until just holding its shape. Place a scoop of vanilla ice-cream in the bottom of each of 4 tall sundae glasses. Top with the sliced banana, some chocolate sauce and a sprinkling of nuts.
- Repeat the layers, finishing with a generous dollop of cream.

Raspberry & passion fruit chinchillas

SERVES 4

INGREDIENTS:

25g/1oz butter (softened)
5 egg whites
150g/5oz caster sugar
2 passion fruit

675g/1¼lb fresh raspberries
250ml/9fl oz custard
2 tablespoons milk

- Preheat the oven to 180°C/350°F/Gas mark 4. With a brush, paint 4 x 300ml/½pt soufflé dishes with a visible layer of butter.
- Whisk the egg whites in a mixing bowl until firm. Add the sugar a little at a time and whisk into a firm meringue. Halve the passion fruit, take out the seeds with a spoon and fold the seeds into the meringue.
- Turn the meringue out into the prepared dishes, stand them in a deep roasting tin, fill with boiling water to halfway up the dishes and bake for 10 minutes.
- Turn the chinchillas out upside-down on to individual plates and leave to cool.

- Refrigerate for 20 minutes.
- To serve, top with the fresh raspberries. Thin the custard with the milk and pour around the edge.

Raspberry fool

SERVES 4

INGREDIENTS:

300g/11oz fresh raspberries
50g/2oz icing sugar
300ml/¹/₂pt crème fraîche

¹/₂ teaspoon vanilla essence
2 egg whites

- Put the raspberries and sugar in a blender or food processor and process until smooth.
- Reserving 1 tablespoon of the crème fraîche for decorating, put the vanilla essence and crème fraîche in a bowl and stir in the raspberry mixture.
- Whisk the egg whites in a separate bowl until stiff peaks form. Gently fold the egg whites into the raspberry mixture using a metal spoon, until fully combined.
- Spoon the raspberry fool into individual serving dishes and chill for at least 1 hour. Decorate with the reserved crème fraîche.

Frozen egg nog

SERVES 4

INGREDIENTS:

2 egg yolks
25g/1oz caster sugar
2 tablespoons rum

1 tablespoon brandy
300ml/¹/₂pt double cream

- Place the egg yolks, sugar, rum and brandy in a bowl over a pan of simmering water and whisk until the mixture is thick and creamy. Remove from the heat and continue whisking until the mixture has cooled slightly. Then transfer to a freezer container.
- Whip the cream until it stands in soft peaks and then fold carefully into the egg mixture. Freeze for at least 4 hours.

Lemon cream with summer fruit

SERVES 6

INGREDIENTS:

225g/8oz curd cheese
75g/3oz icing sugar
1 teaspoon finely grated lemon zest
1 tablespoon lemon juice
300ml/½pt double cream

675g/1¼lb soft summer fruit (sliced strawberries, cherries, blackberries, raspberries, redcurrants and blackcurrants)
2 tablespoons crème de cassis

- Beat together the curd cheese, icing sugar, lemon zest and juice. Whip the cream until it just holds its shape and fold into the cheese mixture.
- Line a sieve with muslin. Fill with the cream mixture and smooth the top. Set it over a bowl to catch the drips and leave to drain in the refrigerator overnight.
- Turn the cream on to a large plate and remove the muslin. Mix the summer fruit with the crème de cassis and spoon around the cream.

Pineapple sorbet

SERVES 4

INGREDIENTS:

850ml/1pt 8fl oz unsweetened pineapple juice
375g/13oz granulated sugar

3 tablespoons lemon juice
1 egg white (lightly beaten)

- Stir the pineapple juice and sugar in a large pan over a low heat until the sugar has dissolved. Bring to the boil, reduce the heat and simmer for 5 minutes. Skim off any scum.
- Stir in the lemon juice and pour into a metal tray. Cover with a sheet of greaseproof paper and freeze for 2 hours. Transfer the mixture to a blender or food processor and process to a slush, then return to the tray and the freezer.
- Repeat the beating and freezing twice more, then beat it for a final time, adding the egg white. Process until smooth. Return to the tray, cover with greaseproof paper and freeze until firm.

White chocolate ice-cream

SERVES 6

INGREDIENTS:

1 egg
1 egg yolk
25g/1oz caster sugar
150g/5oz white chocolate (broken into pieces)

300ml/½pt milk
150ml/¼pt double cream

- Beat the egg, egg yolk and sugar into a heatproof bowl.
- Place the chocolate in a bowl with 3 tablespoons milk and melt over a pan of simmering water.
- Heat the remaining milk until almost boiling and pour on to the eggs, whisking. Place the bowl containing the eggs, milk and sugar over a pan of simmering water and cook, stirring, until the mixture thickens. Whisk in the chocolate. Remove from the heat, cover with a piece of dampened baking parchment and leave until cold.
- Whip the cream until just holding its shape and fold into the custard. Transfer to a freezer container and freeze the mixture for 1 to 2 hours until frozen 2.5cm/1in from the sides. Scrape into a bowl and beat until smooth. Scrape back into the freezer container and freeze until firm.

Brazilian coffee bananas

SERVES 4

INGREDIENTS:

4 bananas
1 tablespoon instant coffee granules
1 tablespoon hot water

25g/1oz dark muscovado sugar
250ml/9fl oz Greek yogurt
2 teaspoons flaked almonds (toasted)

- Peel and slice 1 banana and set aside. Peel and mash the remaining 3 with a fork in a large mixing bowl. Dissolve the coffee in the hot water and stir into the mashed bananas.
- Spoon a little of the mashed banana mixture into 4 serving dishes and sprinkle each with sugar. Top with a spoonful of yogurt, then repeat the layers until the ingredients are all used up. Finish with banana slices and flaked almonds.
- Refrigerate for 30 minutes, then serve.

Apricot and orange jellies

SERVES 4

INGREDIENTS:

225g/8oz ready-to-eat dried apricots
300ml/¹/₂pt unsweetened orange juice
2 tablespoons lemon juice

3 teaspoon clear honey
1 tablespoon powdered gelatine
4 tablespoons boiling water

- Place the apricots in a saucepan and pour in the orange juice. Bring to the boil, cover and simmer for 15 to 20 minutes, until the apricots are plump and soft. Leave to cool for 10 minutes.
- Transfer the mixture to a blender or food processor and blend until smooth. Stir in the lemon juice and add the honey. Pour the mixture into a measuring jug and make up to 600ml/1pt with cold water. Dissolve the gelatine in the boiling water and pour into the apricot mixture.
- Pour the mixture into 4 individual 150ml/¹/₄pt moulds. Leave to chill until set.

Chocolate brandy cream

SERVES 4

INGREDIENTS:

175g/6oz plain chocolate (broken
into pieces)
300ml/¹/₂pt whipping cream

2 tablespoons brandy
1 teaspoon coffee essence
1 egg white

- Place the chocolate in a heatproof bowl placed over a saucepan of simmering water and leave to melt slowly, stirring occasionally. Leave to cool slightly.
- Pour the cream into a small bowl and whip until soft peaks form.
- Gently stir the brandy and coffee essence into the chocolate. Mix together gently until blended, then fold in the whipped cream with a metal spoon.
- Briskly whisk the egg white in a small bowl until stiff, then fold in the chocolate mixture with a metal spoon. Mix gently.
- Spoon into 4 tall glasses and chill for at least 2 hours.

Quick apricot whip

SERVES 4

INGREDIENTS:

400g/14oz canned apricot halves in juice
1 tablespoon Grand Marnier

175ml/6fl oz Greek yogurt
1 tablespoon flaked almonds (toasted)

- Drain the juice from the apricots and place the fruit and Grand Marnier in a blender or food processor. Process until smooth.
- Alternately spoon fruit purée and yogurt into 4 tall glasses. Top with almonds.

Fresh fruit

This chapter includes classics such as Banana split, Strawberries Romanoff and Eton mess. Offering different types of fresh fruit salads and richer, creamier fruit desserts such as Bananas with chocolate marshmallow sauce, it provides a range of delicious recipes for you to choose from, no matter what the time of year.

Strawberries Romanoff

SERVES 4

INGREDIENTS:

750g/1lb 11oz strawberries (quartered)
2 tablespoons Cointreau
½ teaspoon finely grated orange zest
15g/½oz caster sugar

125ml/4fl oz double cream
20g/¾oz icing sugar

- Combine the strawberries, Cointreau, orange zest and caster sugar in a large bowl, cover and refrigerate for 1 hour. Drain the strawberries, reserving any juices.
- Purée about a quarter of the strawberries with the reserved juices.
- Divide the remaining strawberries among 4 glasses. Beat the cream and icing sugar until soft peaks form, then fold the strawberry purée through the whipped cream.
- Spoon the mixture over the top of the strawberries, then cover and refrigerate until required.

Coffee & peach creams

SERVES 4

INGREDIENTS:

4 peaches (halved and stoned)
50g/2oz caster sugar
50ml/2fl oz water

2 tablespoons coffee essence
200ml/7fl oz Greek yogurt
300ml/½pt custard

- Place the peaches in a large bowl, cover with boiling water and leave for 2 to 3 minutes. Drain the peaches, then carefully remove the skins.
- Place the caster sugar in a saucepan and add the water. Bring to the boil, stirring occasionally, until the sugar has dissolved. Boil rapidly for about 2 minutes.
- Add the peaches and coffee essence to the pan. Remove from the heat and allow to cool.
- Mix together the yogurt and custard until well combined.
- Divide the peaches between 4 glass dishes. Spoon over the custard mixture then top with the remaining peach juices. Chill for 30 minutes, then serve.

Chargrilled apples on cinnamon toasts

SERVES 4

INGREDIENTS:

4 sweet dessert apples
Juice of ½ lemon
4 large round bread rolls

15g/½oz butter (melted)
25g/1oz caster sugar
1 teaspoon ground cinnamon

- Core the apples and cut them horizontally in 3 or 4 thick slices. Sprinkle with lemon juice.
- Cut the rolls in half horizontally. Brush sparingly with butter on both sides.
- Mix together the sugar and ground cinnamon. Preheat the grill to medium.
- Place the apple and bread slices under the grill and cook them for 3 to 4 minutes, turning once.
- Sprinkle half the cinnamon sugar over the apple slices and toasts and cook for 1 minute more, until they are a rich golden brown.
- To serve, arrange the apple slices over the toasts and sprinkle them with the remaining cinnamon sugar.

Summer fruits with ricotta & vanilla dip

SERVES 6

INGREDIENTS:

250g/9oz ricotta cheese
250g/9oz Mascarpone cheese
150ml/¼pt crème fraîche
A few drops of vanilla essence

Grated zest of 1 lemon
50g/2oz caster sugar
900g/2lb mixed fresh summer berries

- Beat the cheeses together with the crème fraîche, vanilla essence, lemon zest and sugar. Spoon into a serving dish, cover and chill for at least 30 minutes.
- Pile the berries on to a serving plate and spoon the ricotta and vanilla dip on top.

Eton mess

SERVES 6

INGREDIENTS:

150ml/¼pt double cream (lightly whipped)
200ml/7fl oz Greek yogurt

500g/1lb 2oz strawberries (hulled)
2 tablespoons crème de cassis
5 meringue nests

- Fold the cream into the yogurt and chill for 30 minutes.
- Put 250g/9oz strawberries in a blender or food processor, blend to a purée, then stir in the crème de cassis. Measure out 75ml/3fl oz of the purée and reserve.
- Slice the remaining strawberries into a bowl, reserving 6 for decoration, then pour the purée over and chill in the bowl for 20 minutes.
- Break up the meringue nests and carefully fold into the cream mixture with the strawberry mixture. Divide between 6 glasses, then drizzle over the reserved purée.
- Decorate with the reserved strawberries.

Baked peaches with raspberry sauce

SERVES 6

INGREDIENTS:

25g/1oz butter
50g/2oz granulated sugar
1 egg (beaten)
25g/1oz ground almonds
6 ripe peaches

For the sauce:
225g/8oz raspberries
1 tablespoon icing sugar

- Preheat the oven to 180°C/350°F/Gas mark 4. Beat the butter and sugar together, then beat in the egg and ground almonds.
- Cut the peaches in half and remove the stones. With a spoon scrape out some of the flesh, slightly enlarging the hole left by the stone. Save the excess flesh for the sauce.
- Stand the peach halves on a baking tray flesh-side up, supporting them with crumpled aluminium foil to keep them steady. Fill the hollow in each peach half with the almond mixture. Bake for 30 minutes.

- To make the sauce, combine the raspberries and icing sugar in a blender or food processor. Add the reserved peach flesh and process until smooth. Press through a sieve.
- Let the peaches cool slightly. Spoon the sauce on each plate and arrange 2 peach halves on top. Serve immediately.

Mulled Florida cocktail

SERVES 4

INGREDIENTS:

2 grapefruit
2 oranges
150ml/¼pt apple juice

1 tablespoon brandy
2 fresh cherries (halved)

- Over a saucepan to catch the juice, remove all zest and pith from the grapefruit and oranges, and separate each into segments.
- Place the segments in the saucepan. Add the apple juice and brandy. Heat through until almost boiling.
- Spoon into 4 glass dishes and top each with half a cherry. Serve warm.

Exotic fruit parcels

SERVES 4

INGREDIENTS:

1 papaya
1 mango
1 star fruit

1 tablespoon grenadine
3 tablespoons orange juice
200ml/7fl oz natural yogurt

- Cut the papaya in half, scoop out the seeds and discard them. Cut the flesh into thick slices.
- Prepare the mango by cutting it lengthways in half either side of the central stone. Score each mango half in a criss-cross pattern, then push each mango half inside out to separate the cubes and cut them away from the peel.
- Using a sharp knife, thickly slice the star fruit. Place all of the fruit in a bowl and mix together.
- Mix the grenadine and orange juice together and pour over the fruit. Leave to marinate for at least 30 minutes.

→

←

- Divide the fruit among 4 double-thickness squares of aluminium foil and gather up the edges to form a parcel that encloses the fruit.
- Place the foil parcel on a rack set over hot coals and barbecue the fruit for 15 to 20 minutes, or place under a medium grill for the same amount of time.
- Serve the fruit in the parcel with the yogurt.

Banana split

SERVES 4

INGREDIENTS:

200g/7oz dark chocolate
175ml/6fl oz double cream
25g/1oz butter

4 bananas
12 scoops vanilla ice-cream
Mixed chopped nuts, to serve

- Put the chocolate, cream and butter in a pan and stir over a low heat until smooth. Cool slightly.
- Split the bananas in half lengthways and arrange in 4 glass dishes. Place 3 scoops of ice-cream in each dish and pour the chocolate sauce over the top.
- Sprinkle with the chopped nuts.

Muscat grape frappé

SERVES 4

INGREDIENTS:

½ bottle Muscat wine
150ml/¼pt water

450g/1lb Muscat grapes

- Pour the wine into a stainless steel baking tray, add the water and freeze for 3 hours or until completely solid.
- Scrape the frozen wine with a tablespoon to make a fine ice. Combine the grapes with the ice and spoon into 4 shallow glasses.

Mango & melon ginger salad

SERVES 4

INGREDIENTS:

2 avocados (peeled, stoned and flesh cut into slices)
1 mango (peeled and cut into slices)
1 cantaloupe melon (peeled and cut into slices)

Grated zest and juice of 2 limes
100g/4oz Stilton cheese (crumbled)
2 tablespoons finely chopped stem ginger
2 passion fruit (halved)

- Arrange the slices of avocado, mango and melon decoratively on a serving plate.
- Sprinkle the fruit with the lime zest and juice, Stilton and ginger. Spoon the passion fruit over the salad and serve.

Summer berries in champagne jelly

SERVES 8

INGREDIENTS:

900ml/1½pt champagne
1½ teaspoons powdered gelatine
250g/9oz granulated sugar

250g/9oz strawberries (hulled and chopped)
250g/9oz blueberries

- Pour half the champagne into a large bowl and let the bubbles subside. Sprinkle the gelatine over the top in an even layer. Do not stir. Leave until the gelatine is spongy. Pour the remaining champagne into a large saucepan, add the sugar and heat gently, stirring constantly, until all the sugar has dissolved.
- Remove the saucepan from the heat, add the gelatine mixture and stir until thoroughly dissolved. Cool completely.
- Divide the berries among 8 x 125ml/4fl oz stemmed wine glasses and gently pour the jelly over them. Refrigerate until set. Remove from the refrigerator 15 minutes before serving.

Indian fruit salad

SERVES 4

INGREDIENTS:

For the sauce:
50g/2oz cashew nuts
50g/2oz almonds
50g/2oz pistachio nuts
75g/3oz granulated sugar
125ml/4fl oz single cream

For the fruit salad:
1 mango (peeled and diced)
½ pineapple (peeled and diced)

2 bananas (peeled and finely sliced)
2 apples (peeled and diced)
2 cheekoo (peeled and diced)
1 kiwi fruit (peeled and finely sliced)
1 small guava (peeled and diced)
8 white grapes (halved)
Seeds and flesh of 1 passion fruit
Juice of 1 lime
2 tablespoons chopped mixed nuts

- Place the ingredients for the sauce into a blender or food processor for 2 to 3 minutes or until smooth.
- Transfer the mixture to a small saucepan and heat for 5 to 7 minutes over a medium heat, stirring slowly. Remove from the heat and set aside.
- To make the fruit salad, place the prepared fruit in a large bowl and pour the lime juice over. Mix well, then pour the sauce over the fruit or serve on the side.
- Sprinkle the salad with chopped nuts.

Fresh figs in wine

SERVES 6

INGREDIENTS:

450ml/¾pt dry white wine
75g/3oz clear honey
50g/2oz caster sugar
1 small orange

8 whole cloves
450g/1lb fresh figs
1 cinnamon stick

- Put the wine, honey and sugar in a heavy-based saucepan and heat gently until the sugar dissolves.
- Stud the orange with the cloves and add to the syrup with the figs and cinnamon.
- Cover and simmer until the figs are soft. Transfer to a serving dish and leave to cool before serving.

Californian baked pears

SERVES 4

INGREDIENTS:

25g/1oz butter
1 teaspoon granulated sugar
Grated zest of ½ lemon
4 pears (peeled)

300g/11oz canned fruit cocktail
in syrup
½ teaspoon mixed spice

- Preheat the oven to 190°C/375°F/Gas mark 5.
- Melt the butter in a flameproof casserole dish. Add the sugar and lemon zest and turn the pears in this mixture. Cover and bake for 30 minutes.
- Add the canned fruit cocktail and syrup and sprinkle with the mixed spice. Return to the oven for 10 minutes. Lift the pears out on to warmed plates. Stir the fruit cocktail well into the pan juices. Spoon around the pears and serve.

Pineapple flambé

SERVES 4

INGREDIENTS:

1 large ripe pineapple (about
600g/1¼lb)
25g/1oz butter
50g/2oz brown sugar

50ml/2fl oz fresh orange juice
25ml/1fl oz vodka
1 tablespoon slivered almonds (toasted)

- Cut away the top and base of the pineapple, then cut down the sides, removing all the dark 'eyes'. Cut the pineapple into thin slices. Using an apple corer, remove the hard, central core from each slice.
- Melt the butter in a frying pan with the sugar. Add the orange juice and stir until hot. Add as many pineapple slices as the pan will hold and cook for 1 to 2 minutes, turning once. As each pineapple slice browns, remove it to a plate.
- Return all the pineapple slices to the pan, heat briefly, then pour over the vodka and light with a long match. Let the flames die down, then sprinkle with the almonds and serve at once.

Mandarins in syrup

SERVES 4

INGREDIENTS:

10 mandarin oranges
15g/¹/₂oz icing sugar

2 teaspoons orange-flower water
15g/¹/₂oz chopped pistachio nuts

- Thinly pare a little of the zest from one mandarin and cut it into fine shreds for decoration. Squeeze the juice from 2 mandarins and set aside.
- Peel the remaining mandarins, removing as much of the white pith as possible.
- Arrange the peeled fruit whole in a large glass dish.
- Mix the reserved mandarin juice, sugar and orange-flower water and pour it over the fruit. Cover the dish and chill for at least an hour.
- Blanch the shreds of mandarin zest in boiling water for 30 seconds. Drain, leave to cool and then sprinkle them over the mandarins, with the pistachio nuts, before serving.

Orange & date salad

SERVES 6

INGREDIENTS:

6 oranges
2 tablespoons orange-flower water
100g/4oz stoned dates (chopped)

50g/2oz pistachio nuts (chopped)
15g/¹/₂oz icing sugar
1 teaspoon toasted almonds

- Peel the oranges with a sharp knife, removing all the pith. Cut into segments, catching all the juice in a bowl. Place in a serving dish.
- Stir in the juice from the bowl with the orange-flower water.
- Sprinkle the dates and nuts over the salad, along with the icing sugar. Chill for 1 hour. Just before serving, sprinkle with the toasted almonds.

Poached allspice pears

SERVES 4

INGREDIENTS:

4 large pears (peeled, cored
and halved)
300ml/½pt orange juice

2 teaspoons ground allspice
50g/2oz raisins
25g/1oz demerara sugar

- Place the pears in a large saucepan. Add the orange juice, ground allspice, raisins and sugar to the saucepan and heat gently, stirring, until the sugar has dissolved. Bring the mixture to the boil and continue to boil for 1 minute.
- Reduce the heat to low and leave to simmer for about 10 minutes. Test to see if the pears are soft and cooked by inserting the tip of a sharp knife.
- Remove the pears from the pan with a slotted spoon and transfer to serving plates.
- Serve hot with the syrup.

Spiced fruit platter

SERVES 6

INGREDIENTS:

1 pineapple
2 papayas
1 small cantaloupe melon

Juice of 2 limes
2 pomegranates
Chat masala

- Cut away the top and base of the pineapple, then cut down the sides, removing all the dark 'eyes'. Cut the pineapple into thin slices. Using an apple corer, remove the hard, central core from each slice.
- Peel the papayas, cut them in half, and then into thin wedges. Halve the melon and remove the seeds from the middle. Cut it into thin wedges and remove the skin.
- Arrange the fruit on 6 individual plates and sprinkle with the lime juice. Cut the pomegranates in half and scoop out the seeds, discarding any pith. Scatter the seeds over the fruit.
- Serve, sprinkled with a little chat masala to taste.

Sesame bananas

SERVES 4

INGREDIENTS:

4 ripe bananas (peeled and cut into 5cm/2in pieces)
3 tablespoons lemon juice
100g/4oz caster sugar
75ml/3fl oz water

2 tablespoons sesame seeds
150ml/¼pt fromage frais
15g/½oz icing sugar
1 teaspoon vanilla essence

- Place the bananas in a bowl, spoon the lemon juice over and stir well to coat.
- Place the sugar and water in a small saucepan and heat gently, stirring, until the sugar dissolves. Bring to the boil and cook for 5 to 6 minutes until the mixture turns golden brown.
- Drain the bananas and blot with kitchen paper to dry. Line a baking tray with baking parchment and arrange the bananas on top.
- When the caramel is ready, drizzle it over the bananas, working quickly. Sprinkle the sesame seeds over the caramelized bananas and leave to cool for 10 minutes.
- Mix the fromage frais together with the icing sugar and vanilla essence.
- Peel the bananas away from the baking parchment and arrange on serving plates. Serve the fromage frais as a dip to accompany the bananas.

Melon & orange cups

SERVES 4

INGREDIENTS:

2 small honeydew melons
1 grapefruit (peeled and segmented)
2 oranges (peeled and segmented)

50g/2oz roasted, unsalted peanuts
25g/1oz light muscovado sugar
¼ teaspoon ground cinnamon

- Halve the melons, scoop out the seeds and discard, then remove and chop the flesh. Reserve the melon shells.
- In a bowl, mix together the melon and citrus fruits. Pile the fruits back into the melon shells.
- Chop the peanuts and mix with the sugar and cinnamon. Sprinkle over the fruit and serve.

Caribbean bananas

SERVES 4

INGREDIENTS:

25g/1oz butter
8 ripe bananas (peeled and halved lengthways)
Juice of 1 lime
75g/3oz demarara sugar

1 teaspoon ground allspice
½ teaspoon ground ginger
Seeds from 6 cardamoms (crushed)
2 tablespoons rum

- Preheat the oven to 200°C/400°F/Gas mark 6. Use a little of the butter to grease a shallow baking dish large enough to hold the bananas snugly in a single layer. Arrange the bananas in the dish and pour the lime juice over them.
- Mix the sugar, allspice, ginger and cardamom seeds in a bowl. Scatter the mixture over the bananas. Dot with the remaining butter. Bake, basting once, for 15 minutes, or until the bananas are soft.
- Remove the dish from the oven. Warm the rum in a small pan, pour it over the bananas and set it alight. Serve the dessert while still hot.

Grilled fresh figs with crème fraîche

SERVES 4

INGREDIENTS:

Butter for greasing
8 ripe figs

225g/8oz crème fraîche
50g/2oz light muscovado sugar

- Preheat the grill to high. Lightly butter a shallow flameproof dish, large enough to accommodate the figs in a single layer.
- Cut the figs into quarters without cutting through the base, and gently open each one out a little. Spoon a dollop of crème fraîche into the centre of each fig.
- Sprinkle the sugar evenly between the figs. Put the figs in the prepared dish and put under a hot grill for 2 minutes or until the sugar has melted and the crème fraîche starts to run. Serve immediately.

Papaya skewers with passion fruit

SERVES 6

INGREDIENTS:

3 papayas
10 small passion fruit
2 tablespoons lime juice

25g/1oz icing sugar
2 tablespoons white rum

- Cut the papayas in half and scoop out the seeds. Peel and cut the flesh into even-sized chunks. Thread the chunks on to 6 bamboo skewers.
- Halve 8 of the passion fruit and scoop out the insides. Purée for a few seconds in a blender or food processor. Press the passion fruit pulp through a sieve and discard the seeds. Add the lime juice, icing sugar and rum, then stir the coulis well until the sugar has dissolved.
- Spoon a little of the coulis on to 6 serving plates. Place the skewers on top.
- Scoop the flesh from the remaining passion fruit and spoon it over.

Pineapple & passion fruit salsa

SERVES 6

INGREDIENTS:

1 small pineapple
2 passion fruit

150ml/¼pt Greek yogurt
2 tablespoons light muscovado sugar

- Cut the top and bottom of the pineapple. Using a large sharp knife, slice off the peel and remove any remaining 'eyes'. Slice the pineapple and use a small pastry cutter or an apple corer to remove the tough core from each slice.
- Cut the passion fruit in half and scoop the seeds and pulp into a bowl. Stir in the chopped pineapple and yogurt. Cover and chill. Stir in the sugar before serving.

Melon medley

SERVES 4

INGREDIENTS:

½ cantaloupe melon
½ honeydew melon

¼ watermelon
Pulp from 2 passion fruit

- Cut the melons into bite-sized pieces, or use a melon baller to slice into balls.
- Chill, covered, for 30 minutes.
- Drizzle with the passion fruit pulp before serving.

Chinese fruit salad

SERVES 4

INGREDIENTS:

75ml/3fl oz Chinese rice wine
Zest and juice of 1 lemon
900ml/1½pt water
225g/8oz caster sugar
2 cloves
2.5cm/1in cinnamon stick
1 vanilla pod
Pinch of mixed spice
1 star anise
2.5cm/1in fresh root ginger (peeled and sliced)

50g/2oz unsalted cashew nuts
2 kiwi fruits (peeled, halved and sliced)
1 star fruit (sliced)
100g/4oz strawberries (hulled and sliced)
400g/14oz canned lychees in syrup (drained)
2.5cm/1in stem ginger (drained and sliced)

- Put the Chinese rice wine, lemon zest and juice and water in a saucepan. Add the caster sugar, cloves, cinnamon stick, vanilla pod, mixed spice, star anise and root ginger to the saucepan.
- Heat the mixture in the pan gently, stirring constantly, until the sugar has dissolved and then bring to the boil. Reduce the heat and simmer for 5 minutes.
- Set aside to cool completely.
- Strain the syrup, discarding the flavourings. Stir in the cashew nuts, cover with clingfilm and chill in the refrigerator while preparing the fruits.
- Spoon the prepared fruit into a dish with the lychees and ginger. Stir through gently to mix. Pour the syrup over the fruit and serve.

Clementines in cinnamon caramel

SERVES 4

INGREDIENTS:

450g/1lb clementines
225g/8oz granulated sugar
300ml/½pt warm water
2 cinnamon sticks

2 tablespoons orange-flavoured
liqueur
25g/1oz shelled, unsalted
pistachio nuts

- Pare the zest from 2 clementines and cut it into fine strips.
- Peel the clementines, removing all the pith but keeping each fruit intact. Put the fruits in a heatproof serving bowl.
- Gently heat the sugar in a pan until it dissolves and turns a rich golden brown. Immediately turn off the heat.
- Protecting your hand with an oven glove or tea towel, carefully pour in the warm water. Bring slowly to the boil, stirring until all the caramel is dissolved.
- Add the shredded zest and cinnamon sticks, then simmer for 5 minutes. Stir in the liqueur.
- Leave the syrup to cool for about 10 minutes, then pour it over the clementines.
- Cover the bowl, cool, then chill for several hours or overnight.
- Blanch the pistachio nuts in boiling water. Drain, cool and remove the outer skins.
- Scatter the nuts over the clementines and serve at once.

Blushing pears

SERVES 6

INGREDIENTS:

6 pears
300ml/½pt rosé wine
150ml/¼pt cranberry juice
Strip thinly pared orange zest

1 cinnamon stick
4 whole cloves
1 bay leaf
75g/3oz caster sugar

- Thinly peel the pears with a sharp knife or vegetable peeler, leaving the stalks.
- Pour the wine and cranberry juice into a large heavy-based pan. Add the orange zest, cinnamon stick, cloves, bay leaf and sugar.

- Heat gently, stirring all the time, until the sugar has dissolved. Add the pears and stand them upright in the pan. Pour in enough cold water to barely cover them.
- Cover and cook gently for 20 to 30 minutes, or until just tender, turning and basting occasionally.
- Using a slotted spoon, gently lift the pears out of the syrup and transfer to a serving dish.
- Bring the syrup to the boil and boil rapidly for 10 to 15 minutes, or until it has reduced by half. Strain the syrup and pour over the pears.

Red fruit salad

SERVES 4

INGREDIENTS:

250g/9oz strawberries (hulled and halved)
100g/4oz raspberries
250g/9oz cherries (pitted)

1 tablespoon Cointreau
1 tablespoon brown sugar
2 tablespoons water

- Put the strawberries, raspberries and cherries in a bowl, drizzle with Cointreau, cover and set aside for 20 minutes.
- Stir the sugar with the water in a small pan over a gentle heat for 3 minutes, or until dissolved. Cool, pour over the fruit, and serve.

Snow-capped apples

SERVES 4

INGREDIENTS:

4 small cooking apples
75ml/3fl oz orange marmalade

2 egg whites
50g/2oz caster sugar

- Preheat the oven to 180°C/350°F/Gas mark 4.
- Core the apples and score through the skins around the middle with a sharp knife.
- Place the apples in a wide ovenproof dish and spoon 1 tablespoon marmalade into the centre of each. Cover and bake for 35 to 40 minutes, or until tender.
- Whisk the egg whites in a large bowl until stiff enough to hold soft peaks. Whisk in the sugar, then fold in the remaining marmalade.
- Spoon the meringue over the apples, then return to the oven for 10 to 15 minutes.

Bananas with chocolate marshmallow sauce

SERVES 4

INGREDIENTS:

4 medium bananas (slightly unripe)   *24 mini marshmallows*
50g/2oz chocolate chips

- Preheat the oven to 160°C/325°F/Gas mark 3.
- Trim the ends of the bananas, leaving on the skins. Using a sharp knife, make a lengthways slit in each one.
- Gently prise open each banana and fill with chocolate chips and marshmallows, then wrap each one in aluminium foil. Bake for 15 to 20 minutes.

Baked apples in red wine

SERVES 6

INGREDIENTS:

50g/2oz sultanas
350ml/12fl oz red wine
Pinch of ground nutmeg
Pinch of ground cinnamon

50g/2oz granulated sugar
Pinch of grated lemon zest
25g/1oz butter
6 cooking apples

- Put the sultanas in a small bowl and pour the wine over them. Stir in the nutmeg, cinnamon, sugar and lemon zest. Cover and leave to stand for approximately 1 hour.
- Preheat the oven to 190°C/375°F/Gas mark 5. Use a little of the butter to grease a baking dish. Core the apples, without cutting right through to the bottom.
- Divide the sultana mixture among the apples. Spoon in a little extra spiced wine.
- Arrange the apples in the prepared baking dish.
- Pour the remaining wine around the apples. Top the filling in each apple with 1 teaspoon of the remaining butter. Bake for 40 to 50 minutes, or until the apples are soft but not mushy. Serve hot.

Grapefruit in apricot brandy

SERVES 4

INGREDIENTS:

3 grapefruit
125ml/4fl oz apple juice
1½ teaspoons granulated sugar

2.5cm/1in piece cinnamon stick
3 tablespoons apricot brandy
3 ready-to-eat dried apricots (chopped)

- Cut off all the zest and pith from the grapefruit over a shallow pan to catch any juice. Push out the white core using the handle of a teaspoon. Then thickly slice the grapefruit.
- Put the apple juice and sugar in the pan with the cinnamon stick. Bring to the boil and simmer for 3 minutes. Add the fruit and simmer for 6 to 8 minutes.
- Remove the fruit from the pan and transfer to the warm plates. Add the apricot brandy to the juice. Bring back to the boil, then spoon over the fruit, and sprinkle with the chopped apricots.

Grilled apple stack

SERVES 4

INGREDIENTS:

4 large dessert apples (cored and peeled)
25g/1oz butter

1 x 400g/14oz jar lime marmalade
4 scoops vanilla ice-cream

- Cut the apples into thin slices across the core and place on a lightly greased grill tray. Top each slice with a small piece of butter and ½ teaspoon lime marmalade.
- Cook under a hot grill until the butter has melted and the apple is golden brown.
- Serve 4 to 5 slices stacked on top of each other with a scoop of vanilla ice-cream.

Sweet-stewed dried fruit

SERVES 4

INGREDIENTS:

500g/1lb 2oz mixed dried fruit salad
450ml/³/₄pt apple juice
2 tablespoons clear honey

2 tablespoons brandy
Grated zest and juice of 1 lemon
Grated zest and juice of 1 orange

- Place the fruit salad, apple juice, honey, brandy, lemon and orange zests and juices in a small saucepan. Bring to the boil and simmer for about 1 minute.
- Remove the pan from the heat and allow the mixture to cool completely.
- Transfer the mixture to a large bowl, cover with clingfilm and chill in the refrigerator overnight. Spoon the stewed fruit into 4 shallow dishes and serve.

Wild strawberry creams

SERVES 4

INGREDIENTS:

4 tablespoons grenadine
4 eggs
50g/2oz caster sugar

½ teaspoon vanilla essence
400ml/14fl oz milk
75g/3oz fraises des bois

- Preheat the oven to 150°C/300°F/Gas mark 2. Pour 1 tablespoon grenadine into each of 4 x 200ml/7fl oz moulds.
- Beat the eggs and sugar in a bowl with the vanilla essence. Scald the milk in a saucepan and slowly stir it into the egg mixture. Strain into a jug, then pour into the moulds. The grenadine will mix into the milk, but then sink back to the bottom. Hull the fraises des bois and divide them between the moulds.
- Place the moulds gently in a roasting tin of hot water and bake in the oven for 30 to 40 minutes, until just set. Leave to cool, then cover and chill in the refrigerator for at least 4 hours. Serve chilled.

Strawberries in grape jelly

SERVES 4

INGREDIENTS:

500ml/18fl oz red grape juice
1 cinnamon stick
Pared zest and juice of 1 small orange

1 tablespoon powdered gelatine
225g/8oz strawberries (hulled and chopped)

- Pour the grape juice into a pan and add the cinnamon stick and orange zest.
- Cook over a very low heat for 10 minutes, then remove the flavourings.
- Sprinkle the powdered gelatine over the orange juice in a small bowl. When the mixture is spongy, stir into the grape juice until it has completely dissolved.
- Allow the jelly to cool in the bowl until just beginning to set. Stir in the strawberries and pour into a 900ml/1½pt mould. Chill until set.

Fruit canapés

SERVES 8

INGREDIENTS:

350g/12oz puff pastry
225g/8oz white almond paste
2 tablespoons apricot jam
1 small mango
2 kiwi fruit (sliced)
225g/8oz strawberries (sliced)

1 star fruit (sliced)
20 seedless black grapes
3 tangerines (segmented)
1 tablespoon powdered gelatine
25g/1oz caster sugar
300ml/½pt water

- Preheat the oven to 220°C/425°F/Gas mark 7. Roll out the pastry very thinly and stamp out about 30 6cm/2¼in rounds. Prick each with a fork and bake for 8 to 10 minutes until crisp. Leave to cool.
- Roll out the almond paste and cut out an equal number of rounds, slightly smaller than the pastry. Stick on top of the pastry using the apricot jam.
- Slice through the mango and remove small balls with a melon baller. Use a variety of fruits to decorate the pastries.
- Dissolve the gelatine and sugar in the water to make a glaze. Brush over the fruits, chill for 30 minutes, then serve.

Fresh fruit with caramel rice

SERVES 4

INGREDIENTS:

50g/2oz short-grain rice
Butter for greasing
75g/3oz demerara sugar
Pinch of salt
400g/14oz canned evaporated milk
(made up to 600ml/1pt with water)

2 apples
1 small pineapple
2 teaspoons lemon juice

- Preheat the oven to 150°C/300°F/Gas mark 2. Wash the rice under cold water.
- Drain well and place into a large greased soufflé dish.
- Add 2 tablespoons sugar to the dish with the salt. Pour on the diluted evaporated milk and stir gently. Bake for 2 hours, then leave to cool for 30 minutes.
- Meanwhile, peel, core and cut the apples and pineapple into thin slices, then cut the pineapple into chunks. Toss the fruit in lemon juice, coating thoroughly, then set aside.
- Preheat the grill and sprinkle the remaining sugar over the rice. Grill for 5 minutes to caramelize the sugar. Leave to stand for 5 minutes, then serve with the fresh fruit.

Peach melba

SERVES 4

INGREDIENTS:

300g/11oz fresh raspberries
25g/1oz icing sugar
375g/13oz granulated sugar
1 vanilla pod (split lengthways)

600ml/1pt water
4 peaches
4 scoops vanilla ice-cream

- Purée the raspberries and icing sugar together in a blender or food processor.
- Pass through a sieve and discard the seeds. Stir the sugar, vanilla pod and the water in a pan over a low heat until the sugar has completely dissolved.
- Bring the sugar syrup to the boil and add the peaches, ensuring they are covered with the syrup. Simmer for 5 minutes, or until tender, then remove the peaches with a slotted spoon and carefully remove the skin.
- Put a scoop of ice-cream on a plate, add a peach, then spoon the purée on the top.

Persian melon cups

SERVES 4

INGREDIENTS:

2 small cantaloupe melons
225g/8oz strawberries (hulled
and sliced)
3 peaches (peeled and cubed)
225g/8oz seedless white grapes

25g/1oz caster sugar
1 tablespoon rose-water
1 tablespoon lemon juice
Crushed ice to serve

- Carefully cut the melons in half and remove the seeds. Scoop out the flesh with a melon baller, taking care not to damage the skin. Reserve the melon shells.
- Place the strawberries in a large mixing bowl with the melon balls, peaches, grapes, sugar, rose-water and lemon juice.
- Pile the fruit into the melon shells and chill in the refrigerator for 2 hours.
- To serve, sprinkle with crushed ice.

Pear halves with cranberry sauce

SERVES 8

INGREDIENTS:

1.2 litres/2pt cold water
225g/8oz granulated sugar
Thinly pared zest and juice of
3 lemons
6 large pears

225g/8oz cranberries
75g/3oz caster sugar
4 teaspoons arrowroot
Finely grated zest of 2 limes

- Put the water into a saucepan with the granulated sugar and lemon zest and juice. Heat slowly until the sugar dissolves, then bring to the boil. Boil gently for 10 minutes.
- Peel the pears, leaving the stalk on. Very carefully cut each pear in half lengthways, cutting right through the stalk, so that each half retains a stalk. Using a teaspoon, scoop out the core from each pear half.
- Put the pear halves into the hot lemon syrup and cook very gently for about 20 minutes, until they are only just tender. Pour the pears and the syrup into a

→

←

large bowl and allow to cool, then cover and refrigerate.

- Put the cranberries and caster sugar into a saucepan with the remaining water.
- Cover the saucepan and cook the cranberries gently for 15 to 20 minutes, until soft. Pour the cranberries into a sieve over a mixing bowl to drain off the juice.
- Return the cranberry juice to the saucepan. Dissolve the arrowroot in a little cold water to make a smooth paste, then stir it into the cranberry juice. Bring to the boil, stirring all the time until the sauce thickens and clears. Stir the cranberries and lime zest into the sauce. Pour the sauce into a bowl and cover with greaseproof paper, cool, then refrigerate.
- To serve, lift the pear halves from the syrup with a slotted spoon and drain them on kitchen paper. Fill each pear half with a little cranberry sauce. Put any remaining sauce into a serving bowl and serve separately.

Nectarines with marzipan & yogurt

SERVES 4

INGREDIENTS:

4 nectarines
75g/3oz marzipan

75ml/3fl oz Greek yogurt
3 Amaretti biscuits (crushed)

- Cut the nectarines in half, removing the stones. Cut the marzipan into 8 pieces and press one piece into the stone cavity of each nectarine half. Preheat the grill.
- Spoon the Greek yogurt on top. Sprinkle the crushed Amaretti biscuits over the yogurt. Place the fruits under the grill for 3 to 5 minutes, until the yogurt starts to melt. Serve immediately.

Fruit fondue

SERVES 2

INGREDIENTS:

50g/2oz soft cheese
150ml/¹/₄pt hazelnut yogurt
1 teaspoon vanilla essence
1 teaspoon caster sugar

Selection of fresh fruits for dipping
(such as strawberries, satsumas, kiwi fruit, grapes, all cut into bite-sized pieces)

- Beat the soft cheese with the yogurt, vanilla essence and sugar in a bowl.
- Spoon the mixture into a glass serving dish set on a platter. Arrange the prepared fruits around the dip and serve immediately.

Port fruit salad

SERVES 8

INGREDIENTS:

300ml/¹/₂pt water
100g/4oz caster sugar
1 cinnamon stick
4 cloves
Pared zest of 1 orange
300ml/¹/₂pt port

2 oranges
1 small honeydew melon
4 small bananas
2 dessert apples
225g/8oz seedless grapesa

- Put the water, sugar, spices and orange zest into a pan and stir over a gentle heat to dissolve the sugar. Bring to the boil, lower the heat, cover and simmer for 10 minutes. Leave to cool, then add the port.
- Strain the liquid into a bowl. With a sharp knife, cut off all the skin and pith from the oranges. Then, holding each orange over the bowl to catch the juice, cut it into segments, allowing them to drop into the syrup. Squeeze the remaining pulp to catch any juice.
- Cut the melon in half, remove the seeds and scoop out the flesh. Add to the syrup.
- Peel the bananas and cut them diagonally in 1cm/¹/₂in slices. Quarter and core the apples and cut the wedges into small cubes. Halve the grapes if large. Stir all the fruit into the syrup, cover with clingfilm and chill for 1 hour before serving.

Gooseberry cheese cooler

SERVES 4

INGREDIENTS:

500g/1lb 2oz fresh gooseberries
Finely grated zest and juice of 1 small orange

1 tablespoon clear honey
250g/9oz cottage cheese

- Top and tail the gooseberries and place them in a pan. Add the orange zest and juice to the pan and cook gently, stirring occasionally, until the fruit is tender.

$\rightarrow$

←

- Remove from the heat and stir in the honey. Purée the gooseberries with their juice in a blender or food processor until almost smooth. Then allow to cool.
- Press the cottage cheese through a sieve until smooth. Stir half the cooled gooseberry purée into the cheese.
- Spoon the cheese mixture into 4 serving glasses. Top each with gooseberry purée. Serve chilled.

Lime sherbet

SERVES 6

INGREDIENTS:

8 limes
75g/3oz caster sugar
Pinch of salt

1.5 litres/2½pt cold water
Crushed ice (to serve)

- Squeeze the limes and pour the juice into a large jug. Add the sugar and salt and stir until dissolved, then pour in the water and top up with plenty of ice to serve.

Poached peaches with ginger

SERVES 4

INGREDIENTS:

4 peaches (halved and stoned)
125ml/4fl oz water
2 tablespoons lemon juice
1cm/½ in root ginger (peeled and grated)

1 cinnamon stick
225g/8oz seedless white grapes (halved)

- Preheat the 180°C/350°F/Gas mark 4.
- Place the peach halves skin-side up in a baking dish. Combine the water, lemon juice, ginger and cinnamon stick and pour over the peaches.
- Bake for 30 minutes. Remove from the oven and place the peaches on 4 dessert plates. Top with the cooking juices, add the grapes and serve.

Grilled pink grapefruit

SERVES 4

INGREDIENTS:

2 pink grapefruit
1 teaspoon granulated sugar

4 scoops vanilla ice-cream

- Halve the grapefruit and cut round the edge of each, between the pith and the flesh. Separate the segments. Sprinkle each grapefruit with sugar.
- Place in ramekins to keep them flesh-side up and put on a grill pan. Grill for 2 to 3 minutes, until lightly browning. Put a scoop of vanilla ice cream on top of each and serve immediately.

Conversion
tables

Weights

Imperial	Approx. metric equivalent	Imperial	Approx. metric equivalent
$1/2$oz	15g	$1\,1/4$lb	600g
1oz	25g	$1\,1/2$lb	700g
$1\,1/2$oz	40g	$1\,3/4$lb	850g
2oz	50g	2lb	900g
$2\,1/2$oz	60g	$2\,1/2$lb	1.1kg
3oz	75g	3lb	1.4kg
4oz	100g	$3\,1/2$lb	1.6kg
5oz	150g	4lb	1.8kg
6oz	175g	$4\,1/2$lb	2kg
7oz	200g	5lb	2.3kg
8oz	225g	$5\,1/2$lb	2.5kg
9oz	250g	6lb	2.7kg
10oz	275g	$6\,1/2$lb	3kg
11oz	300g	7lb	3.2kg
12oz	350g	$7\,1/2$lb	3.4kg
13oz	375g	8lb	3.6kg
14oz	400g	$8\,1/2$lb	3.9kg
15oz	425g	9lb	4.1kg
16oz (1lb)	450g	$9\,1/2$lb	4.3kg
1lb 2oz	500g	10lb	4.5kg

The Imperial pound (lb), which is 16 ounces equals approximately 450g (g).

Oven temperatures

°C	°F	Gas mark	Temperature
130	250	$1/2$	Very cool
140	275	1	Very cool
150	300	2	Cool
160–170	325	3	Warm
180	350	4	Moderate
190	375	5	Fairly hot
200	400	6	Fairly hot
210–220	425	7	Hot
230	450	8	Very hot
240	475	9	Very hot

Fluid measures

Imperial	Approx. metric equivalent	Imperial	Approx. metric equivalent
1fl oz	25ml	9fl oz	250ml
2fl oz	50ml	10fl oz (½pt)	300ml
3fl oz	75ml	12fl oz	350ml
3½fl oz	100ml	15fl oz (¾pt)	450ml
4fl oz	125ml	18 fl oz	500ml
5fl oz (¼ pt)	150ml	20fl oz (1pt)	600ml
6fl oz	175ml	1½ pt	900ml
7fl oz	200ml	2pt	1.2 litres
8fl oz	225ml	2½pt	1.5 litres

The Imperial pint (20 fluid oz.) measures slightly more than ½ litre – approx. 575ml.

Spoon measures

All the measurements given in the recipes are for levelled spoonfuls (British Imperial Standard)
1 teaspoon = 5ml
1 tablespoon = 15ml

The tablespoon measurements below are equivalent to approximately 1oz (25g) of the following ingredients:

Breadcrumbs (dried)	3	Flour, unsifted	30
Breadcrumbs (fresh)	7	Rice (uncooked)	2
Butter/margarine/lard	2	Sugar (granulated, caster)	2
Cheese, grated (Cheddar)	3	Sugar (icing)	3
Cheese, grated (Parmesan)	4	Honey/syrup	1
Cocoa powder	4	Yeast (dried)	2
Cornflour/custard powder	2¾		

Index